Sweet
LOU
and the
CUBS

Also by George Castle

Entangled in Ivy: Inside the Cubs' Quest for October

Baseball and the Media

Where Have All Our Cubs Gone?

Throwbacks: Old School Players in Today's Game

*The Million-To-One Team: Why the Chicago Cubs Haven't Won
the Pennant Since 1945*

The I-55 Series: Cubs vs. Cardinals

Sammy Sosa: Clearing the Vines

I Remember Harry Caray

Sweet
LOU
and the
CUBS

A Year
Inside the
Dugout

GEORGE CASTLE

The Lyons Press

Guilford, Connecticut

An imprint of The Globe Pequot Press

CONTENTS

PROLOGUE
LOU PINIELLA'S VEXING QUESTION

THERE'S NO OTHER MORE GENTEEL, HIGHBROW, DIGNIFIED, proper-English way to state it: Reaching, and then winning, the World Series is a real bitch.

Cautioning against premature giddiness over winning spells while employed in Chicago, manager Lou Piniella knew this stark fact all too well. In the brave new contending Cubs world into which he had directed his long-laggard team, a whole new set of problems replaced the tiresome goals of playing "competitive games" in September, as the infamously conservative Cubs management had proclaimed not long ago. Breaking the .500 mark had now been replaced by the quest to win the World Series after two seasons with Piniella at the helm in Wrigley Field. Yet navigating myriad minefields and trip wires into which the seven-win path to the Fall Classic had evolved had become infinitely more difficult than merely assembling a playoff-worthy team and keeping it at that level for years on end, as was the agreed-upon standard by Piniella and Cubs boss man Crane Kenney for a big-market franchise like the Cubs. The romantic image of a franchise triumphantly marching into the World Series after besting nine other league opponents over 162 games is, unfortunately, four decades out of date.

So many teams had won 97, 100, 103—Piniella's 2001 Seattle Mariners even won 116—and could not win those seven additional games to reach the World Series, let alone the final four to stand alone atop baseball's pinnacle achievement. In 2008, the Cubs earned the dubious status as the ninth team in the past 14 seasons to lead their league in victories, yet not advance past the division series. Their status as an elite contender was too new to comprehend this phenomenon that had ground up so many excellent, proud teams for eons. So first shock, then unremitting anger followed the second-straight three-game National League Division Series elimination—and an utterly ineffectual one at that—of the Cubs from the postseason. It was incomprehensible to millions who had witnessed the best Cubs regular-season team in their lifetimes dominate the NL for most of the 2008 season. Shouldn't that massive upper hand have translated into an express ticket to the World Series that all natural law had owed to the Cubs for decades? And, failing to reach that destination, weren't the Cubs themselves worth John Nance Garner's pitcher of warm spit despite the dramatic improvement Piniella had forecast when he hired on?

Renowned for his unique malaprop-filled homilies during his Cubs tenure, Piniella made the most sense of all with his best stream of consciousness of the year when he held court soaked in celebratory champagne from the Cubs' second consecutive NL Central title late in the afternoon on September 20. He stood at the bottom of the staircase leading to his Wrigley Field office, a perch at which the likes of Jim Riggleman and Don Baylor once held their postgame talks before the manager was shifted to a dungeonlike interview room.

"We're a talented bunch, but there are a lot of talented bunches that go into the postseason," Piniella said. "Do I like our chances? Yeah, I like our chances. Saying [of] our team, if it doesn't win the World Series, it hasn't been a successful year is nonsense."

Piniella cited the case of one cagey manager who has been downgraded because he does not have an excess of championship rings.

"Bobby Cox in Atlanta won 14 divisions in a row," he said. "Bobby Cox is a Hall of Fame manager. And he's won one World Series. What the hell does that tell you? It's not the easiest thing in the world to do. You've got to have fortune, you've got to have a little luck, you've got to stay healthy."

The first realization comes with the sheer numbers involving the postseason. The five-game division series becomes, in effect, a one-game elimination round that often swallows whole the game's best teams and undoes all they've accomplished in 162 games. Losing the first game when there's no wiggle room in a short series often starts bad momentum that can scarcely be reversed with the urgency at hand, resulting in a three-game sweep rather than a competitive, down-to-the-wire five-game series. That's what happened with the Cubs in both 2007 and 2008. And they had plenty of company.

From 2004 to 2008, only two of 20 division series went the full five games. That contrasts with fully one-half of the 10 National and American League Championship Series going the complete seven contests during the same period. Only a last-ditch rally in 2008 in Game 3 at Fenway Park prevented the Angels—after having led the American League in wins—from being swept out similarly by the Red Sox, who had swiped the first two games at The Big A. The division series also has proven a graveyard for other good teams. The Oakland Athletics were ousted in four consecutive opening-round playoffs from 2000 to 2003, wasting their best teams, which had compiled 102 and 103 wins, respectively, in 2001 and 2002. The Houston Astros were knocked out in three straight division series from 1997 to 1999. Even in a hotly contested five-game duel, a seemingly lesser team can knock off a statistically superior one. The Cubs did it themselves, their 88-win entry from 2003 upending the 101-victory Atlanta Braves by riding the hot arms of Kerry Wood and Mark Prior.

"Anything happens in the postseason," Wood said. "If you throw the Pirates automatically in the postseason to see what happens, they might be able to [win a five-game series]."

Might it be time to lengthen the division series to seven games?

"The first [round] would be important to have best-of-seven because it's really a tough situation to adjust to," said Dodgers manager Joe Torre, one of baseball's ranking postseason experts. "Usually, the best teams get in after 162. And then to send them out for that crapshoot, I think it's lucky a lot of times if you win."

But concerns over an overly long season, which has devalued a World Series already played late at night and often in inclement weather in late October, seem to trump the competitive angle.

Piniella differs with Torre, desiring "a pair of five-game series"—both the division series and championship series—and then the World Series. His general manager, Jim Hendry, sees merits in extending the division series to seven games. The flip side, though, is possibly extending the season to November, which nobody in baseball wants.

Cubs lefty Ted Lilly said, "You're going to probably get a better read on what club is deeper if you play a best-of-seven." But he opposes further lengthening of the season. "Obviously if that happens do we end up playing in the middle of December or what?" he said. "I don't know if that's the best thing to do. But the way it is fine, I guess. It's definitely a long season to begin with. We get there in February."

Thus the question morphs into how to properly prepare a team for the rigors of October baseball after they've been drained physically and mentally over seven-plus months, starting with pitchers and catchers reporting just after Valentine's Day?

"This is a business where you learn to stay on the edge," Piniella said. "Once you get comfortable, once you get sassy, you get beat. So you've got to have a team that's always on the edge. You can't get to the point to where [players automatically assume] it's in our reach, it's ours."

Once again, as champagne stung his eyes, Piniella proved prescient about what did not happen—much of it laid at his feet, as he was unable to fine-tune his players to prevent their second successive playoffs fiasco. Beyond the obvious nonproduction that featured a cumulative 5-for-51 performance from leadoff man Alfonso Soriano and cleanup hitter Aramis Ramirez, the Cubs as a team appeared against the Dodgers like a deer caught in head-lights, their "Cubbie swagger" of late summer, as Piniella sketched it out, long gone. It was obvious to all witnesses, ranging from fans to savvy baseball honchos, through jit-tery actions and catatonic body English that ranged from errors to an utter failure of control by normally mentally disciplined pitcher Ryan Dempster. No wonder ex-Cub icon Mark Grace, covering part of the series as a Fox TV analyst, suggested the team "laid down." Accusations that the Cubs "choked" abounded.

Chicago Tribune feature writer Lou Carlozo, a renais-sance man as a professional musician and radio-show pro-ducer, would not wrap up the Cubs' on-field deportment in euphemisms. "They looked like they were stoned," he said.

The sea change in player behavior was apparent even on TV. Former Cub Joe Borowski, closer for the near-miss 2003 World Series team, saw the hint of a tight team by the players' facial contortions.

"It just seemed like they were flat on their heels," Borowski said. "They were waiting for something to do something to them. Their expressions looked like they were scared. You could tell just by watching their expressions. There's nobody in baseball who lays down. But what you can see is a little bit of doubt, a little bit of frustration. I don't know if they thought the NLDS was a formality."

A longtime scout who watched all three Cubs-Dodgers division series games in person would not use the word *jittery*, but was still noncomplimentary in backing up some of Borowski's analysis.

"They looked lackadaisical, like they almost didn't care," the scout said. "They looked flat. Almost like they already celebrated, a given like they were going to the World Series. They were going through the motions. In any kind of job, you have to get to the finish line, finish it off. Sure, the Dodgers peaked at the right time. But the Cubs appeared as if they thought they were going all the way. They were a team early on that didn't look right."

Getting down to the bottom of things was a respected National League executive who spied telltale signs of players ranging emotionally far out of their games.

"I'm sure some guys were too amped up for their own good," the executive said. "Some guys were not prepared mentally. You've got to treat it with some sense of urgency. You can't sit there and lose two, three games in a five-game series. Right from pitch one, there's got to be some sense of urgency. Pitch one, you're ready, more alert. As soon as that first pitch is thrown, you can't be falling behind.

"It's about reaching inside and getting that little extra. Mistakes are microscoped in a situation where you're facing your opponent's numbers 1, 2, and 3; everything is under a microscope. It's a controlling of emotions."

The physical preparation, or lack of the same, preceded the mental aspect. There's something to be said about
charging into the playoffs with momentum. The 2007 and
2008 Cubs left "big mo" behind in the regular season. Late-
season malaise does not commonly translate into postseason success, the 2000 New York Yankees and the 2006 St.
Louis Cardinals being the exceptions to the rule.

In Piniella's debut season, an 11–3 September surge
brought them from one game behind the Milwaukee
Brewers to a 3½-game lead with a season-high 83–73
record with six games to go. But a startling three-game
sweep by the last-place Marlins in Miami in front of heavily pro-Cubs crowds delayed the NL Central clincher to
a Friday night in Cincinnati against the hapless Reds.
Although the Cubs had a playoff berth locked up with
two games to go, they had peaked at Wrigley Field before
the ill-fated trip to Florida—one that prompted Piniella's
urge to caution about distractions 11 months later on
their next visit to Dolphin Stadium. The week without
playing at Piniella's preferred "edge," including the negatives of the sweep by the Marlins, took away the Cubs'
mojo against an apparently inferior Arizona Diamondbacks NLDS opponent.

The braking of good baseball in the homestretch was
even more striking in 2008. The Cubs reached their season
high point of 35 games over .500 at 85–50 on August 29
after a 3–2 win over the Philadelphia Phillies at Wrigley
Field. That culminated the Cubs' best stretch—25–6—of
the season. But the eventual world champions' starters put
the Cubs hitters into a slump from which they never really
recovered. Coasting to the finish, the Cubs were 12–14 the
rest of the season, including a 1–8 slide immediately after
the August 29 victory. Only a modest one-week revival
coinciding with Carlos Zambrano's September 14 no-hitter

and the Brewers' 4–15 slide to open September enabled the Cubs to clinch with eight games to go.

Finishing out the string, the Cubs were 3–4 with some sloppy play against the Brewers and New York Mets. Overall, in September, they finished with their lowest on-base percentage (.329) and highest team ERA (4.58) of any month in the regular season. They were outscored 117–112, the runs-allowed total the highest for the Cubs for any month of 2008. Derrek Lee, who had trouble driving in runs consistently all season, led with 13 RBI in the final month. Alfonso Soriano, Geovany Soto, and Mark DeRosa all hit under .244 for the month, while left-handed hitters Jim Edmonds and Kosuke Fukudome continued slides that began a month earlier. Never speed demons, the Cubs nevertheless did not tune up their small-ball game by stealing just five bases in eight attempts in September.

The Cubs' newfound patience at the plate, the major lineup improvement throughout 2008, was thrown to the wind against the Dodgers. During the regular season, the Cubs averaged 156.6 pitches seen per game. But the three-game NLDS totals were 141, 145, and 143 pitches. Aramis Ramirez, renowned for the most improved patience of his career through September (4.03 pitches seen per at-bat) slipped to 3.45 per at-bat in the postseason. Table-setter Ryan Theriot, who averaged 3.75 pitches seen per at-bat in the regular season, dropped to 2.9 against the Dodgers.

Savvy players who pay attention realize that Wrigley Field—and the season itself—requires two different offensive styles, sometimes concurrent, but always with the ability to implement the styles as the environment changes.

"When you're a Cubs player, you have to realize what's going on in the game," said Ron Coomer, a Cub infielder in 2001 and a childhood Cubs fan growing up in the Chicago area who is now a Minnesota Twins TV analyst. "Early in the season, you manufacture runs. Midseason, you hit three-run homers. In September and going into the playoffs, you manufacture runs again."

The near-miss Cubs' World Series team in 2003 apparently was able to eke out runs with speedster Kenny Lofton and bat-handler Mark Grudzielanek at the top of the lineup. That ability enabled the Cubs to catch fire at just the right time, going 19–8 in September to overcome first the St. Louis Cardinals, then the Houston Astros. They clinched the NL Central with one game to go, keeping their momentum going for the postseason and permitting them to slot in Wood as a Game 1 NLDS starter against the Braves. They outlasted the Braves in a quintet of well-played games before playing similarly well enough to grab a three-games-to-one NLCS lead against the Marlins—and then came the fateful eighth inning of Game 6.

"[Momentum] plays a big part," said Borowski. "A team plays meaningful baseball at the end, it's still in a competitive mode. You might lose that competitive balance [clinching too early]. It's not how you start, it's how you finish."

HardballTimes.com writer Chris Jaffe suggested Lou Piniella himself contributed to the loss of the competitive edge through a flaw in his managerial game in the final week of the regular season. Piniella, who eschews the "cerebral" side of baseball, fell short in mentally preparing the Cubs, drawing unneeded attention to the fact that the playoffs might be different than the regular season after he lectured the team to block out the 100-year championship drought stories and media questions. Jaffe's logic was that wholesale benching of regulars and using "bullpen potluck" to pitch the final game of the season against the Brewers—one that Milwaukee needed to win to snare the wild-card spot—actually proved counterproductive.

"His decision to prioritize physical preparation has likely helped cause their mental shortcomings," Jaffe wrote as a season postmortem in October 2008. "The decision to treat players differently because the postseason is coming up sends the team some signals. First, it loudly pronounces to the players that the upcoming games are fundamentally different from everything they've experienced before. Second, it implies that they can't be trusted to win unless they approach this somehow differently.

"If you think the team can just keep playing as they have all year and win, there's no need for any fancy adjustments on the verge of the postseason. Instead, these notions can make a team self-conscious. That's the single worst thing that can happen to a team. If you have to think about what you're doing, it won't be done properly. It should come naturally."

The only player who actually verbalized how he changed his game in the postseason was Dempster, analyzing why he walked seven Dodgers prior to James Loney's grand slam homer in Game 1—after he had walked seven in 30 September innings spread over five starts, while serving up just four homers in 17 starts in the second half of the season.

"I could have been a little bit more aggressive, throw the ball over the plate a little bit more than I did," Dempster said. "You're trying to be a little too fine."

"It can't carry the weight of all the past failures on its back," Piniella said of his team. "It can't. It's too much pressure. I'm trying to alleviate that so these kids can relax and play baseball . . . I've got to put the pressure on me to take it off the players."

Before the playoffs, Kerry Wood emphatically threw out the 100 years angle as a factor in the Cubs' demeanor.

"I don't let it [affect me], I don't talk about it," Wood said. "I don't do a whole lot of interviews about it. I pretty much stay away from that. I stay with my daily routine. We're not idiots. We know there's pressure on this team to win, but not 100 years' worth of pressure on our shoulders.

"It's this year's pressure," he continued. "There's enough pressure of winning as many games as we've won this year and playing as well as we've played because of how good we are, regardless of what happened in the past. I can tell you win, lose, or draw, the guys on this teams and myself included. We're not going to say, 'Oh, it's 101, we didn't get it done.' There's enough pressure to worry about, once you get in between the lines than worrying about how long it's been since this team's won. It's a good storyline, something to write about, something for fans to hope for. From fans' standpoint; it's irrelevant to us."

In the end, each season is self-contained. But postseasons can develop a trend. The first crop of Piniella teams turned out not to be playoff-worthy, through a combination of circumstances, physical and mental. And when that happens, changes must be inevitable.

Few consistent contenders keep their core together for more than a few years in 21st-century baseball. The Yankees of the Jeter-Posada-Rivera-Williams-Pettitte era are a standout in this respect. Fine-tuning is necessary. The Cincinnati Reds were first called the Big Red Machine when they won the 1970 NL pennant after a half-decade of building. But they truly weren't the all-time dominating team worthy of the Red Machine tag until they traded favorites Lee May and Tommy Helms to the Astros for Joe Morgan more than a year later. Morgan set the tone for the Reds' dominance, complemented by an entirely new outfield of Ken Griffey Sr., Cesar Geronimo, and George Foster. The bunch was an exquisite balance of speed and power that the 1970 Reds did not possess.

In the Cubs' instance, eventual World Series success, building upon health and good fortune will require not only such lineup versatility but also a devil-may-care mental toughness.

"You trade for a guy who plays above average when it counts," said the National League executive who doubted the Cubs' readiness from "pitch one." "You can't have that, 'I'm going to come here, we're the champions, I'm not going to change a damn thing.' "

Perhaps history is a guide, even though too many baseball types pretend yesterday never happened. How 'bout all those blue-collar-type players on the 2003 Cubs who overachieved and did not appear a bit nervous till Dusty Baker's lack of confidence in his bullpen and the Marlins' comeback-kids style simply overwhelmed them?

"We actually believed we were going to win that series," Joe Borowski said of the '03 NLCS. "We not ever brought it up once [not winning]. I know that we were confident going into the playoffs. It seemed like we were going out there, it was us versus everyone else. Nobody thought we'd be there."

The successful playoff performer needs to elevate his game without allowing pressure to seep in. That's where the Cubs' long-term fine-tuning in this new era of playoff contention must concentrate.

And they should be hopping mad if they don't get it done, as Wood was in the locker room after Game 3 in Dodger Stadium. Several key Cubs, such as Soriano and Ramirez, did not appear crestfallen. Ramirez later said that the Cubs experienced a team failure while not explaining his own clutch failures two postseasons in a row. Wood knows what has to be done. Do his 2007 and 2008 team-mates have a similar awareness?

"It [a playoff game] all boils down to just another game in the season," Wood said earlier. "It just means a lot more. When the bells rings, everybody feels it, everybody knows it. A lot of guys feed off that extra adrenaline. That's why you see so many one-run games in the postseason. You don't see blowouts. There's not a sequence in pitches where there's a mental lapse, there's not an at-bat where there's a mental lapse. This is the best baseball."

The debate is intellectually invigorating once the anger over 2007 and 2008 subsided. Better yet, it's far better sub-ject matter than the typical recriminations over yet another losing season and management platitudes about becoming competitive.

In his first press conference as manager in 2006, Lou Piniella said the Cubs eventually would win, and "that's the end of the story." He knew that significant improvements would not automatically snare rings for him and his play-ers. But it is indeed a new era from which there cannot be any turning back. This time, the fans will not permit it.

"Chicago is a major city," Piniella said. "I've said this and I've told Jim Hendry this, I've told [Cubs chairman] Crane Kenney this, this team here should dominate the NL Central the way the Yankees and Red Sox have domi-nated the American League. That's not to take away from the teams in our division. This is a big city. There's no rea-son why our team can't be in a position for a long time to come."

How Piniella started on his fiery path that in turn has likely put the Cubs in such a position will be the entertain-ing journey to follow on these pages.

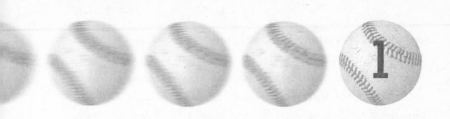

MEET LOU PINIELLA

LOU PINIELLA AND THE LATE CHICAGO MAYOR RICHARD J. DALEY WERE kindred souls when it came to the King's English.

Both put their own spin on pronunciation and usage. You simply had to go beyond the simple verbal utterances to understand what each man meant. Who can ever forget Daley proclaiming amid a riot that "the police are not here to create disorder, the police are here to preserve disorder"?

In the annals of Chicago public life, Daley had only one rival in such pronouncements: Sweet Lou.

Take, for instance, the spring day in 2008 when Piniella stammered for about 15 seconds, trying to grasp the right terminology for an ongoing Cubs issue.

"What do you call it, something in motion?" he asked assembled media, who are always eager to help Piniella expand his linguistic horizons. "Progress in motion? There you go, I love that."

How about *poetry* in motion?

"Not poetry," Piniella replied. "It's a progress in motion. When you see things you make adjustments.

'Progress in motion,' is that a good word or a bad word? A 'work in progress,' what the hell. 'Work in progress.' What's the difference? You all know what I'm trying to say."

Then, days after mangling the term *svelte* to describe outfielder–first baseman Daryle Ward's trimmer physique, requiring a writer to spell out "s-v-e-l-t-e" on his notebook and show it to Piniella, he searched for the proper phrase to describe a hitter working a pitcher for a walk. He finally settled on one suggestion from the peanut gallery—"coax a walk, like svelte."

How about the time when he used the trainer's official term *contusion* for Ryan Theriot's foot malady when something simpler would have done better? If anything, Sweet Lou loves his layman's language. "He's got a bruise, that's what he's got. You've got the contusion, so I used it [as his audience burst out in laughter]," he said with a huge grin.

From Day 1 of his managerial tenure, on October 17, 2006, when he sweated through his white dress shirt on the 55-degree day of his introductory press conference at Wrigley Field, Piniella became endearing to anyone who was not hard of hearing. Of all the faces he displayed to the public, his verbal syntax side became the most prominent and the most appealing. Nine miles south, White Sox manager Ozzie Guillen turned the air blue with his rapid-fire, Spanglish pronouncements. In contrast, profanity was just about the only aspect of speaking Piniella did not provide for public consumption. To his players, especially a pitcher struggling on the mound, he was different, making lip-reading a useful talent. But Piniella possessed good brakes on cuss words, with *hell* and *damn* as far as he'd go.

The malapropisms and misidentifications flowed freely in that first press conference. He referred to Cubs then–media relations director Sharon Pannozzo as "Sherry." He told of wonderful afternoons as a Chicago visitor spent strolling and shopping the "Michigan Mile." That was the same side of town, apparently, where the White Sox won the World Series on the "North Side." The 20-year-old Cubs Convention was "FanFest."

And when asked how he would promote working the count from a traditionally impatient Cubs lineup, he suggested fielding a lineup of "midgets." Oops—that was a journey into politically incorrect territory from which Piniella was fortunate to extricate himself.

In spring training 2008, Piniella said he'd take a rare Arizona off day with the family in the "Superstitious" Mountains east of Mesa—they are in reality the Superstition Mountains. The retro 1980s Cubs theme song, 'Go Cubs Go" revived and readopted by the Wrigley Field fans in 2007, intrigued Piniella so much that he called it "Go Cubs Win." He wondered about what to call that metal protrusion from the top of the bleachers after Geovany Soto hit a crucial homer into it. Again, he asked for nominations from the floor and it came up as "the basket," erected in 1970. What was the green, clingy stuff underneath the basket? Piniella at least twice called it the "ivory." Guess he never had to fish a ground-rule double out of the "ivy," so what's two more letters to make your point? Later, on September 6, 2008, Piniella was relieved that Alfonso Soriano did not take a curtain call in a road ballpark for his three-home-run outburst against the Cincinnati Reds. "I think I would've grabbed him if I'd seen him," Sweet Lou said. "That's what you'd call evicting road rage." Translation: "evoking" road rage. And let's not get into Sweet Lou's opinion of the 17-year cicadas that took up residence in the vines in 2007.

When Piniella discussed ace Carlos Zambrano's balky shoulder in late summer 2008, he must have "evoked" a second opinion from a physician because he kept referring to a "Dr. Griswald." The team orthopedist who actually examined Big Z was Stephen Gryzlo.

But it was describing one of his own pitchers where Piniella outdid himself in 2007. Lefty Scott Eyre (last name pronounced A-yer) had been a prominent reliever for half a decade, but Piniella apparently added yet another southpaw to complement the colorful Eyre. He referred to a "Stevie Ire" working his bullpen.

That was typical Piniella, who falls short in the name game, recalled Lee Elia, one of his longtime coaches with Seattle and Tampa Bay.

"Nicknames were awesome," said Elia. "One guy we nicknamed Mule. Lou would call him Moose. Everyone knew what he meant."

With Spanish his first language growing up in Tampa, Piniella has professed to understand the Latin player better than most.

Of the criticism swirling around Alfonso Soriano early in the 2008 season: "Thank God he doesn't read English very well. He doesn't let it bother him. His demeanor and disposition doesn't change. He works hard, takes BP, he gets his stretching in, he gets in his running, he does a few dances, and he's ready to play."

Of letting ace Carlos Zambrano throw 130 pitches in a 2008 victory: "[Not a problem] for a big, strong kid from Venezuela. [You can do it] once in a while. The game dictates you need to do that. I would have been booed out of the park if I took him out. Carlos wouldn't have been happy if I had taken him out."

Now, what does Piniella *really* think? Only a handful of family and close friends will get the truly "A" material, perhaps over an after-hours "cocktail," as Piniella calls his libation. Having worked as a stockbroker and in marketing for

Jantzen swimwear in the off-seasons of his baseball youth, he never was a one-note Baseball Jones. Could it be interesting to chat up politics and American history with Sweet Lou?

"He can make examples and correlations with World War II," Elia said. "He has unbelievable ways of getting his point across. There's a part of Lou that's very, very knowledgeable and intelligent. He can be complex at times."

Off the field in Chicago, he kept a relatively low profile in and around his two-bedroom condo in a historic North Michigan Avenue building. He dined at the likes of Gibson's and Smith and Wollensky steakhouses—the latter at which Piniella childhood buddy Tony La Russa would slip in alone to read a book in a darkened corner—or Ballo's Italian restaurant. Companions were wife Anita when she commuted up from Tampa, other family members or side-kick/first-base coach Matt Sinatro. On an August 7, 2008, off day, after 20 straight days of baseball, Piniella did something so basic and simple as taking his grandchildren for a boat ride on Lake Michigan. Living in a hotel a few blocks away, Sinatro often drove Piniella to Wrigley Field. Sweet Lou put very few miles on his own car in Chicago.

Sinatro easily found his way to Wrigley Field with his celebrity passenger. But he became the Wrong Way Corrigan of his era the morning of September 6, 2008. Instead of taking the most direct route by zipping right down Interstate 65 through Indianapolis while driving Piniella to a road series in Cincinnati, the coach followed directions he'd found on the Internet. He headed east on the Indiana Toll-way with the intention of turning south at Interstate 75 at Toledo—definitely the long way. One problem—Sinatro missed the turn and continued heading east. Taking a nap in the car, Piniella awoke as they got within 80 miles of Cleveland. Sensing something was not right, Piniella got a map and the dynamic duo backtracked through Columbus, finally arriving at Great American Ballpark just a bit more than two hours before first pitch.

Sinatro is 17 years younger than Piniella, but he has been treated like an age cohort. He knows when to humor the boss.

"He always had a good backup guy, Matt Sinatro, to laugh at his joke if nobody else did," Tampa Bay reliever Trever Miller said. "And everything flowed well. He's got a good group there. He's got Ed McMahon in Matt."

While out in public, Piniella absolutely diverged from managerial mentor Billy Martin. There will be no fights with his pitchers or marshmallow salesmen.

"I like to stay in my hole, as I say it," Piniella said in 2007. "I like my privacy. I don't like the limelight at all. I'm basically a little bashful and a little shy. I'm courteous to people. If I'm out to dinner and somebody wants an autograph or somebody wants to talk a little baseball, as long as it's not too long, that's fine.

"The one thing with these public jobs," he continued, "if you go to a place where those things occur, you better at least be prepared to be courteous and hospitable. If not, just stay home. I enjoy having a beer from time to time. But I'm not going to places where I'm going to be put in a situation where something ugly can happen."

Piniella has always liked his food and drink. Diagnosed before the 2004 season with type 2 diabetes, and he apparently struggles with his weight. He professed exhaustion after the stressful 2007 Cubs season, adding that it took him six weeks to recover. He started walking for exercise in the off-season and shed some pounds, but the late-night eating and restaurant meals took their toll during the season with the reappearance of an ample belly. "Each year in spring training," said a longtime Piniella observer in the industry, "Lou starts out looking good, but by midseason it looks like he's gained weight again." Several postgame media sessions after night games in both 2007 and 2008 were called off, ostensibly because Piniella was tired. And before a Saturday afternoon game in 2007, Piniella reported he was still feeling the after-effects of a bigger-than-normal portion of spirits consumed the previous night.

He had long fought the battle of the bulge, a less-publicized duel with a Piniella trait than his famed temper. Throughout his Yankees playing career, Piniella was famed for letting himself go in the off-season. Yankees owner George Steinbrenner tapped former Heisman Trophy–winner Hopalong Cassady to pick up Piniella three times a week at his Tampa home and lug him to the gym for weight-training machines and to go running.

Hitting, not possessing a body beautiful, was his main motivation.

"They don't pay me for my speed," he said in 1982 after trimming five pounds from his accustomed 205. "I get paid to hit a baseball. The day I stop hitting a baseball is the day I will be out of baseball."

The Yankees took his weight so seriously that they threatened to fine Piniella, then 38, $1,000 every day he was over 200 pounds and threatened a breach-of-contract charge as 1982 spring training opened. The fine was not necessary; Piniella made his weight at 199. "When I leave here, I'm going to have a big pizza and a keg of beer. Only joking, George," he said then. He had reached the prescribed weight goal by eating two hard-boiled eggs for breakfast, a cup of soup and celery for lunch, then a piece of broiled chicken and string beans for dinner.

But if Piniella could turn over a new leaf by curbing his temper, maybe he could become a gym rat, huh? Well, that might be going a bit too far, just like a Piniella totally purged of his old red-ass side. The latter persona will follow him to the end of his baseball days and beyond. At least he can laugh at himself. He turned the temper angle into an Aquafina bottled-water TV commercial in 2008, in which he pretended to be arguing with the third-base umpire to keep up his reputation. The real dialogue has Piniella asking the arbiter about his family. To ensure the proper visual effects for the faux dispute, Piniella dislodged third base and tossed it, just as a close-up shows him guzzling a bottle of water.

Another TV spot in 2008 had him teaming with Ozzie Guillen to plug Chevys. Doubles obviously did most of the body English shots, including the two supposed managers jumping on a trampoline and dashing into a photo booth to pose together. But a brief sequence in which Piniella rapped was real.

"I had fun doing it," he said. "It's all right. You didn't like it? It's not my type of music. I did what I was asked to do."

Piniella set himself up with that line of logic. Would he next like to compete in *Dancing With The Stars?* "In India," he replied. "I don't think so. I don't have that [kind of] dexterity."

Life was simpler and more defined when the vintage Piniella would jack up his team and dominate ESPN highlights with the ultimate sight gag—the base toss. His all-time throw on September 18, 2002—exactly 11 years after he grappled with reliever Rob Dibble in the Reds clubhouse—hurt his hamstring and right shoulder. Protesting a bang-bang play in which catcher Ben Davis was called out and frustrated over a late-season collapse by his Mariners, Piniella first ran onto the field and threw his cap to the ground as he screamed at umpire C. B. Bucknor. Piniella was immediately ejected, but Bucknor exacerbated the situation with an apparent smirk. Sweet Lou kicked his cap, screamed at first-base coach Johnny Moses to return it, and then threw it again. Seconds later, amid more 100-decibel diatribes, he ripped first base from its mooring, raised it high, and heaved it down the rightfield line. Piniella then caught up with the errant base, grabbed it, and threw it again.

In Cincinnati he also had tossed first base after being angered by a Dutch Rennert call.

"Lou pulled the base out of the ground and threw it into rightfield," Reds announcer Marty Brennaman recalled, "and went out to get it and threw it again. My line was, 'That's the greatest act we've seen in this ballpark in a long time.' He wore his emotion on his sleeve, the fans loved it and the players loved it.

"He's mellowed since 18 years ago; you don't see it as much now. You'll see the old Lou occasionally, but not as readily as we saw it."

Indeed, except for the contrived dirt-kicking on third-base ump Mark Wegner on June 2, 2007, to divert attention from the Carlos Zambrano–Michael Barrett two-round brawl, Piniella apparently had retired from physical comedy.

"I've created my own bed in a lot of situations and I recognize that, so I have to live with it," Piniella said six weeks after the Wegner episode. "Quite frankly, when I have one of my little tirades or whatever you want to call 'em, I get embarrassed by it. This last one I had in Chicago will be the last one I ever have on the field. I get a little miffed because you don't win as many games as I have or get as many jobs as I had in baseball just because you put on a show once in a while.

"The new hierarchy in baseball would rather have no arguments and no fights on the field, and just play the game. I would rather be recognized as a good baseball man as opposed to just a colorful baseball man."

That leaves Sweet Lou the Philosopher, Sweet Lou the Elocutionist, and Sweet Lou the Preacher Man as his social security age personality. And to most fans and media weary of stale platitudes in connection with the long, strange journey of the Cubs, that's good enough.

"Look, I'm basically a guy who's just making a living," Piniella said. "It just so happens I'm a baseball manager, that's all. I've had a wonderful career, a long, long time. I've said this many times. This is my last job in baseball. In the short period of time I've been here, it would be very, very special for the Cubs to finally get in a Fall Classic."

Everything he ever learned about the nuances of our most fascinating and talked-about sport would be needed in what he termed his last job in baseball with the Cubs, one in which the desired goal would far overshadow anything else he ever accomplished.

A BUTT AND A BAT ON FIRE

A QUICK LOOK AROUND LOU PINIELLA'S SMALL, CINDER-BLOCK-WALLED WRIGLEY FIELD OFFICE DURING the 2008 season was all that was necessary. There was nothing to capture your gaze for more than a few seconds—or give a clue to the personality and history of the room's occupant.

Piniella sat behind a small desk, with a couch set against it at a 90-degree angle. On the desktop: some scouting reports, a Chicago newspaper crossword puzzle [a pregame work in progress], and a cell phone.

No laptop whirring. No digital mini-bytes of baseball popping up on-screen. "I only know how to turn it on," he said. "It might make me look good; it might make me look more intelligent. I don't get too involved in a laptop. I don't use e-mail." Yet on September 29, 2007, in the visiting manager's office at Great American Ballpark, just minutes before the Cubs clinched the NL Central title, Piniella was spotted surfing the Internet on a laptop for the latest scores. Perhaps an aide had logged on and clicked Piniella over to the scoreboard site then. But there were no mouse clicks here at home.

And there were few items on the office bookshelf: just a couple of books involving Pete Rose, George Will, and the New York Yankees. Not a single photo or other memento graced the walls. The physical evidence was cold on Piniella's colorful four-decade career that netted three World Series rings and crossed paths with a roster of all-time baseball personalities. In the middle of his first Cubs season in 2007, Piniella had said that his wife, Anita, would decorate the office. But almost a year later, her interior-design touch had not been felt. The lack of decor was in stark contrast to predecessor Dusty Baker's photo-museum design that mimicked Tommy Lasorda's old Dodger Stadium office. Baker displayed his journey through baseball history, his love of music, and his other eclectic tastes via images of personalities as diverse as Henry Aaron and John Lee Hooker, along with a packed bookshelf and a CD hookup on the wall.

Nearing age 65 and smack-dab in the middle of a three-year contract for his professed final managing job, Piniella obviously was renting short-term, not buying, in Chicago.

"Anita decorated his Seattle office," said Larry LaRue, baseball writer for the *Tacoma News-Tribune,* who had covered Piniella his entire 10-year run with the Mariners. "There were a lot of family photos, pictures of Lou with the Yankees, and a photo of Lou with President Clinton, who had thrown out the first ball."

You could make a case that Piniella's laser focus on his toughest-ever assignment—transforming the Cubs into winners—caused the spartan office decor and absence of personal artifacts. This is an uncomplicated man who simply emphasizes winning each day's game and setting up the Cubs for near-future success, with no time for reflection on the good ol' days—or analysis of how the Cubs' past melded with the present.

Throughout his Chicago tenure to date, Piniella hardly ever sat back and waxed nostalgic. He had been at the center of the 1970s Yankees "Bronx Zoo," but rarely brought up his role in the collisions of George Steinbrenner, Billy Martin, and Reggie Jackson. Such experiences almost had to be pried out of him. He insisted he did not watch *The Bronx is Burning*, the 2007 ESPN dramatic series about the 1977 Yankees season.

"I'm not a storyteller," Piniella claimed, offering up the difference between him and, say, Don Zimmer. Hardly an anecdote escaped from his mouth about managing the "Nasty Boys" Cincinnati Reds bullpen to an upset World Series win over the Athletics in 1990. Requests to make comparisons between top baseball achievers of today and the greats he had witnessed decades previous often were met with too-short answers and changes in subject matter. Once in a while, Piniella would react to a present-day event with an anecdote about a time he destroyed a water cooler, then bought the damaged contraption and moved it to his garage. But he never sought the past as a refuge; his no-frills focus was on creating a "new culture" of winning for the Cubs.

Did Piniella share a philosophy with Mike Ditka, the bard of Bears-dom, who once proclaimed, "living in the past is for cowards and losers"? Probably not. Maybe Piniella simply disdained "cerebral" questions and observations tossed his way. Or maybe he did not want to rub all his past success in the faces of his new employers and their worldwide, long-suffering fan base. Who wants to hear about Yankees glory days and World Series rings when his first Cubs team had to recover from a 22–31 start and play like maniacs just to finish 85–77 and barely scrape into the playoffs?

He wouldn't have had the time to properly reminisce through a full life anyway, with his task at hand. Piniella's experiences were complex, at once an American success story and an old-school baseball journey. He moved from an upbringing in a sports-crazy family in which his father played in Sunday semi-pro doubleheaders in 1950s Tampa to an apprenticeship with four different baseball organizations that delayed big-league success until 1969. Add on a single-minded devotion to hitting that included trying out batting stances in front of mirrors at all hours of the night to a white-hot temper when he fell short in a sport chock-full of failure. The story would also include a 20-year managerial resume.

The incubator for the baseball junkie who would pick up his Sweet Lou nickname in Kansas City in the early 1970s was a close-knit family in a neighborhood of hard-working people of Spanish and Italian descent. They lived their lives in the baseball hotbed of Tampa, which produced generations of big leaguers starting with catcher-turned-manager Al Lopez (born in 1908) all the way through the likes of Dwight Gooden and Gary Sheffield. In the semi-tropical climate, baseball skills could be honed outdoors year-round.

Piniella followed in the athletic path of his father, also named Louis, and mother, Margaret, a good athlete in her own right in softball and basketball. Working long hours, the elder Louis Piniella ran a distributorship while Margaret worked the company's books. When they could get away to play sports, they went at it full-bore as a family. The ties that bind were still close in 2008: Margaret Piniella still lived in the old family home on Cordelia Street, across the road from a park that was home to family athletic feats.

"My dad was a pitcher," Lou Piniella recalled in an uncommon look-back moment in 2008. "He could have played pro ball. He was offered a contract. But they made

more money in the shipyards than they offered playing baseball. He played in an intersocial baseball league in Tampa.
They had some real good teams. The Cuban club, the Italian club, the Loyal Knights. Six to eight teams, they'd play
every Sunday and sell out. They played doubleheaders on
Sunday and it was fun."

Fun—and punctuated with fights. Hot blood runs
through Piniella's genealogy. One time the elder Piniella
disagreed with his catcher on the selection of pitches. He let
go what his son called a "haymaker" and the battery went at
it, the fans joining in. Twenty minutes later, after the combatants had gone several rounds, both pitcher and catcher
resumed their positions on the field and play continued as
if the fight never took place.

Surprisingly, a Piniella kinsman suggested that Sweet
Lou acquired most of his intensity from his mother, who
was notable for riding referees and umpires in her sons'
games. Boston Red Sox hitting coach Dave Magadan is
Piniella's first cousin and godson, so he got an up-close-
and-personal view of family dynamics.

"No question it was his mom," Magadan said. "She
was very passionate about Lou and Lou's brother [Joe]. She
took a personal interest in their athletic careers."

Lou Piniella first crossed paths with future baseball
celebrities as a youth in Pony League. Teammates on the
West Tampa Pony League team were Tony La Russa and
future catcher Ken Suarez.

A few years later, Piniella first gained fame as an all-
American basketball player at Jesuit High School in Tampa.
He was a load on the court, scoring from everywhere. A
very young Jim Hendry, who would go on to hire Piniella
as Cubs manager 45 years later as the team's general manager, looked up to the Basketball Jones then.

"My older brother [John] went to Jesuit, two grades behind Lou," Hendry said. "I was about six years old. My brother would take me every few weeks to see him play. We lived 20 miles away in Dunedin. Jesuit was located where the Bucs stadium is now. I was a young sports fanatic and worshipped guys at Jesuit who were sports stars. Lou was a tremendous scorer, a great shooter who could score from all over the place."

Success in basketball slowed down Piniella's baseball progress. He was asked to start pitching by Jesuit High coach Jack O'Connell only one day after the basketball season ended. Piniella refused, claiming his arm was not ready. He would not relent, so O'Connell barred him from playing the 1961 prep baseball season. That cost Piniella a potential lucrative signing bonus from scouts who already had taken notice of him, but cooled on him when he sat out the season.

He'd have to wait another year, after he took a basketball ride from the University of Tampa. Piniella's freshman hoops season, however, was cut short by an ankle injury suffered jumping from a roof trying to escape a police raid on a local college hangout where underage drinking—including by Piniella—was taking place. Piniella recovered in time to have a good 1962 baseball season for Tampa, and the scouts' interest resurfaced.

Cleveland Indians scout Spud Chandler signed Piniella to a $25,500 bonus. He broke in with the Class D Selma (Alabama) Cloverleafs. But after one season, the Washington Senators selected him in a minor-league draft. He did not stay long, moving on to the Baltimore Orioles organization in a trade. Orioles general manager Lee MacPhail, father of future Cubs president Andy MacPhail, promised Piniella a call-up to the Orioles for the final month of 1964. He only got into a total of four games with just one at-bat in his big-league debut pinch-hitting for Robin Roberts on September 4, 1964, at Dodger Stadium. He had prepped for that cup of coffee via a minor-league stop in Aberdeen, South Dakota, playing for manager Cal Ripken Sr., whose namesake son was the team batboy. Piniella's minor-league teammates in '64 included pitcher Jim Palmer and short-stop Mark Belanger.

Consignment to the minors again in 1965 meant a clash of strong-willed men—the young Piniella playing for a feisty, rising manager, Earl Weaver, in Elmira, New York. The inevitable took place with Piniella drawing a suspension, later rescinded, from Weaver. Despite their conflicts and Weaver's initial doubts about Piniella's talent, Piniella credited Weaver with teaching him the importance of winning. Weaver ended the 1965 season telling Piniella he wanted the young hitter with him when he'd manage Triple-A Rochester in 1966.

The second year of Piniella-Weaver never took place. Piniella was traded back to the Cleveland organization. The move was fortuitous: After a brief, failed attempt to convert Piniella to catching, the Tribe sent him to play for a more reserved manager named Johnny Lipon at Triple-A Portland, Oregon. The two clicked as Lipon worked with Piniella early each day, having the then 23-year-old outfielder hitting hundreds of baseballs.

"This was serious business," Piniella said in his 1986 autobiography *Sweet Lou,* co-written with Maury Allen. "I had a manager who cared about me and was willing to give up his free time to help me, so I sure was going to take advantage of it."

Piniella had trouble hitting the slider, stalling the upward progress of his career. Lipon got Piniella to move away from the plate, change his stance, use a heavier bat, and forget about being a power hitter. Soon he could hit to rightfield and hit-and-run. He became the kind of bat handler for which he would earn notoriety in a long big-league career.

The new, improved Piniella caught the eye of minor-league opponent Lee Elia. An infielder who would one day work as Piniella's top aide with the Seattle Mariners and Tampa Bay Rays, Elia noticed how he was "a pretty good hitter, aggressive as hell. You could see then he'd settle for nothing less than success. He became a rightfield gap hitter, and that made him more profound in the clutch."

Veteran minor leaguers entering their mid-20s in the 1960s often spent multiple seasons in Triple-A, and Piniella was no exception. He finally nudged his average to .308 in 1967 under Lipon's tutelage, part of a memorable year that included his marriage to Anita Garcia, a former Miss Tampa beauty queen. Cleveland was not brimming with talent, but Piniella did not yet fit in. After a .317 season in 1968, he got his second September call-up, logging five at-bats (no hits) over six games. Piniella felt he did not mesh with taciturn Cleveland manager Alvin Dark.

Finally, just before the 1969 season, his career break came. Piniella was taken by the new Seattle Pilots in the expansion draft. They sent him to spring training, where he rubbed shoulders with aging pitcher Jim Bouton, slyly gathering information for his groundbreaking book *Ball Four*. But like meat on the hoof, Piniella was part of yet another trade—this time with the Kansas City Royals, the other American League expansion team of '69.

"They drafted Lou, we drafted [outfielder] Steve Whi-taker," recalled Atlanta Braves president John Schuerholz, then administrative assistant to Lou Gorman, the Royals' player development chief. "Then we traded them. Lou was a sweet-swinging, natural hitter. We felt like he had major league tools, he was a young guy we could have.

"He could really hit, it distinguished him. He had intensity and passion for it, a real competitor. He knew hitting mechanics and nuances."

Piniella was an immediate hit at old Municipal Stadium in Kansas City. Inserted at the leadoff spot and in centerfield for the Royals first-ever game, on April 8, 1969, against the Billy Martin–managed Minnesota Twins, he was flanked by a natural catcher in Ed Kirkpatrick in leftfield and a natural first baseman in Bob Oliver in right. But he was not bothered by hard-hitting, weak-fielding, slow defensive alignment. Facing rail-thin Twins lefty starter Tom Hall, Piniella was 4-for-5, including a leadoff double, in the Royals' 4–3, 12-inning victory before 17,688.

Within days, manager Joe Gordon moved Piniella back to his more comfortable position in leftfield, where he settled in to make up for lost time spent in the minors.

Royals management soon discovered they got the long end of the Piniella-Whitaker trade. John Schuerholz became fast friends with Piniella in 1969 in the mom-and-pop operations that were big-league franchises then, and even pulled strings to get Piniella and pitcher Roger Nelson into his Army Reserve unit. He echoed his bosses' opinion in describing a money hitter in the making.

"The good ones have passion, have that flair, that fire," Schuerholz said. "If they can't channel it in a positive way, it works to their detriment. Lou had his share of outbursts and confrontations, but he also was able to channel that in a quiet way, into his hitting.

"Before Sabermetrics were cool, there was an analysis of actions—who were the clutch players? Who got better in late-inning runs-scoring situations, who got better with two outs—especially in tough, big games? It didn't take long after that analysis to figure out this guy really shined when his team really needed him to. You needed to have good hand-eye coordination and a short swing. And you had to be confident. That combination described Lou."

Piniella simply immersed himself in the science of hitting, and went deeper the further he progressed in baseball, including bedroom-mirror batting-stance practice. One night he inadvertently startled Anita awake when, groggily, she saw a man standing over the bed with a bat in hand. It was her husband, practicing instead of sleeping.

Piniella did not change through the years and mounting success.

"Two hours after the game, he'd still be in the shower going through batting stances and helping other guys out. All baseball," said longtime Yankees trainer Gene Monahan. Every chance he'd get, sometimes just standing in the middle of the clubhouse, Piniella practiced his stance— with or without a bat.

Turned loose in The Show after all those years of being hemmed up in Triple-A, Piniella thrived within his self-prescribed hitting regimen. Without much of a supporting cast on a last-place expansion team, he won the American League Rookie of the Year award for 1969. By latter-day standards, Piniella's numbers seemed modest—11 homers, 21 doubles, 68 RBI, and a .282 average. Yet old Municipal Stadium was a big ballpark and unkind to would-be sluggers. And this was an era without injected artificial stimulants, when 20 homers had real value—at 20 you were a certified basher. Just two years previous, before the mound had been lowered after the much-derided "year of the pitcher," Carl Yastrzemski's .301 had led the American League.

Piniella matched that average in 1970, while his RBI total climbed to 88, thereby dodging the age-old "sophomore jinx." Lou and Anita Piniella planted year-round roots in the Kansas City community, with Lou investing in a restaurant and a Honda motorcycle dealership.

In 1970, a 19-year-old Minnesota Twins rookie with a crackling curveball began dueling Piniella.

"He was a very good breaking-ball hitter," recalled a now-middle-age Bert Blyleven, working as a Twins announcer. "He sometimes sat on the curveball. A lot of them sit on it, but whether they hit it is another issue. Lou did.

"He could stay with my curveball, he could go the other way or if I hung it, he could hit it a long way. Lou had a very good eye at the plate. Lou knew what a strike was and what a ball was. You watch a guy like Joe Mauer, who has so much patience and knows the strike zone. Lou was a lot like Joe—as far as knowing the strike zone, not going out of his element to chase a pitch. He had a short, compact swing, didn't like to extend his arms. He was quick inside and covered both sides of the plate."

The American League's dominant team during the early 1970s was the Baltimore Orioles, who had their way with the Royals. In 1971 the Orioles fielded four 20-game winners. One, though, remembered Piniella's intensity as his teammate back in Elmira in 1964 and took his threat seriously when he faced the Royals star.

"He could use the whole field," said Hall of Famer Jim Palmer. "He was capable of hitting home runs. But he was a line-drive hitter, right-center, left-center. Occasional power. Knew how to hit, he was very smart. He was a student of the game. He could hit it over the first-base bag. If you hung a breaking ball, he could hit it over the leftfield wall."

The savvy Palmer understood Piniella's devotion to the game by his hitting approach and other mannerisms.

"Low and away, you could get most guys out," he said. "Lou could hit quality pitches, that's why he was such a great hitter. He didn't like to give away at-bats. He might have taken it to an [emotional] extreme, but for him, that worked. He understood the game. He was smart enough to be able to take that game plan to home plate. A lot of guys are fog banks between the on-deck circle and home plate. He was able to skirt around that."

Piniella's already-sound approach at the plate was further enhanced when he began working with legendary hitting instructor Charley Lau in 1971. Lau—who would later follow Piniella to the Yankees—emphasized putting the batter's weight on his back foot. Piniella and his teammates took to the Lau style quickly. It paid off when the entire Royals outfield—leftfielder Piniella, centerfielder Amos Otis, and rightfielder Richie Scheinblum—were named to the American League All-Star team in 1972. Piniella was the fourth-leading American League vote-getter during a season in which he batted .312 with 33 doubles.

All-Star status, of course, did not cool Piniella's inner fire, which frequently bubbled up in spectacular style. Piniella simply was baseball's worst loser, and his explosions finally got notoriety in the majors after alternately scaring and entertaining those who crossed his paths going all the way back to his childhood.

"The problem that I've had in life more than anything else is my temper," Piniella reflected back in 2007. "I've had to really fight my whole life to curtail it. As a player, I was considered a little bit of a red ass. I'd rather have some tranquil moments and have no problems at all. I like to be as meek and humble as I possibly can. I think those are really good traits for people."

But in his teens and 20s, Piniella did not have this perspective of maturity.

Although good prospects in talent-laden organizations often spent three seasons in Triple-A well into the late

20th century, Piniella heard that his long tenure in the high minors was largely due to his temper.

"Everywhere I played," Piniella told *New York Times* confidant Murray Chass in 1974, "they talked to me about it [the temper]. 'We know you can do this and that.' they said, 'but you've got to control your temper.' People have told me it kept me out of the majors a couple of years."

But he could not change his basic nature. Even as big leaguer in his mid-30s, Piniella believed the tantrums improved his concentration.

"At times, I need something to get me going," he told Chass in 1979. "If I become passive, I don't play as well. I need an outburst to get my adrenaline gong. Some players, if they have an outburst, lose their train of thought. I think better because of my outburst."

Piniella produced on the field most of his career, so his tantrums were tolerated. Longtime Yankees trainer Gene Monahan, once sprayed by a busted cup of Gatorade knocked off the bat rack when Piniella slammed his bat on it, is used to providing a bedside manner to his players. He figured Piniella was better off venting than keeping his frustrations confined.

"I think it's better out than in for a lot of guys," Monahan said. "As long as Lou had the capability to vent, no matter who was around, that made him more comfortable. It made him play the game more relaxed."

In fact, the venting, whether on the field, in the dugout or in the clubhouse—attacking the food spread, for example—loosened up his teammates and provided more grist for those who wanted to author sequels to Joe Garagiola's *Baseball Is a Funny Game*. In keeping with his here-and-now style, Piniella rarely told such volcanic anecdotes, but did chuckle early in the 2008 season when the subject of his frequent destruction of dugout water coolers was recalled. Piniella bought several of the damaged coolers over the years and shipped them home to Tampa. He said if he had more foresight, he would have sold them on eBay.

Piniella throwing his bat or punching a dugout wall after an out was a staple. Johnny Lipon installed a punching bag in the corner of the dugout in Portland as an alternative to hitting concrete.

But sometimes, Piniella got far more creative in channeling his anger over failure. One day in Selma, Alabama, in 1962, he was peeved over taking a called strike three with the bases loaded. As a teammate tossed him his glove to run to the outfield after that half-inning, he heaved it in a water barrel from which the players drank. Leaning into the barrel to retrieve the glove, Piniella stumbled in headfirst. As the teammate tried to pull him out, the barrel tipped over and the soaked outfielder was on display for the entertainment of the fans.

A year later, playing for the Senators in the minor leagues, Piniella was so upset at striking out to end a loss that he ripped an adjoining showerhead out of the wall in the locker room, stranding manager Archie Wilson in mid-stream. Equally angered, Wilson made Piniella fetch six buckets of water so he could complete his shower. Sweet Lou also kicked the trainer's bag in the dugout, breaking a jar of acid that burned a hole through the bag's fabric. When the trainer picked up the bag after the game, the contents spilled to the floor, several of the items breaking.

In 1967 Piniella went after even bigger game—the outfield fence. After one inopportune rally-killing strikeout for Portland, he charged off full speed when he took his defensive position. Piniella gave the portable fence a good, swift kick, and it gave way, crashing down around him.

Two other players were required to rescue Piniella by pulling the boards off him.

There seemingly was no end to the creativity of Piniella's temper as he established himself in the majors.

"There was a little commode right around the corner of the dugout in the runway to the Kansas City clubhouse," said longtime Royals announcer Denny Mathews. "It was a phone-booth-sized commode for the convenience of the players. The story goes that Lou grounded into double plays twice in two at-bats. Frustrated, he threw his batting helmet into the toilet and flushed it. Of course the helmet was spinning around and didn't go anywhere. He took his bat and started to plunge it [again to no avail]. The guys in the dugout were waiting for the next explosion; they were rolling around. They loved it."

One day, anyone walking behind the leftfield fence at Kansas City's Municipal Stadium would have had a unique souvenir, remembered Bert Blyleven.

"Lou got so frustrated he drop-kicked his glove over the fence," he said. "They didn't have any bleachers. The game was delayed because Lou had his tantrum. We all signaled field goal. He took every at-bat like it was his last. I would love to have a guy like that play behind me."

Blyleven also talked his way out of seeing Piniella's anger very up close and personal.

"He was the only one who made a couple of steps out toward the mound on me," he said. "I threw a fastball up and in, and then came back with a breaking ball that accidentally went over his head. He said something to me. We exchanged words and I told him if I'm going to hit you, I'm going to hit you with a fastball."

Piniella did not desire to fight Jack McKeon in the same manner, but he did the next best thing—a sit-down strike at the end of the 1973 season. The future "Trader Jack" and Piniella simply did not get along well after McKeon took over as Royals manager in '73, at a time when Piniella's performance slipped.

"I didn't like his manner, his tone of voice, his sarcasm—and the feeling was mutual," Piniella said in *Sweet Lou.* "He didn't like me very much. I just couldn't play for the man."

The conflict came to a head when McKeon started young outfielder Jim Wohlford in place of Piniella against three White Sox lefties in September 1973. But when Rangers right-hander Jim Bibby, whose sometimes awry control meant risking being hit, was scheduled to start, Piniella was put back in the lineup. Piniella told McKeon he'd refuse to play. The Royals took the field minus a leftfielder that night, because McKeon had not told Wohlford he was a last-minute starter due to Piniella's jab action.

A path out of Kansas City was inevitable, and it turned out to be lucky for Piniella. He got entrée to the biggest stage in baseball via a deal with the Yankees that swapped elderly reliever Lindy McDaniel to the Royals for Piniella and pitcher Ken Wright.

"There will be a lot of fur coats, a lot of special things for us, in New York," Piniella told his wife during his first Bronx Bombers spring training in '74. "It's great to be young and a Yankee."

Piniella's arrival followed that of George Steinbrenner as majority Yankees owner. The fiery outfielder quickly became a Steinbrenner favorite after only two minor irritating events. Steinbrenner, a stickler for military-style neatness and grooming, ordered Piniella to trim his 1970s-style modish long hair. The owner also dissuaded Piniella from suing the *New York Daily News* over inadvertently showing the player naked in the background of a front-page locker-room photo.

The always-tough Yankee Stadium fans quickly joined Steinbrenner in a huge Piniella fan club. Chants from thousands crooning "Lou-u-u-u" for the outfielder's heroics became a ballpark staple. Hitting .305 in his first New York season in 1974 did not hurt his image.

"The fans in New York are so knowledgeable," Gene Monahan said. "They could see the game within the game—how he played rightfield."

Piniella would face only one setback in his eventual 11-season run as a Yankees player. Due to an inner-ear problem, he suffered his worst season in 1975, batting just .196 in 74 games. His time on the pines rankled him so much that two months into the season, he asked general manager Gabe Paul for a trade to the Los Angeles Angels. Fortunately, for the well-being of Piniella's career, Paul did not follow through.

Piniella's immediate salvation was the arrival of Billy Martin as Yankees manager, his Martin's dream job, for the final 56 games of the 1975 season. The biggest Piniella fan also would be the most controversial Yankee of his era—and a kindred soul, competitively. Piniella and Martin quickly had a meeting of the minds.

"Billy would migrate to these kind of guys," Monahan said of the resident students of baseball. "And they would migrate back, picking up little things about the game. Billy would share things about the game. Lou would be thinking about the other seven, eight guys in the lineup. He was like another coach."

Piniella treated his time in baseball as a continuing-education process. Martin was a gifted teacher tutoring a gifted student.

"Billy was also the kind of guy who recognized talent in people," said Yankees then–media relations director Mickey Morabito, now the Oakland Athletics' traveling secretary. "I've never been around a manager who could get the best out of teams by adapting himself to the kind of players he had. He just recognized Lou was an intelligent player.

"Lou was the kind of guy who soaked everything in as a player. Billy was probably the most brilliant one he played under. He'd glean things from everyone. Just sitting around and talking to him, he was like a sponge. He was always willing to learn new things."

While Piniella soaked up the game's nuances from Martin, he also made friends with the biggest-name Yankees, such as Thurman Munson, Catfish Hunter, Sparky Lyle, and Graig Nettles. He served as a top cutting wit in the clubhouse and beyond, a talent he'd display in give-and-take with the media three decades later.

"He was just so quick," Morabito said. "Some of the best lines you'd hear on the bus would be from Lou. It's a famous story—he and Mickey Rivers went back and forth. They talked about your IQ. Lou said, 'Mickey, you couldn't even spell *IQ*.' Lou also told Catfish Hunter they'd give away construction helmets to all fans in the outfield to protect them from the home runs Catfish gave up."

Piniella contributed with a .281 mark to the Yankees' return to the World Series in 1976 after a 12-year absence. Then he really moved into mainstay status with a .330 mark for the rollicking 1977 team that emblazoned the Bronx Zoo nickname on the franchise amid constant conflict between Martin and newly imported prima donna slugger Reggie Jackson. The constant soap opera made for entertaining summer viewing in 2007 via ESPN's *The Bronx Is Burning* mini-series—an epic tale that Piniella professed not to watch as part of his misdirection style.

One of the funnier segments depicted a late-night visit by Piniella and Thurman Munson to Steinbrenner's suite at Milwaukee's Pfister Hotel, where only two years previous legendary broadcaster Harry Caray and White Sox third baseman Bill Melton engaged in a shoving match over Caray's on-air criticism. Piniella and Munson urged Steinbrenner to return Jackson to the cleanup spot from which Martin had dropped him. In an adjoining suite, Martin somehow overheard the wee-hours conversation, pounded on Steinbrenner's door, and demanded entrance. Piniella and Munson hid in the bathroom, but were discovered by Martin, who felt betrayed by his stars. In 2007 Piniella denied ever hiding in the bathroom, but he consented to the story being included in *Sweet Lou* more than two decades earlier.

Obviously, Piniella took mental notes about how not to run a baseball team from all the Yankees infighting.

"I used to call the whole Billy-George-Reggie thing the 'Vicious Triangle,'" Morabito said. "Each day, you didn't know who was mad at who. One day it would be George and Billy mad at Reggie, another it would be Reggie and George mad at Billy. Lou watched that kind of stuff."

The Martin-Jackson rift was patched up in time for the Yankees to win their first World Series in 15 years in 1977. Piniella then cemented his folk-hero status with a .314 mark frequently batting third in front of Jackson and pulled off perhaps the greatest play of his career—on defense—in the famed October 2, 1978, AL East "Bucky Dent" playoff game in Fenway Park, after the Yankees had stormed back from a 14-game deficit on July 19, under the direction of Bob Lemon, the first of many relief managers for Martin.

With the Yankees holding a 5–4 lead over the Red Sox, Rick Burleson walked with one out in the bottom of the ninth. The late-afternoon sun had been blinding for Piniella in rightfield for three innings. Jerry Remy then lined a ball to right. Piniella lost track of the ball right off the bat in the glare. Almost deking Burleson into thinking he had the ball in sight, Piniella backtracked in the outfield in a desperate attempt to locate the ball. At the last second, Piniella saw the ball land a few feet to his left. He lunged with his glove hand and speared the ball, firing it on a line to third to keep Burleson from advancing beyond second. Piniella called the throw the best of his career.

"He saved the ball game," Gene Monahan said. "Our fans knew that and really took a liking to him."

In keeping with his personal style, the modern-day Piniella doesn't talk about that play nostalgically unless he's interrogated.

Jim Rice's fly to Piniella seconds later would have scored Burleson with the tying run had Piniella not tracked down Remy's hit. Goose Gossage then inflicted one of the worst moments in Red Sox fans' lives by getting Carl Yastrzemski to pop up for the final out.

Piniella also developed a reputation for postseason clutch hitting. He was 10-for-30 against the Royals in the American League Championship Series in 1977 and 1978. He slugged a three-run homer to match Graig Nettles' feat as part of a seven-run fourth inning in a 13–3 victory over the Athletics in the ALCS on October 14, 1981. Six days earlier, his fourth-inning homer against Milwaukee stood up as the winning run in a 3–0 victory in the AL East division playoff. He batted .305 with 2 homers and 6 RBIs in 18 ALCS games.

Piniella also had his World Series moments. He drove in the winning run off the Dodgers' Bob Welch in the 10th inning in a 4–3 victory in Game 4 on October 14, 1978, at

Yankee Stadium. He also was 7-for-16 (.438) with 3 RBIs in 1981 against Los Angeles. Piniella batted .319 with 10 RBIs in 22 World Series games.

The '81 performance was his last in the national spotlight. While a lot of the 1970s New York stars moved on, Piniella would be allowed to retire as a Yankee. Steinbrenner, though, had other plans for him. And the path The Boss prescribed eventually would take Piniella to that little office, stripped of any telling historical artifacts, in Wrigley Field.

BILLY LITE

THERE'S NO ROOM FOR FORMAL SPORTS PSYCHOLOGY OR CEREBRAL ANALYSIS, ACCORDING TO LOU PINIELLA. Just like there's no crying in baseball.

Don't make the mistake of asking Piniella if a team is emotionally ready to win. To the man who has lived almost two-thirds of a century, with the majority of that swinging a bat or matching wits against other managers, baseball is boiled down to basics—pitching, hitting, baserunning, executing.

"I think invariably baseball is not as complicated as you seem to make it," Piniella said on May 17, 2008, smiling as he feigned mock exasperation in his tiny office at Wrigley Field.

"Emotional? Why do we get into the emotional aspects?" he continued. "We can get into the emotional aspects of being married. About making a decision on where you're going to eat. Baseball, you let these guys play and stay out of their way."

But wasn't there an emotional aspect to the Bronx Zoo Yankees, including clutch-hitting outfielder Piniella, in how they alternately dominated, fell back, and rushed from far behind to win a memorable pennant race.

"We had talent and we had confidence, and we expected to win," Piniella said. "Is that emotional? I don't know how to correlate between that and emotion. Do you sob before the ball game? Do you sing out loud? I don't know. Let's drop that subject and go to something else."

But Piniella, the original hyperemotional player, is fated to hear that question repeatedly, as he did a week later.

"Emotion to me is good pitching and good hitting, and solid defense," he said. "I call that emotion. If you want the other kind of emotion, you go to a rock concert . . . or to church. OK? All right."

Even though Sweet Lou disregards creeping intellectualism and psychology in his beloved game, he has succeeded beyond the scope of most managers all-time. With the exception of Tampa Bay from 2003 through 2005, he has crafted winners of all his teams. There is no special formula at work—just a single-minded devotion to winning at all costs. He is a self-professed nonexpert on the fine points of pitching. But put all other aspects of baseball into a percolating stew, and Piniella somehow has the means to nudge it to a delectable final form.

His handling of teams and players has, with a few exceptions, provoked rave reviews from those he has managed. The best endorsement of all comes from a player Piniella groomed from teenage prospect to superstardom.

"I just think he's the best manager in the game, a Hall of Fame manager," said the Yankees' Alex Rodriguez, whom Piniella broke in as a Mariner at the tender age of 18 in 1994. Swamped by the Yankees beat writers in the daily suffocating coverage of the Bombers and eager to retreat to an off-limits area for a mental break one evening in April 2008, A-Rod froze in his tracks and loosened his lips at the opportunity to praise Piniella.

So why is Piniella the best manager in the game?

"Smartest, strategic, recognizes talent, roster evaluation, Lou Piniella's magic. He's the best," Rodriguez said.

And there's more.

"If you want to win and be consistently great, he's the perfect guy," Rodriguez added. "There's no one like Lou Piniella as far as strategy, bullpen management, getting the most out of his players, motivating. He's the greatest."

How Piniella attained such praiseworthy status was through a balancing act that combined a sharp eye, a master's expertise in hitting mechanics, and a fiery attitude that somehow has been fine-tuned over the decades, plus an apprenticeship to a savvy practitioner of managing techniques who himself was tutored by a grand master of the dugout.

"It's a 24-hour job for Lou," said former Cubs manager Lee Elia, who went on to become his hitting and bench coach in Seattle. "He has an insatiable desire to win. Lou can put together a ball club and knows the components to have continuity to score runs and win. He's gifted that way.

"Lou knows how to make pitching changes where the other manager can't counter. He knows matchups. He knows percentages, but has an unbelievable gut feeling. He's just a very, very instinctive, intuitive, intelligent guy. He feels, 'I've got to get this right, I've got to get this right.'"

Confidence, certainly a definable emotion—there's that word he doesn't like in connection to baseball—enabled Piniella to get to the juncture where the Cubs zeroed in on him as the man who would lead them to a World Series, after previous ballyhooed hirings of Don Baylor and Dusty Baker backfired. To get to the point where he's perceived to stand out above all his contemporaries, he had to purge much of his infamous "red-ass" emotion—that cursed word again. Heaving bases down the rightfield line, tossing his cap and kicking dirt on umpires makes for good theater, but it doesn't by itself win a World Series.

To succeed, he has also exorcised two, well, emotions that most of us are only able to mask: fear and doubt. No one ever called his managerial style "safety first." One underplayed example took place on August 14, 2007, when he left an ineffective Carlos Zambrano in the game an extra inning, in the seventh at Wrigley Field, to work out the kinks in Zambrano's arm slot. The only place to properly fine-tune such mechanics, Piniella reasoned, was live game action—even if Zambrano would give up six runs and 13 hits in an eventual 6–5 Cubs loss. Maybe a fresh reliever shuts the Reds down if Piniella pulls Zambrano earlier. Maybe not. The manager moves ahead without caution flags dotting his path.

"Let me tell you something about managing up here," Piniella said in an aside in his dugout five days after the Zambrano outing. "If you're scared to lose a game, you're going to lose a whole lot of them. Sometimes you lose a little skirmish to win a battle, and sometimes you lose a battle trying to win a war. You can't be scared to lose up here on a particular day."

A related philosophy, verbalized in 2008, used the old battle analogies.

"I'm from the school that you try to win a war," he said. "You don't want to win a little battle here, a little skirmish there. You try to look at the longer-term picture and what the ramifications are of the things you do or don't do. My job as manager of this team is to ensure the long-term prospects, to be on top at the end. I've got to weigh all these things. If corrections need to be made, they'll be made."

Baseball 101 is the only class Piniella ever took—no advanced courses full of thick analysis and politicking. That education was reflected in his daily persona around the clubhouse at Wrigley Field and on the road. His presence is felt but not seen until the Cubs take the field to stretch before batting practice.

Piniella holes up in his office with his scouting reports, lineups, and crossword puzzles. The lone daily exceptions seem to be a couple of forays, adorned in a T-shirt and skivvies, into the lounge for a snack. He doesn't flit about the locker room like Ozzie Guillen, his 2007 and 2008 White Sox counterpart and admirer, who often could be found encamped by a player's locker or entertaining media with impromptu, rapid-fire diatribe.

"My philosophy on the clubhouse—it's the players' domain," Piniella said. "It's their second home. I want to make it as comfortable as I can for them. You won't see me in the clubhouse very much at all. I'll be in my office or the coaches' quarters. When I was playing, I didn't want the manager coming around all the time. The least I saw of the manager, probably the better I liked it."

And, yes, he disdained taking the daily temperature of locker room—can't we use another word?—emotions.

"We play so many games that if you needed to do that, you'd need a team of psychologists and psychiatrists in that clubhouse," he said. "The best way to look at a baseball is cut your season into ten 16-game segments, and you see how they do over a 16-game span. Daily, you can't measure it, too many ups and downs."

He is not Howard Hughes, isolated in the penthouse in Las Vegas, but Piniella is unseen much of the pre- and postgame time. His coaches, just like Hughes' assistants, scurry about to do his bidding, and they scarcely have time to stop to chew the fat in the manner of tobacco-chewin',' Jack Daniels-lovin' coaches since the game began. Piniella does not come out, and in turn few turn the corner into his office.

"I've only had two players in my office since I started here," he said in the spring of 2008. For a player, a Piniella office visit must be an Adult Depends experience, given the man's decades-long reputation for temper. One confirmed visit was Kerry Wood in spring training 2007 to explain comments in a *Chicago Sun-Times* story. Another was closer Ryan Dempster later that season, summoned to be informed he was to become a starter, but with that decision rescinded 15 minutes later.

Piniella conducts most of his one-on-one communication with players outside. After time spent on the bench doing his pregame media session, pregame radio show with Ron Santo, and additional small talk, he moves about the field, starting out at the batting cage, then wandering out to third base, shortstop, and eventually leftfield as he checks out his Cubs. After batting practice he quickly returns to his office, leaving the players to their own style of preparation. With the exception of Don Baylor, he might be the most distant manager in Cubs history to all but a trusted circle of coaches and team officials. There is no entrée by the media to his office without prior arrangement or the occasional decision to hold his pregame briefing on day games after night games, or when rain washes out batting practice.

But there were necessary tradeoffs. The Cubs hired Piniella to drag them to the World Series, not to be the No. 1 ballpark politician. They hired him for his baseball intellect twinned with his famed intensity. With the exception of Tampa Bay, his teams have typically been on the far side of .500, often in the playoffs and once a world champion.

"Yes, I'm intense, but no, I'm not as intense as I used to be," he told Frank Deford on HBO's *Real Sports.* "I've changed. People in Chicago probably expect me . . . I'm going to throw a base or something. No. I don't like that part of me. I get envious a little. My good buddy Tony La Russa, Hall of Fame career manager . . . they describe him [as] pensive, studious. Describe me—fiery. I won 1,500 games as a manager, not because I throw bases, but because I know what the hell I'm doing."

He professes to be even-keeled, to be immune to the ups and downs of the season. Working in the Cubs environment, unlike any other in baseball due to the franchise's crazy-quilt history, was a true culture shock. After winning as a player with the Yankees and a manager in several other locales, he just could not understand the premature venture into nirvana. He just shrugged while urging caution.

"You people make too much out of first place, first of all," he said on the night of August 1, 2007, when the Cubs finally climbed to the top of the National League Central by percentage points after trailing by 8½ games six weeks previously.

"Right now it looks good, but we got a lot of baseball to play. You can't get caught up in this. You got to keep focused on the game in hand, on the team you're playing and forget everything else. It works much better that way."

Then, when the Cubs zoomed to a hot start six weeks into 2008, he argued against the townsfolk and media getting too giddy—or giggly.

"We're only in May," he said. "You don't win pennants in May, you win them in September. You get in position to win them in May, and that's what we are—in position. Nothing more, nothing less. You can get giggly before you clinch, but that's in September.

"We're a little more of a marked team. For people to make those conclusions [the Cubs are the pennant favorite], if they feel that good about it, they should load up in Vegas. But I don't feel that way. I prefer to be a little more cautious, a little more sane, and just play these games one at a time. Continue to play good baseball. If you continue to do these things and not get too carried away, the press clippings, what people say, you're much better suited to win."

Yankees owner George Steinbrenner was so impressed with Piniella's intensity and baseball savvy that the Boss suggested to Billy Martin that he take the outfielder under his wing to train him for an eventual managing job. The volatile Martin had learned much of the game's nuances in the 1950s from Casey Stengel, who regarded Martin almost as a son. So some of what Piniella knows—and maybe even, spiritually, his sometimes fractured syntax—filtered down by osmosis from Ol' Case.

"Billy was Casey's protégé and Lou was Billy's," said Gene Monahan. "It [managerial savvy] was passed down through the generations."

Piniella was a willing student who took mental notes. His teammates, who had witnessed Piniella incessantly practicing his batting stance, even in the outfield between batters, picked up on his student-of-the-game stance and figured he might be their dugout boss one day.

"I think the guys knew someday it could happen," said then-Yankees lefty Dave Righetti, now Giants pitching coach. "He just had the personality for it."

"Billy was a really good field manager," Piniella said. "I thought he ran a baseball game as well as anyone in that era. He was sharp. He knew when to pull a pitcher, when to steal a base. He knew when to squeeze in a run. He had a great sense for the unexpected. I learned a lot of baseball from Billy. I played for Bob Lemon, Yogi Berra, Dick Howser, I played for some real good managers. I played for Joe Gordon. You learn something from everybody.

"The guy I probably manage more like anybody else is Billy. I like an aggressive style of play. I like to take chances. I play my entire roster and pitch everyone who's available. I differ from Billy in one regard. Billy used to pitch the hot reliever, where I tend to try to pick and choose a little bit more and try to keep everybody fresh."

While certainly at home with beer and other stronger libations, Piniella never adopted Martin's excesses with the bottle or quick-trigger temper with his fists.

"Off the field, Billy had his problems, obviously," Piniella said. "It's a shame, because he was a good person. He couldn't control one of his vices, and that was really his downfall. But he was a good man. We won a lot of games. I played for him three different times. I coached for him as a manager. I replaced him as a manager, he replaced me. I was his general manager. I knew Billy really well. A good person with one vice that caused him problems. It's a shame. If it hadn't been for that, he'd have won a lot more ball games and he'd be in the Hall of Fame."

But Martin was not the only World Series–winning managerial mind that Piniella tapped.

"One guy that I have a particular fondness for and would take time to talk to me as a young manager on what to do and what not to do was Sparky Anderson with the Tigers," he said. "He gave me nice pointers when I could take some liberties, when I didn't need to run, the ins and outs of the ball game, talked to me about the bullpen. He was good."

Piniella's formal apprenticeship had taken place as a much-praised hitting coach under Yogi Berra in 1984 and '85. He finally advanced to the manager's job at age 42 for the 1986 season. Piniella still had his player's fiery behavior ingrained when he took over a team, saddled with high-priced free agents, past the prime of the Bronx Zoo era. He was still smack-dab in an era in which Steinbrenner micromanaged the Yankees baseball operation. Piniella fielded phone calls in the dugout during games from Steinbrenner.

"I know that one of the things he had to learn is patience, pitching patience, young players patience," Monahan said.

If Piniella the player was formerly just tough on him-self, as manager he imposed his fiery persona on 25 players. He was not afraid to call any of them out.

"If he was mad at a player or mad at a situation, he'd just let it out," said Yankees coach Bobby Meacham, then a New York infielder. "As players, we'd just deal with it."

If a Yankee got called into Piniella's office, he was being taken to the woodshed.

"I was one of them," Meacham said. "He was talking to me about different things, my reaction to making errors, worried about me not caring out there. He wanted me to show my emotions like he did."

So when Meacham might blow a bubble after he made an error, Piniella objected. "You want me to throw my glove or something?" Meacham remembered asking. Piniella said why not—just show some emotion.

"Lou was one of those guys who you felt he was like your brother and he was fun," Righetti said. "In one sec-ond, though, if you were unprofessional about something, he would get your ass. He didn't care who you were. He liked emotion. He liked guys who showed emotion."

In the end, however, players could handle a tough manager better than a milquetoast who sits back and lets things spin out of control.

"One thing that it was clear, he wants to win," Meacham said. "I really don't think players care whether their manager yells at them or puts his arms around them. I don't think they care if he yells at an umpire. They just want a guy who wants to win. That's why players want to play for Lou. A team sees how bad Lou wants to win, and that team exudes the same attitude."

Yankees players soon discovered Piniella had their back during a stressful time when Steinbrenner micromanaged and second-guessed freely.

Righetti, by then one of the game's best closers, recalled a tumultuous day in 1986 when he served up a game-tying grand slam in Toronto after he had not warmed up. Piniella's first choice in relief suddenly was unable to work due to a tight arm, necessitating that Righetti be rushed into the game. Already under fire from Steinbrenner, an upset Righetti fired the ball over the rightfield wall, earning an ejection from plate umpire Don Denkinger.

"We ended up winning the game, but it unfolded that everyone wants my head—the writers, the front office," Righetti said. "It was a big deal. But Lou came right out to say this is my guy, I'm sticking with him. He put his career on the line, especially in New York. Every year there was a different manager. For him to do that, you never forget that. I also felt a responsibility, not only for the team and myself, but for this guy, one way or another. It helped a lot of guys. It lifted the whole team. He did a helluva job with us."

But Piniella couldn't tell Steinbrenner he could win it all. He endured poor timing in trying to win and thus placate the owner during his first two managerial seasons. The Yankees were stuck in baseball's toughest division, with strong competitors in Toronto, Boston, and Milwaukee. It was a decade too soon for a great, second-best record to gain rewards through the wild card. The 1986 Yankees won 90 and finished second. A year later, as Toronto and Detroit played out a nerve-racking race to the final day, the Yankees finished in fourth with 89 wins.

"We needed the wild card," said Meacham. "If it wasn't for the wild card, the Red Sox would have never won their first World Series. We were in a great division. In our division, the leader had to win 95 games. We missed out. It's just the way it goes.

"It would have lifted a lot of pressure from a lot of great people who deserved to play in those postseasons," Righetti said. "In spring training, we heard all the interviews—we got to win 95 to 100 games this year, we have to, we have to. It was a tough, tough division."

Since the Yankees did not come in first despite the game's biggest payroll, the ever-restless Steinbrenner made the inevitable change, knowing Martin was always around like the ultimate managerial comfort food. Piniella was kicked upstairs to the general manager's job for 1988 with Martin returning again to the dugout for a staggering fifth time since 1975.

But Martin's last stint as Yankees skipper lasted only through a series of one-run losses at Detroit, after which Piniella came back down from the executive suite for a less successful 93-game stint as manager. He then served as a front-office advisor in 1989, after which he caught his first bit of wanderlust away from the familiar chaos of New York—reviving the Cincinnati Reds, crippled by Pete Rose's gambling scandal.

Piniella arrived at just the right time as manager. The Reds and New York Mets had traded left-handed closers in the 1989 off-season, hard-throwing Randy Myers coming to the Queen City in exchange for fellow southpaw John Franco. Myers soon joined homegrown Reds Norm

Charlton and Rob Dibble to form an impregnable bullpen nicknamed the Nasty Boys. But Piniella was the missing link, an all-business, all-winning manager without the side-shows and distractions of Rose.

"I always loved a manager who was into a game winning or losing as much as the players," said then-Reds rightfielder Paul O'Neill. "When Lou came over, we won immediately. We fed off his emotion. He brought an atmosphere of winning. He brought that from New York—the attitude that winning every single day was important."

Piniella had a period of adjustment to managing in the National League after never working for an NL franchise either as a player, coach or manager.

"He didn't know how the game was played in this league," said longtime Reds announcer Marty Brennaman, who became close with Piniella and to this day rates him as his favorite Reds manager. "So he was smart enough to surround himself with National League coaches and keep his mouth shut and listen to their advice about the way the game was played in this league, until he knew how it was played. Then, it was his baby. He accepted the fact he had to learn."

Once Piniella grasped the National League, he plunged full-steam into its style. The '90 Reds featured four players—Barry Larkin, Eric Davis, Billy Hatcher, and Chris Sabo—with at least 21 stolen bases. Only two, Davis and Sabo, slugged more than 20 homers. Piniella verbalized such a preferred style for all his teams 17 years later.

"I like certain types of teams to manage," he said. "I'm basically a guy who doesn't like to sit and wait for a three-run homer. I like to be able to force the issue a little bit, I like to be able to hit and run a little bit, I like to be able to steal a little bit. That does a lot of different things for a baseball team. It makes the infielders bunch a little more. It makes pitchers throw more fastballs, it makes them slide-step, they don't have as much stuff to the plate. The catcher doesn't want guys running on him, so he invariably wants more fastballs. It makes it easier from an offensive sort of thing."

With the speedy, hustling lineup, the high-octane bullpen and decent starting pitching, the Reds shocked Piniella's childhood chum Tony La Russa. After upsetting the Pittsburgh Pirates, managed by former La Russa aide Jim Leyland, in the National League Championship Series, La Russa's much-favored Oakland Athletics were swept away in four games in the World Series. Piniella finally had his ring as a manager to match his pair won as a Yankees player.

Although the world championship should have bought him a near-lifetime pass in Cincinnati, Piniella would be gone within two years. His ultimate boss was thrifty, clumsy-mouthed widow Marge Schott, who loved her pooping-on-Astroturf St. Bernards far more than any of her employees. A poor year in 1991 was followed by a revival to a 90–72, second-place NL West finish in 1992. Schott would not discuss a contract extension during the season. So immediately afterward, Piniella quit—and set the pattern for the remainder of his managerial career. Unless the situation suited him to a T, he would not linger or let aggravations fester. He'd just walk away.

"I truly believe his run in Cincinnati would have been a whole lot longer had he been treated with greater respect by Marge Schott," Brennaman said. "Lou was a very sensitive guy. He needed the person who signed his paycheck to say every now and then you're doing a great job. She [Schott] was not that kind of person. She didn't say that to anybody. It was a terrible loss. He made up his mind to leave and she tried to talk him out of it, but he made his mind up he was leaving.

"I don't think he'd say it today because he's managing in Chicago, but he said Cincinnati was his favorite city of all time. His wife [Anita] said the same thing. She loved it."

Two days after season's end, Schott met Piniella in his office. He delivered his parting shot to Schott: "Stick the job up your ass," according to *Dayton Daily News* veteran Reds beat writer Hal McCoy.

Piniella had no problem finding gainful employment quickly. Needing a jolt once and for all, the struggling Seattle Mariners hired him. He was now a six-hour flight from home in Tampa, but he could not resist the challenge of jump-starting a franchise that had just one winning season in its previous 16 years of existence.

He was blessed with two of the best players in the game—Ken Griffey Jr. and Randy Johnson. Both came through big for Piniella in 1993, when the Mariners cracked the break-even mark again at 82–80. Griffey belted 45 homers, while Johnson went 19–8.

Piniella first had to purge the losing atmosphere. In his first spring training, the new Peoria, Arizona, stadium had not yet been built. All the Mariners' Cactus League games were on the road. After one bad loss, the team bus was stuck in traffic on its way back to Peoria. In an empty field off the highway, some kids were playing baseball. Spotting the pick-up game, Piniella asked the driver to stop. He stood up, flipped his cap on backward, and began yelling at the players that he should let them play with the kids, and they'd get their "asses beat" by the kids the way they were playing now. Piniella then sat down, the bus drove on, and all was quiet except a few snickers from veterans near the back.

"He didn't like losing, from Day One," Griffey Jr. said. "He didn't accept losing. He felt if you don't play hard for me, I'll sit you. Give me 100 percent, I'll back you. If you don't, I won't back you."

Piniella would not easily forget Junior, especially after he clubbed his 600th homer in 2008. He believed Griffey should have been way past 700, anyway.

"I really enjoyed the years I spent with him in Seattle," he said. "There's no question in my mind he would have [challenged the home-run record with good health]. Just the time he was with me he suffered a couple of serious injuries. They took their toll on him. When I had him in Seattle, he was the best player in baseball in my opinion, and that was when Barry Bonds was in his prime. That's a pretty strong statement. Junior was a special player."

Griffey and Johnson would be joined to form a triumvirate of stars on July 8, 1994, when Alex Rodriguez, then just the third 18-year-old shortstop to play since 1900, made his big-league debut. Despite status as baseball's top prodigy at the time, Piniella did not coddle him, screaming at him in "tons" of instances, Rodriguez said. "So do Bobby Knight and Coach K [Mike Krzyzewski]. Most of the great ones get on your ass a little bit."

A-Rod would not have had it any other way.

"He was great," he said in hindsight 14 years later. "He gave me tough love. He made me the player I am today. I loved him."

When informed of Rodriguez's "tough-love" compliment, Piniella had a slightly different description.

"When you care about a person and you know he has the ability," he said, "you try to extract it from him and put out the realities. Don't sugar-coat. I don't think I'm tough. There's certain things you have to do as a young player to establish yourself. We try to get you to that point as quickly as possible.

"If I didn't think a player had the ability or talent [he would not be tough]. When you realize how talented the possibilities Alex had at a young age, you want to extract that as quickly as possible."

Piniella had a bad-cop/tender-cop moment with A-Rod on August 4, 1995. The 20-year-old shortstop struck out on three pitches against Oakland's Dennis Eckersley. "Gosh, son, I love you and all that, but you've got to give me better swings than that," Piniella hollered from the other end of the dugout at Rodriguez. Tears began welling up in Rodriguez's eyes after the put-down and he put on sunglasses to hide his emotions. Suddenly, Piniella walked over to Rodriguez and kissed his forehead—just about the last thing anyone would expect the firebrand manager to do. "In that one moment, he showed me toughness and he showed me love," Rodriguez recalled.

Most players on Piniella's teams voice similar opinions as Rodriguez, Griffey, and the 1980s Yankees about the manager. Some pitchers' ears may have been singed by Piniella's verbal dressing-downs, and reliever Rob Dibble was literally jumped by the manager in 1992 in a rare physical outburst. But few negative reviews and fewer instances of clubhouse dissension have marked Piniella's stewardships.

One notable exception was outfielder Jacque Jones, who refused to talk about his 2007 Cubs days with Piniella early in the 2008 season while briefly playing for the Detroit Tigers. A 27-homer producer as the Cubs' shaky-fielding rightfielder in 2006, Jones totally crumbled at the plate in the first two months of the next season, was busted all the way down to 25th man, and was nearly traded in early June to the Florida Marlins. Reporters kept a vigil by Jones at his locker before one game when the trade seemed moments away from being official. When the deal fell apart,

Piniella announced Jones would play and become an integral part of his roster. During the remainder of the season, Jones was the regular centerfielder and revived all but his power, becoming one of the top second-half clutch hitters in the NL Central title season.

"I really hurt for a player who's not playing much," Piniella insisted a month after the aborted Jones trade. "My coaches can tell you that. I find every way possible that I can to figure out how I can get them into a major-league lineup. I know they work hard and I know they want to get a chance to perform also. As a player I wasn't an All-Star [except once, in 1972]. I was a solid player. There were times I rode the bench, too. It's no fun when you sit on the bench. Like I tell the players, stay ready because if you go out there and you help us win a baseball game, you're going to get a chance to play."

The players found few shades of gray with Piniella. They knew if they produced, he'd find a spot for them. If not . . .

"With the players, I am a little demanding," he said. "But my mom told me when I was young, 'The baby that doesn't cry doesn't get the milk.' You have to be fair, honest, open, available. I have no doghouse at all. If I have a problem it's over with. We go forward. Be ready to play at any time. I take pride in teams going out there playing hard, having fun and going out there in a very professional way and trying to beat the other team."

Piniella put this philosophy into practice to enable the Mariners to finally grow up as a franchise. With Sweet Lou at the helm, they were no longer a poorly run, obscure club, despite ranking as the most geographically remote in the majors off in the Pacific Time Zone. Seattle burst onto the scene in the strike-truncated 1995 season, fashioning one of the greatest late-season comebacks in history.

Dropping to a season-low 43–46 record, 13 games behind the Anaheim Angels on August 2, the Mariners suddenly charged forward 1951 New York Giants–style as the Angels collapsed. They finally tied the Angels for the lead on September 20, took a three-game lead in a 10–2 victory over the Angels six days later, and ended up in a dead-heat at season's end October 1. Then, there was a one-game playoff at the Kingdome on October 2. Johnson came through magnificently, winning 9–1 before 52,356.

Then the Mariners solidified Seattle major-league baseball with a stunning divisional series comeback that delayed the start of the late-20th-century Yankees mini-dynasty. After dropping the first two games at Yankee Stadium, the Mariners stormed back to win three in a row at the Kingdome, with Johnson pressed into service in the ninth inning of Game 5 to nail it down. The Mariners' four-games-to-two loss to the Cleveland Indians in the championship series was almost anticlimactic. Better yet, other than a couple of seasonal dips, they remained a contender for the rest of Piniella's managerial tenure, surviving the trades of Griffey and Johnson and the free-agent defection of Rodriguez to the Texas Rangers. They racked up a record-tying 116-victory season in 2001, the year after A-Rod's departure.

During his time in the Emerald City, Piniella shaped the modus operandi that he'd take with him as manager of Tampa Bay and Chicago. He assembled his own posse of coaches—a staple of long-running managers—who would move on with him to his future employers. They included John McLaren, Lee Elia, Matt Sinatro, and Gerald Perry. The latter two eventually came with him to the Cubs.

The best portrait of the Piniella style, first clearly displayed with the Mariners, is a chief executive officer type who does not micromanage and often seems above the fray, yet sees all and hears all. By the best estimate, Piniella is the opposite of Dick Vermeil, the maniacal coaching archetype who'd sleep in his office. He doesn't keep the longest ballpark hours. He has delegated to all his coaches, who spend valuable time working with players rather than exchanging hot air in meetings with the manager.

"I'm a little bit of a perfectionist," Piniella said in 2007. "I prepare myself very well. I have a real, real good coaching staff. I give them all the autonomy I can to do their jobs. My posture with them is, 'How can I help you do your job better?' "

Sinatro, a former backup catcher who became the Cubs' first-base coach, has been with Piniella the longest, since 1995. Piniella's right-hand man in Chicago, he seconded his boss's description of the flow chart.

"He's very demanding, but gives coaches their space," Sinatro said. "He lets us take charge of our area. If it's not doing well, he'll tell us to pick it up.

"In spring training, the coaches all meet. He'll come in, but it's our show. He'll tell us what he expects and then gives us full reign to do what we need. He lets us be accountable for our area. I think it's healthy. If an area is not working the way he wants it, he'll sit us down and ask how we['re] going to get this right. He's not a big meetings guy at all. He's very prepared, but he's not a big computer guy.

"You'll see him at spring training walk out [onto the field]. Trust me, he doesn't miss a beat. You may think he's not watching your area, and a week later he'll bring up something, with the catchers. He's very much in control, but the nice thing about it is he lets the coaches have their area."

Piniella has no problems turning over the reins of his team's most vital area to a younger, less experienced big-league coach. Bryan Price was promoted at age 38 to the

Mariners' pitching coach's job in 2001 after a long stint in that team's minor league system. Price obviously was ready, as the M's improved their ERA by nearly a run from 2000 to win the AL ERA title with a 3.54 mark in 2001, a major component of Seattle's astonishing 116-victory regular season.

"My first year, my first day I was hired, Lou said you have total autonomy to run spring training the way you want to, their conditioning, throwing programs," said Price, whose tenure as Arizona Diamondbacks pitching coach began in 2008. "As we get to the back end of spring training, we want to get these guys lined up in order that he was going to set as manager for rotation. We didn't talk much [about] their throwing schedules, how many pitches they were throwing, developing their breaking balls. That was my job, to get them in shape by Opening Day."

Interestingly, Piniella's coaches haven't been cronies from the old neighborhood in Tampa or his Yankees playing or managing days. He simply linked up with them on his long managerial road and added them to his kitchen cabinet. Lee Elia, his first bench coach with the Mariners who stuck with Piniella through his Tampa days, met him while he was Yankees' third-base coach in 1989. Piniella, by then a part-time broadcaster and team consultant, was sent out to Seattle to work with a slumping Don Mattingly. Elia and Piniella got to talking and hit it off. Three years later, Piniella hired him as bench coach. "We became hand and glove," Elia said. "They wanted a former manager [Elia had piloted the Cubs and Phillies] as bench coach. He'd listen to my suggestions, for sure."

Sinatro had just finished a decade-long career as a backup catcher with the Mariners when Piniella arrived as manager. He was given a choice to manage in the minors or work as Piniella's advance scout. Sinatro picked the latter job "and I made the right choice," he said. In 1995, Piniella asked Sinatro to join the Mariners coaching staff, and as of 2008 he had been with him ever since. Meanwhile, Cubs hitting coach Gerald Perry's first year in such a job was with the Mariners in 2000, five years after he retired as a player who had never previously crossed paths with Piniella. The only holdover coach from the Dusty Baker era to Sweet Lou's Cubs regime was pitching coach Larry Rothschild, with whom Piniella had a longtime connection. Rothschild, a transplanted Chicagoan to Tampa, had broken into the majors as a coach working the bullpen for Piniella's Reds in 1990.

Both Sinatro and Price said one of Piniella's strengths has been understanding matchups both ways—hitter-to-pitcher and pitcher-to-hitter. The matchups would go into Piniella's lineups, with which he constantly tinkered in his first season running the Cubs.

"He's always thinking," Sinatro said. "I've been with him before where he's writing up 10 different lineups on a piece of scrap paper, moving it around and staring at it."

Piniella always had two lineups ready for each game. If his team just recalled a position player from the minors, he'd often put him in the lineup immediately to see what he could do and avoid rustiness on the bench.

"It doesn't take that long," he said. "I usually think about the lineup the night before, so by the time I get to the ballpark, I've got a lineup that's made out. And then I have a backup lineup just in case I need to change it. If somebody has an injury or somebody needs a day off, whatever, I have a backup lineup. If the team is playing well, you just come back and duplicate the lineup from the day before and that's the end of it."

Admittedly, the technicalities of pitching were never Piniella's strength, and he admits it. He has constantly deferred questions about mechanics and command to the pitching coach.

"I rely on my pitching coach to handle the pitching," he told the *New York Times'* Murray Chass in 2001. "All I do is utilize it. We've got a darn good pitching coach here in Bryan Price. He does an outstanding job with our pitchers. I basically stay out of it. My only involvement is using the pitchers and sometimes telling them how to pitch hitters. Outside of that, that's an area I stay away from.'

"You give me good pitching, I can handle it. You give me bad pitching, I'm going to struggle with it just like everybody else."

Price actually learned from Piniella about the art of the matchup.

"He taught me a lot, especially a lot about bullpen usage," Price said. "He runs a great bullpen. He matches up really well. He's thinking about what the other manager's potentially doing with his left-right combos off the bench. He's outstanding."

The Piniella style can work with a competitive roster. His only failure came when he took a calculated risk to leave Seattle after the 2002 season to return home to Tampa to assume the manager's job with the Rays, then called the Devil Rays. He was promised a financial commitment to upgrade in the roster by founding owner Vince Naimoli. But the only upgrade was Piniella himself. While Naimoli busied himself screaming at fans who chided him for his thrifty ways and kicked a Mets scout out of Tropicana Field for using the owner's suite bathroom, Piniella got increasingly more despondent over his first stint dwelling in a divisional basement. The surge of home-grown talent that coalesced into the Rays' surprising 2008 season would not come fast enough to help Piniella.

His biggest accomplishment in the three seasons he managed Tampa Bay was setting a franchise record for victories with 70. That's not the Piniella everyone knew, and he soon acted very much unlike his fiery personality.

"It was eatin' on him," said catcher Toby Hall, who played across town from Piniella for two years with the White Sox. "The frustration started after the first year. After the 70 wins, you'd figure they'd step up. They didn't. He lost his fire. Those days you go out there, [he should be] yelling and screaming, it stopped. You thought, Gosh, it's eatin' on him. You'd see three days' growth of beard. When you get a guy who has a résumé like his and is a born winner come into his hometown, and all he does is lose, it's tough."

By the end of the third season, Piniella was "very quiet," said Hall. "He wasn't the same Lou. There'd be some days I'd hit him on the side of butt, say 'Here we go.' "

But the only "go" was out the door for Piniella with a year remaining on his contract. There wasn't enough money in the world that could compensate him for another year of losing.

The Rays' loss ended up the Cubs' gain after a season of Fox Game of the Week analysis.

Piniella was able to properly put his philosophies into practice. He talked of changing the Cubs' culture, to make it like the winners he had often known. Other managers with winning systems had said the same thing and had been consumed just the same by the intractable syndrome of losing and mismanagement from above.

"I agree with you [about consuming the manager]," Piniella said. "I said if I don't change the culture, I'll be swallowed up here, too. I'm no different than anybody else."

THE LIBERATED FRONT OFFICE

On back-to-back days at the end of the 2006 season, the Cubs allowed team president Andy MacPhail to fall on his sword—actually, they pointed him directly to the tip—and then told manager Dusty Baker he would not be considered for a new contract for 2007. What next?

First, marketing chief John McDonough, the Cubs' top nonbaseball spokesman, was immediately elevated to MacPhail's job. But the process of hiring Baker's successor would take a bit longer. Just-cashiered Florida Marlins manager Joe Girardi, a childhood Cubs fan in Peoria, Illinois, interviewed and became the favorite of many fans and media. But the vote that counted was general manager Jim Hendry's, who strongly favored Lou Piniella, who had just engaged in a favorite between-jobs pastime of managers: the network TV color analyst.

Once burned, a million times careful—Piniella had heard enticing ownership promises of roster upgrades when he interviewed with his hometown Tampa Bay Rays four years previous. This time, however, Piniella picked up the assurances as genuine. The deal was struck relatively quickly.

Piniella would be the hired gun come to town to clean up the mess that had gotten away from Baker.

But to back up Piniella's on-field and clubhouse efforts, the corporate plan to improve had to go deeper than mere commitments to open the exchequer to upgrade the roster.

Piniella could not hope to pull the team out of the morass into which it had fallen in 2005 and '06 if the front-office underpinnings were substandard.

So while under the glare of the media light, the Cubs acquired on-the-field contributors Alfonso Soriano, Kosuke Fukudome, Ted Lilly, and Mark DeRosa; behind the scenes they added an assistant general manager, a supervisor of Far East scouting, a Taiwan-based scout, a baseball operations assistant, a national scouting coordinator, and a Miami-based scout assigned to Latin America.

And, to boot, both Piniella and reporters who would give him the third degree were given an expanded, air-conditioned interview room. Both sides of the questioning process wouldn't be sweating buckets after tough losses, when Piniella's own hot-under-the-collar emotions jacked up his own postgame temperature even more.

These and other upgrades were part of an effort by Cubs chairman Crane Kenney to mimic the Boston Red Sox's spending, organizational chart, and success. Kenney's effort, of course, meant increasing the front-office payroll dramatically.

"I feel like staffwise, we have it very, very good now," Hendry said in April 2008. "I don't need anybody else in the office. I'm very comfortable with the layering I have under me."

Hendry might have said something similar two years earlier, but he would not have meant it. Former Cubs president Andy MacPhail had approved hiring Hendry to his first pro baseball department-head position as farm director in 1994. Six years later MacPhail began formally grooming Hendry to become the general manager, elevating him to that position by title in July 2002. So anybody who tried to get an honest, public answer from Hendry about why the MacPhail-era Cubs couldn't keep up with the premier big-league teams found that the GM retained too much loyalty and gratitude to the man who promoted him to his current post. Besides, Hendry typically shies away from excuses about not having all the financial and personnel resources he realistically needed.

"The budget wasn't unworkable," he said. "I'll never use the budget as an excuse for not being better. It wasn't an issue. You'll never find a GM who doesn't want more money, more staff, more scouts. Andy was the boss. It was a very good working relationship. I didn't fault him because the payroll wasn't higher or we didn't have an extra scout. It was not an excuse for not succeeding."

No, the MacPhail style was not an excuse. Rather, it was a factor even more profound—an underlying reason for the Cubs' continuing failure, featuring five seasons of 94 or more defeats in MacPhail's 12 seasons as president from 1994 to 2006.

No economic reason existed for the Cubs' constant dips to near-laughingstock status, as if it was the early 1960s and owner Phil Wrigley was foisting the college of coaches on both an unwilling organization and a skeptical fan base. "It's the Yankees, Red Sox, and Cubs," ESPN's baseball maven Peter Gammons said of baseball's three elite teams—and then there's everyone else.

"We're a superpower in this [National League Central] division," Crane Kenney, the Tribune Company corporate counsel–turned–Cubs chairman, said in the spring of 2008. Kenney was a childhood Boston fan who thus had multiple motivations to benchmark the Cubs on the Red Sox organization, considered one of the game's most dynamic.

Kenny went on: "We play with all middle-market teams. We can grow this business to allow us to do things on Jim's [Hendry's] side and also on the business side, to do some extraordinary things. We've doubled our revenue from 2003 and we feel we can double it again in three to four years [no matter who is the owner]."

The laggard condition of the Cubs on the management end had to be a philosophical bent. The general public, through uninformed or incomplete media accounts, believed the roadblock came from the Kenney corporate level—and it once did. By hiring MacPhail in 1994, then-Cubs overseer Jim Dowdle desired to "cut the cord" between Tribune Tower and Wrigley Field. Dowdle wanted a baseball executive with full authority to run the team and concoct the budget without any micromanaging from 435 North Michigan Avenue.

MacPhail was given such authority. He needed only his corporate overseer to sign off on his budget. But his bosses would be surprised at the relatively modest figures he turned in for approval. The blue-blooded third-generation scion of a legendary family of baseball executives had widespread personal popularity with his own personality that centered around old-school manners, thus tipping the balance toward the good. Yet he had become reflexively conservative in his view toward how a 21st-century baseball operation should be run. Once a boy wonder running the Minnesota Twins amid two World Series victories and just 41 years old when appointed Cubs president, he had a vision that had devolved into a throwback of a baseball executive from a bygone generation as he passed age 50. "The antique" was one scout's description of MacPhail's reputation throughout the game. History students might have likened him to a Robert Taft, the Mr. Conservative of baseball.

"I am reasonably conservative," MacPhail said in September 2006. "People make a lot of assumptions as a result of that, which I really don't think are accurate.

"Conservative to me—don't let it take on a political tone—I'd like to think it doesn't necessarily, when you get down to it, has to impact the approach you have on building your franchise. . . . Conservative doesn't have to mean you're averse to change."

Only in MacPhail's final years as president did his Cubs crack the top five in player payroll. The priciest free agents were never signed. In 1997, the Cubs ranked 13th in payroll, matching their major-league status in revenue, with MacPhail tying the two together. Yet the fiscal restraint extended into the core of the Cubs organization. MacPhail constantly trumpeted his desire to build a good player-development system. But in 1999, when asked how the development expenditures ranked in baseball, as the Cubs weren't putting that money into free agents, MacPhail responded, "middle of the pack." That philosophy would have opposed MacPhail's stated desire to mold the Cubs into the image of the development-savvy Atlanta Braves organization, which at first passed on signing overpriced free agents at the big-league level to marshall the finances into a game-pacing scouting and farm system.

Neither MacPhail's budget nor his personnel roster would ever be rated as an industry leader. And the shortfall was never more critical than in MacPhail's baseball operations department. The ranks of the front office did not change much over his tenure—and never expanded to the standards of almost every other team, especially the high-budget consistent contenders operating in big markets.

From a historical perspective, during his final seasons running the championship-starved franchise, MacPhail actually developed a management style similar to that of Phil Wrigley, minus the late chewing-gum magnate's eccentricities and abject ignorance of the game's nuances.

"Slow, steady, and unspectacular" had been MacPhail's motto for improving the Cubs back in 1994. He still used that line on his colleagues more than a decade later, much to their astonishment. MacPhail's office was described as a place "where new ideas go to die."

After the Cubs missed a golden chance to reach the World Series in 2003, MacPhail's philosophy increasingly clashed with his Tribune Company superiors, who disavowed their perceived skinflint stance, and wanted to step on the gas financially to help the Cubs catch up to the Yankees and Red Sox, baseball's biggest spenders.

After MacPhail formally stepped down as president, the Cubs executives discovered the team ranked 29th out of 30 teams in front-office staffing. A rumor had long circulated that the Cubs had the smallest scouting staff in baseball, but that proved to be false. The Cubs employed the same number of area scouts as other teams in the United States, but they had shortfalls in evaluators in the talent-rich Caribbean and the new-frontier areas of Asia. The shortfalls didn't end with international scouting: In the early autumn of 2006, MacPhail's successors realized that they employed far fewer people in their front office than could adequately run a winning, big-market, big-revenue franchise.

In the summer of 2005, MacPhail admitted he did not mind being understaffed. The following statement practically shocked others throughout baseball when it was repeated to them.

"I would rather be one man too short than one man too heavy," MacPhail said. "People would like to be engaged, want to have areas that they're responsible to, and they're happier in some activity than having too many people with too few tasks, people fighting over who's doing what."

In reality the Cubs baseball operations were stretched too thin. The lack of additional bodies, minds, and second opinions called into question whether the franchise was properly evaluating talent. The short staffing compounded poor Wrigley Field facilities for players, team employees, and media members. The Cubs were way behind other teams in most facets of baseball operations. How could they compete with teams who benefited from spacious, modern ballparks and an adherence to modern sabermetrics analysis that enlightened franchises like the Red Sox had long embraced?

Word had spread through the two seasons after MacPhail's departure about his financial self-restraint. When he made his first visit back to Wrigley Field as Baltimore Orioles general manager on June 24, 2008, he was grilled by reporters in the visitors' dugout. He was asked if he did not use all the resources at hand while he ran the Cubs.

After acknowledging again that he was "conservative" and "old-fashioned," MacPhail sidestepped the issue of underfinancing his former baseball operation, claiming that whatever budget he concocted each fall was approved by his corporate superior—be it Jim Dowdle, Crane Kenney, or Dennis FitzSimons. He left out one important fact—the Tribune Company execs had expected MacPhail to submit bigger budgets than he did. Based on team revenues and the top-end desire to win, the appropriations likely would have been approved.

Despite repeated questioning on the issue during the dugout session, MacPhail continued to refuse to admit he had left resources on the table in his annual budget planning, while hinting the fault lay elsewhere.

"It's hard to answer that without putting the finger on someone else," he said, the someone else obviously being a Tribune Company man. "We would go in and determine in October what our operating parameters were going to be. We had freedom to operate within those without restriction. If you exceeded those, you needed their permission. I cannot think of a time where I was not given permission. It was not like we were banking millions either, at the time. That's the best answer I can possibly give you."

As other teams like the Red Sox expanded their front office, and specifically scouting, the Cubs remained static, not growing with the times, as baseball ballooned its global reach and delved increasingly into sabermetics analysis. They became a throwback to a darker era in Cubs history.

In essence, the immediate post-MacPhail era was 1981, '82 redux. The Cubs had to radically upgrade their business just as when the team transitioned from the mossified Wrigley family ownership to the bombastic, change-hungry Dallas Green, the first general manager under Tribune Company. The Cubs needed a similar radical shakeup in MacPhail's wake.

"At the end of '06, we had a terrible no-show rate in September, and season-ticket holders were questioning the direction of the organization," Kenney said. "We had to do something in '07. We had a successful team on the South Side [as an alternative for corporate sponsors]. I told Jim [Hendry], 'What resources do you need, I'll go get them.' We will find the resources on the business side to support the payroll and the front office we need. Jim came back with recommendations, and we worked it through with John [McDonough]."

Thus Piniella's arrival in October 2006 was perfectly timed. He could not have worked under the restraints of a year previous. The win-at-all-costs, brook-no-failures Piniella could not have existed in the same universe as the cautious, unaggressive MacPhail.

Kenney and Hendry refuse to lambaste MacPhail. They had pleasant conversations when the Orioles made their June 2008 Wrigley Field visit. Hendry and MacPhail, who talked for months over the previous off-season but failed to complete a trade for Baltimore leadoff man Brian Roberts, dined together. But it is clear Kenney imposed a sea change in philosophy once MacPhail fell on his sword.

John McDonough, tapped by FitzSimons, then Tribune Company CEO, and Kenney in 2006 to take over for MacPhail, emphasized the Cubs' one goal of winning the World Series as with almost the first words out of his mouth in his introductory press conference. The franchise symbol soon became a blue capital *W* impressed upon a white background, a copy of the victory flag that flew atop the Wrigley Field scoreboard after home triumphs. It was a drastically different attitude than during the MacPhail era.

"You can make the case that the best thing [for baseball] is for the Cubs to win three championships in a row," MacPhail said two weeks before he resigned in September 2006. "It would be great for ratings and it would make [good for] the game. Nothing would be better for baseball than to have the Cubs be world champions next year. It wouldn't matter [if the World Series opponent was the Yankees or the Red Sox]. Go back and look at postseason TV ratings; none were higher than the 2003 NLCS."

But in the 12 years leading up to that statement, MacPhail had never mentioned publicly the Fall Classic as the Cubs' ultimate destination, preferring to carefully refer to being "competitive" and playing meaningful games in

September. And maybe he had been looking at his own big picture—as a long-projected successor to commissioner Bud Selig, playing off his own baseball royal linage. A Cubs president who doesn't promise too much and then doesn't deliver amid the continual financial prosperity of humming turnstiles at Wrigley Field has a measure of job security. But a chief exec who goes for the home run, but fails to reach the World Series and then gets fired isn't a good commissioner candidate.

Erring on the side of conservatism with his budget requests under MacPhail, Hendry had a substantial laundry list ready for Kenney and McDonough. Topping it off was an assistant general manager.

Such a position had become standard in the industry—except with the Cubs. A general manager's work had become so complex and time-consuming that a right-hand man (and in a couple of cases, a woman) was needed to help with scouting, budgets, trade talks, and contract negotiations. Yet under MacPhail, the Cubs employed an assistant GM only in 1999, when David Wilder had the job, and in 2000 through '02, when Hendry was in training for the top job while MacPhail doubled as the GM after Ed Lynch's removal from the role and re-assignment to scouting. After he was promoted to GM, Hendry only had his special-assistant scouts like mentor Gary Hughes and front-office aides Scott Nelson and Chuck Wasserstrom to provide second opinions and engage in the incessant give-and-take of evaluating players.

With most teams, assistant GMs extend their bosses' reach in the 30-team sport. They usually are allowed to initiate trade talks with their counterparts or even talk to other GM's, then turn over the conversations to their own GM if there is a hint of progress. But MacPhail said he wanted only his own GM—Hendry—talking to other GMs.

Hendry is a 24/7 type whose cell phone is like his third ear, but Kenney urged him to bring on some help. "Jim's a tireless worker, but an assistant GM makes sense," he said. Hendry never publicly complained about being overworked. Who needs an assistant GM when you had a former two-time World Series–winning GM to consult at the other end of a connecting office with your own?

"When you have Andy MacPhail across the hall, he's a baseball guy, too," Hendry said. "Andy was very helpful to me in areas I wasn't very proficient. When he left, it became essential to have somebody else in a high-level position."

Two candidates were scout Randy Bush, a former Twins outfielder under MacPhail, and longtime Hendry confidant Oneri Fleita, doubling as farm director and Latin director. Bush won out for one specific reason.

"The reason I went in the direction I went was because in the state we were in at the time, I felt it was more important over the next two, three years for Oneri to keep doing what he was doing in the farm system and Latin signings," Hendry said.

"I don't look at Randy as ahead of Oneri. Randy has a lot of authority here. He has full authority when he's on the road with the club. In spring training, he watches games and is in contact with other teams' high-level scouts. He initiates a lot of info gathering and exchanges ideas on potential deals. He sees our farm system more than I do. That increases our coverage."

And, belying MacPhail's GM-to-GM-only talks, Bush has started trade talks, including ones that have culminated in deals.

"Absolutely," Bush said. "There's a certain level I can take it to [and then turn over to Hendry]. It takes a workload off him. He trusts me that I'm going to take it to a certain point and bring it back to him."

Another Bush routine that eases Hendry's job is processing scouting reports.

"Probably as important as anything is the time I spend going over the pro reports that come in," he said. "We probably get 50 or 60 reports a day. I read over most or all of them. Jim wouldn't have the time in his day. By doing that, it helps me really stay on top of what our people think on a daily basis, not only major-league talent, but minor-league talent. If Jim comes to me and says we're having discussions with this organization, I can right off the top of my head tell him where we're at."

Bush also provides a crucial second opinion in any talent-evaluation scenario. A GM cannot possibly know every angle about a player. Top execs have confirmed they've been dissuaded from deals by an assistant with more and better information, and the conviction to state that publicly.

"Randy will come up with innovative ideas," Hendry said. "Sometimes I can be reactionary, want to do this by tomorrow. He'll slow me down. He was instrumental in [acquiring Kosuke] Fukudome. In October [2007], we were talking about trading for this guy or that guy. Randy always was the guy in back who says, 'Wait a minute, let's try to get Fukudome first.' "

Yet another advantage of Bush's presence is his having played the game at the big-league level.

"I've been in different jobs in my life, but there's one missing link," Hendry said. "Jim Hendry wasn't a major-league player. Is that essential to do this job? Of course not. But you need somebody close to you that did [play]. Randy sometimes gives me a little different perspective that only a big-league player would really have.

"I like to think the players have a decent amount of respect for me. I'm honest with them, don't bullshit them. Randy even adds another dimension. When he's on the road, he can talk to a player on a level different than I can because he did it. I don't act like I'm somebody I'm not. He can engage in a kind of communication I can't. I wouldn't want it any other way."

Bush had participated in the scouting of Fukudome in Japan, another facet of the baseball operations that had expanded in the post-MacPhail era. Also watching Fukudome were Paul Weaver, hired by Hendry to oversee Asian scouting operations, and Gary Hughes. Such expeditions would not have been undertaken under MacPhail, who allowed the Asian talent hunt to wither after Leon Lee, father of slugger Derrek Lee, left as Pacific Rim scout after the 2002 season.

The elder Lee had been a legend for his home run prowess in Japanese pro baseball. He even lived in Japan full-time for several years, exposing his son and future Cub to another culture. Such experiences were deemed vital when Lee was taken on to scout the Far East in 1998, although he was based domestically. Lee made just a little headway, his prize signee being hyped slugger Hee Seop Choi out of Korea. Choi's bat proved too slow for the majors. He faded away, playing in several organizations after the Cubs traded him to the Marlins for, ironically, Derrek Lee after the 2003 season. The only other Leon Lee signee to make the majors was pitcher Jae Kuk Ryu out of Korea, a bit-part starter with the Cubs in 2006.

Even if Leon Lee did not open up a big talent pipeline from Asia to Wrigley Field, he had the right concept. And in 1999, he suggested he'd like to start scouting China to tap a potentially raw talent base from the teeming population. Lee's desire was immediately shot down by MacPhail, who considered it too radical. Just stick to Korea, Japan and other familiar territories was his reasoning. Interestingly, Major League Baseball has been trying to make inroads into China in recent seasons. Lee would have been a baseball pioneer had he been given permission.

After Lee moved out of the organization, the Cubs modest interest in the Pacific Rim was farmed out to a consulting organization. All the while, Japanese talent increasingly began filtering into big-league rosters. By 2006, the Cubs were the only big-market team that had not signed a Japanese player. Even though MacPhail claimed he encouraged transpacific scouting expeditions in his last few years in Chicago to scope out Japanese talent like Fukudome, the team simply did not have a permanent on-site presence in the Far East, and none was forthcoming under MacPhail.

Plugging this big hole in the organization topped Hendry's wish list once John McDonough was named president. The hiring of Weaver—a veteran of the Houston Astros, San Diego Padres, and Arizona Diamondbacks scouting staffs— was announced even before Bush came aboard as assistant GM. Also added was Taiwan-based Steve Wilson, a former left-handed pitcher for the Cubs from 1989 through '91 who had first opened a sports bar in the island nation in the mid-1990s, then married a local woman, learned Chinese, and went into part-time scouting work.

"Paul was essential and Wilson was essential," Hendry said. "They've made tremendous headway in 15 months."

Weaver shuttles to the Far East from the United States on big-picture missions. The daily grind of mining talent falls to Wilson, a native of British Columbia.

"From January to September, I'm basically on the road a lot," Wilson said via an e-mail interview. "I try to keep my trips to 10 days if I can, and then try to be at home with my family for about seven days, before going back out again for another trip."

Wilson works with part-time scouts in Japan, Korea, and Australia.

"For my trips to Korea, I'm usually watching high school tournaments," Wilson said. "The tournaments will have three or four games each day, starting in the morning and ending late in the evening. The tournaments are usually at one stadium, but sometimes multiple locations. I try to schedule time to see pro games in Korea as well, to check up on any possible free agents. Mix that in with going to see specific kids practice, or a workout if Paul [Weaver] comes in to see particular players."

Wilson usually makes six to seven annual trips to Korea. Closer to home, he has plenty to keep him busy.

"In Taiwan, it's the same for high school," he said. "They don't play a season, as in Korea, but have tournaments during the year, with three to four games each day. I try to get all my Taiwan high school and college coverage done for the most part in the fall, September and October, and then in January and February there are more tourneys, so that when the weather gets nice I can concentrate on Korea and Japanese pro coverage."

Oneri Fleita also has a hand in cross-checking Pacific Rim prospects. He journeyed to Australia's MLB Academy in June 2008 with Wilson to look at prospects. Wilson also worked as a pitching coach at the academy. Earlier in the year, the Cubs signed top Korea high school shortstop Lee Hak-Ju, an academy attendee, along with Australian right-hander Adam Spencer and lefty pitcher Cody Hams.

In Japan, Wilson and Weaver are assisted by part-time scouts Danny MacLeith and Junichi Takahashi. All work off a list of possible free agents and "posting" players to be scouted. Wilson makes about six trips a year to Japan.

"For Japan, our main priority is to see the Japanese pro league," Wilson said, "and to scout the entire league so we not only see the upcoming free agents, but also start to build up a good history on all the players in the league so when they do come out, we've seen them, and have a history on them for three, four, five years.

"We also will stay on top of the industrial league and players from there and college who have expressed an interest in coming to play in the States, and try to see them play as well. For the Japanese pro league, I'll go in for a week at a time, and sometimes a two-week trip. They play six days a week, and I try to see two games if possible on Saturdays and Sundays—a day game and shoot over to catch a night game with single games during the week. We cover the high schools to a certain degree in Japan, but not much because it's very difficult to sign a Japanese high-school player."

Wilson's Far East coverage also extends to international tournaments in Asia, such as the 2008 World Cup in Taiwan, Olympic qualifiers, Asian high-school championships, and others. Apparently he is the Cubs' man of the world, as he was also dispatched to the Czech Republic, the Netherlands, and to Germany to watch players. As part of their scouting expansion, the Cubs employ part-timers Bill Holmberg, in charge of a training academy in Italy; Bill Froberg in the Netherlands; and Richard Kania in the Czech Republic.

And if a European fling wasn't enough, Wilson made a trip to the Cubs' Dominican Republic Academy in January 2008 and two visits to Arizona, one for the team's organizational meetings and Fall League scouting in late October, and another during spring training for training of part-time scouts.

Asia and Europe were not the only geographic improvements in Cubs scouting. Much closer to home, domestic amateur prospects got another layer of analysis previously absent at the behest of Tim Wilken, who took over from John Stockstill as scouting director in late December 2005.

By 2007, Wilken added two national cross-checkers in Sam Hughes and Steve Hinton to back up the area scouts and three regional (Eastern, Midwest, and Western) supervisors. Previously, the prime prospects would get at least one look apiece from the local scout, the regional talent evaluator, and the scouting director—and a fourth, from the general manager, if he was at or near first-round material. Now a fifth set of eyes and ears would evaluate prospects.

"[Adding scouts] was more philosophical," Wilken said. "I always refer to it as checks and balances. I did not want yes guys. I wanted people not afraid to state their opinion. Our area guy gets more looks this way. Jim [Hendry] was open to it."

The team also added three pro scouts, including former Pirates general manager Dave Littlefield and ex-Cubs farm director Bill Harford. The net effect is to take a load off area scouts when they have coverage of other team's organizations in the summer. The pro scouts' presence will enable the area scouts to spend more time following amateur prospects in the summer leagues.

"The double coverage on all other 29 organizations was kind of hurting the amateur side," Wilken said. "They couldn't scout these guys in summer. They were stretched too thin. What [the pro scouts' addition] that does on the amateur side is the scouts are able to identify [prospects] earlier in the summer and into the fall. I could see a lull in our [farm] system because it was too difficult to identify guys. It made us late in [scouting and evaluating] each spring."

As an example, under the previous system Hinton and Hughes each had to keep an eye on a total of 24 teams in four organizations. Hinton was responsible for the parent club and all minor-league affiliates of the Athletics and

Giants. Hughes had the same responsibilities for the Braves and Reds.

"Now Sam doesn't have the Reds, and Hinton only has Oakland," Wilken said of the load being shifted to the pro scouts.

Wilken also "cleaned out" some of the part-time scouting ranks. New part-timers include Ramser Correa in Puerto Rico, a talent-rich area oddly undercovered by the Cubs previously; Eric Servais in the Dakotas, which has produced more big leaguers than most figure; Keith Ryman to cover eastern Tennessee; and Eloy Gil to work Florida when Rollie Pino has flown south to look at Caribbean talent.

Wilken's near-future wish list includes adding an area scout for Canada, as the Great White North seems to produce a nice little flow of talent.

The scouting ranks, numbering 29 full-timers, still will need to be bolstered further to bring the Cubs up to the level of the Red Sox. Making use of every last inch of Fenway Park office space, Boston employs two assistant general managers to complement Theo Epstein. The Red Sox employ 24 amateur scouts and 15 pro scouts among a total of 48 full-timers.

Long accustomed to a large player-development staff, the Los Angeles Dodgers employ a total of 39 full-time scouts, including 20 amateur talent evaluators.

However, the Cubs numbers are now similar to that of the Atlanta Braves, which set the gold standard for scouting and player development starting in the late 1980s. Chicago even uses more professional scouts than Atlanta.

Even the elevation of a front-office assistant from intern status made a difference in the efficiency of the front office. Jake Ciarrachi is a Lombard, Illinois, native and baseball junkie whose father, Dave Ciarrachi, used to watch

50 or more Cubs games per year and now is part owner of a minor-league team in Rockford, Illinois. He was promoted from intern to full-time as part of the staff expansion after the 2006 season. Assisting both Oneri Fleita and Tim Wilken, he has taken away much of the grunt work from both, along with Patti Kargakis, the longtime player development assistant.

As part of his dawn to after-dark duties, Fleita formerly had to research and evaluate players released from other teams in case the Cubs had interest. He also had to gather information and analyze the six-year free-agent lists, and research scouting reports and statistics on all potential Rule 5–eligible minor-league players. Now, Ciarrachi handles much of that work, freeing Fleita for more scouting and player evaluation. Ciarrachi also runs the team's college scholarship plan, a duty formerly assigned to Kargakis, a 24-year front-office veteran.

Other parts of Ciarrachi's job are overseeing the Cubs' player development database that has all the game reports and player evaluations, returning calls and e-mails from player agents, assisting in watching and reporting on Cubs minor leaguers, helping coordinate spring training, and working with minor-league training coordinator Justin Sharpe and scouts on medical exams and health history of prospects for the amateur draft. Like a utility player, he'll work wherever he's needed.

"There's no question not only for myself and Patti, but a load off Tim Wilken," Fleita said of Ciarrachi. "He's been attending all the scouting meetings, preparing for the draft. He's done some advance [scouting] work this year [filling in for Brad Kelley, absent due to his wife's illness]. He's helped me with communication with our scouts internationally.

"Jake asked me once, 'How did you do this by yourself?' I don't know. I got up earlier. It's allowed me to be a dad a little bit more, going to my kids' games, knowing he's here at the ballpark, covering a few things for me. It's given me a chance to focus on other areas. I've been a little bit more involved with Paul Weaver and Steve Wilson on international scouting. We've all gotten to do some things that are new.

"Jake's got a bright future, a great ceiling like we say about a lot of players," Fleita continued. "He's got great work ethic and a passion for the game."

Similarly, Wilken is grateful for Ciarrachi's help in organizing prospects' medical information, and for the assistance of 2008 front-office intern Alex Suarez. Both perform the scutwork in which he would have had to be otherwise involved, cutting down on his time watching prospects in the field.

"What's just as important is hiring people with good baseball sense and great common sense, and the combination of these two qualities can only mean good things down the road for Jake and Alex," Wilken said.

Even with added staff, the facilities in which both media and players had to operate under MacPhail would have been far substandard to the big-league norm if not for some quick construction in the winter of 2006–07. The media interview room behind the Cubs dugout was long an embarrassment throughout the game.

The room, hardly bigger than an average-size mid-level executive's office, originally was set up to view weather radar over the Internet, then was pressed into service as an interview room in the wake of the crush of media demands during the Sammy Sosa–Mark McGwire home-run chase in 1998. However, the room was too small for all but modest-size pre- and postgame interview sessions. If a big story took place or huge media contingent was on the premises, the room would turn into a modern-day black hole of

Calcutta. Manager Dusty Baker called the cubbyhole the dungeon. Making matters worse was the inability to use a 1970s-vintage wall air conditioner that cooled the room adequately when just a couple of bodies were inside. But the press of bodies packed together for interviews—sometimes spilling out into a corridor for lack of room—overwhelmed the noisy AC unit, which had to be turned off to avoid interfering with the audio of the interviews being fed into recording devices. The room thus would heat up an additional 10 to 15 degrees in minutes to intolerable levels. After visiting Cardinals pitcher Daryle Kile was found dead in his downtown hotel room in 2002, so much flesh and metal tried to squeeze into the room, heating it past human tolerance, that media relations director Sharon Pannozzo had to dole out bottles of water. In spite of this black eye to the Cubs reputation—and the presence of an unused room next door that was grist for the interview room's expansion—MacPhail never appropriated money to remedy the problem. One anecdote even had MacPhail taking joy in the thought of perspiring media when he was told of an upcoming press conference on a hot day.

However, once MacPhail was forced out, successor John McDonough immediately ordered about a 30 percent expansion of the room—into the next-door space. The grandstand did not collapse amid the construction. Central air-conditioning ductwork was run into the room. Although the space was still relatively crowded, interviewers were not bunched body to body after high-demand games, and the 75-degree or thereabouts temperatures did not add heat to Lou Piniella's mood after a tough loss.

Cubs players were not so lucky in increasing their elbow room. Their home clubhouse, considered relatively spacious when it was built in 1984, was not expanded under MacPhail. Admittedly, the crowded confines of the surrounding ballpark did not permit expansion of the long, narrow room, which had been created through excavation back in the Dallas Green era. Trainer's rooms and weight rooms were too small. The Cubs had to improvise a mini-batting cage with netting hung from the clubhouse ceiling for players to practice their swings during games. In modern ballparks, including U.S. Cellular Field, indoor batting cages are adjacent to dugouts. But Wrigley Field's cage is 360 feet away, under the rightfield bleachers.

Some of the space problems were supposed to be solved through the construction of a triangle-shaped building on the parking lot on the west side of Wrigley Field. The plans, sidetracked when Tribune Company ran into financial problems in 2005, called for team offices, shops, a restaurant, and possibly a Cubs museum as part of a "Wrigley Field Campus." Connecting underground with the building would have been expanded player facilities, including the batting cage and bigger training and weight rooms. The old weight room would have been converted into a bigger player's lounge compared to the present tiny lunchroom. MacPhail had used the lack of space as a partial justification for his modest front-office staff, saying he was somewhat encumbered by the square footage, or lack thereof.

But even with such building plans on the drawing boards, MacPhail was not sympathetic in 2005 when the subject of the cramped home quarters was raised. He lambasted the "extraordinary lavish" wives' lounges and other spacious features of new ballparks, while insisting that the addition of more women's washrooms and other fan amenities had a higher priority at the time.

With the "triangle building" on hold, the media relations staff and traveling secretary Jimmy Bank were moved out to the old Yum Yum Donuts building adjoining Clark Street in 2006. Two years later, media relations shifted again to a trailer next to the old donut shop. Lack of space did not equal lack of staffing for long after 2005.

Acquiring new state-of-the-art equipment to help players was a chore. A suggestion to upgrade the Cubs' video room was met with deaf ears by MacPhail. Bob Albrecht, producer of Comcast SportsNet's Cubs telecasts, tried to interest the chief exec in cutting-edge video equipment. The proposal, like so many others, went nowhere.

One major improvement for the players in the post-MacPhail era took place within the cozy confines of Wrigley Field. The playing surface was much criticized for decades for its "crowned" infield that sloped downward into foul territory to promote natural drainage. Players ranging from Barry Bonds to Kerry Wood also were not fond of an outfield that contained some scattered indentations hazardous to either galloping outfielders or pitchers running before games. When the player complaints were relayed to MacPhail, he protested that there was not enough time in the off-season to re-do the field. And there always was cost. California-based baseball-field builder Chris Krug, a former Cubs catcher whose throwing error resulted in the only run in Sandy Koufax's perfect game against Chicago in 1965, claimed in 2005 that he could re-do the field for under $1 million and before winter hit. Krug did not get the job, though, after MacPhail left. White Sox master groundskeeper Roger Bossard, who has built numerous major-league fields and constructed athletic fields as far away as Saudi Arabia, oversaw the reconstruction of the field, installing drainage ducts below the surface while evening the field from foul territory to the warning track. Bossard finished the job in two months in the autumn of 2007 and beat the first snow.

"We are going to drag this place into the future," Kenney said. "It will take a little time and a little effort, but we are going to get there."

The front office had no choice. From top to bottom, they were forced to be on the same winning wavelength as Piniella.

"The revenues have been available to us for enough time to do it sooner," Kenney said. "It [holding back] was philosophical. Better late than never. Tribune Company in recent years said it's their [Cubs] fortune to be made and their fortune to be spent.

"This is about winning. We can't measure success any longer on having record attendance or great ratings on WGN. The only measurement is 'Did we win the World Series?' This business has only one barometer—did you win or just have an OK year?"

PATIENCE IS REWARDED

THE CUBS NEVER PLAYED AN OPENING DAY AT WRIGLEY FIELD IN THE month of March until 2008. And in keeping with the theme of unprecedented events, the Cubs' astounding offensive production to come would be summed up by a newcomer's patient taking of four pitches before his sweet swing connected for a ballpark-shaking home run.

Yet, a slew of the age-old Cubs negatives marred the rain-delayed "lid lifter" with the young-and-eager Milwaukee Brewers. Hulking starter Carlos "Big Z" Zambrano, a caffeine devotee who loves his Red Bull, had to depart with one out in the seventh because of an arm cramping due to apparent dehydration, later diagnosed as a potassium deficiency. "Drink water," he'd say in his postgame mea culpa, not yet realizing that the prescription would be bananas, loaded with potassium.

Two innings after Zambrano left, amid a scoreless tie, newly minted closer Kerry Wood hit Brewers leadoff hitter Rickie Weeks, a perplexing loss of control for the erstwhile Kid K that would bedevil him on other occasions in the Midwest spring. Inevitably, a free pass to a leadoff batsman ends badly for a late-inning reliever. And it did, as the Brewers put up three runs and handed off a save situation to closer Eric Gagne, a hurler tainted by an injury-riddled downfall from unhittable status years before with the Dodgers and scarlet-letter inclusion in the steroids-accusing Mitchell Report. Cynics knew the Brewers signed the wrong guy in Gagne, and he did not disappoint the Cubs fans by giving up the three-run lead to send the game to the 10th inning. Then, Bobby Howry, the crack Cubs setup man of the 2007 division race who had never pitched well early in the season, performed true to form by giving up the game-deciding run that again sprouted from a Weeks hit-by-pitch. There would be no Willie Smith walk-off pinch homer and a memorable opener talked about for decades to come as there had been in the originally blessed, then star-crossed Cubs season of 1969.

But a subtle game-within-a-game while Gagne was unraveling in the bottom of the ninth would have massive ramifications for the 2008 Cubs. As the disciplined Japanese star Kosuke Fukodome came to the plate in the bottom of the ninth, the crowd roared for something extraordinary. Much ballyhooed since the Cubs signed him for $48 million as their first Japanese player three months earlier, Fukudome was renowned for his patience at the plate. As dozens of rooters wearing Japanese-language headbands with the rising-sun symbol cheered, Fukudome did not stand with bat on shoulder when he saw his first big-league pitch from Brewers ace Ben Sheets in the second inning. He whacked a double to dead center, literally causing Wrigley Field to shake from the frenzy. Only on the most impactful or emotional occasions did the 94-year-old ballpark mimic a 4.9 on the Richter scale, a bigger temblor than the Chicago area received every other decade or so from far-off quakes from the New Madrid fault down around the Missouri bootheel.

Fukudome added a walk and a single to his opening-game line before coming to bat as the tying run against Gagne. Predictably, Gagne had put the first two runners on base via a Derrek Lee single and an Aramis Ramirez walk. The savviest experts about hitting, including Cubs manager Lou Piniella, always counseled that the pressure is on the pitcher in such a situation. But the Cubs of recent vintage, who lacked an organizational hitting philosophy, took an anti-*Moneyball* stance and lacked savvy, count-working players on the roster. They most often responded to such invitations to victory by requiring adult Depends. A typical reaction to first-and-second/nobody out/nervous closer on the mound was to swing at the first pitch, either popping up or slapping the ball right to the third baseman for a neat 5–4–3 twin killing.

Fukudome's mere presence at the plate with the game on the line threw Cubs convention out the window on a higher organizational level, too. The franchise was slow to integrate the roster with African-Americans other than Ernie Banks as the 1950s progressed. Given a chance to keep up with the rest of baseball, they declined, also lagging on signing Latin players until the 1990s, further retarding their talent flow. The Cubs did not even produce a home-grown Dominican player until pitcher Amaury Telemaco in 1996. When the influx of Asian talent sparked by Hideo Nomo began in the late 1990s, the Cubs again were way behind the curve, all big-market teams fielding a Japanese player prior to Chicago's ardent pursuit of Fukudome, the best Japanese free agent on the market, in the fall of 2007. Now the Cubs were current with the rest of the game, and the fans sensed progress toward the Holy Grail of a World Series.

His muscle memory kicking into gear, Fukudome gauged the struggling, straining Gagne, who peered at his catcher through gogglelike glasses. Ramirez, notoriously aggressive, had just waited him out for a walk. Fukudome took one pitch, then another. Gagne kept caving in to the stress. Ball three. The closer would have to try to come in with the automatic strike, a fastball down the middle. If he missed, ball four. Fukudome dutifully took it. But now at 3-and-1, he could expect a hitter's pitch and set up for it. Again, a Cub of other times probably would not have risen to the occasion. But Fukudome represented a clean break with the past. He got his fastball and connected with a smooth, level swing. The ball rocketed toward the right-centerfield bleachers as the entire ballpark practically lifted off its foundation, the Richter scale shooting past 5 as the Cubs tied the Brewers 3–3.

Fukudome did double duty with his Hollywood heroics. He midwifed the 2008 Cubs even more so than did Lou Piniella, Jim Hendry, $400 million in player-payroll commitments, or the exile of Andy MacPhail. Even though Fukudome eventually would fade in the heat of summer, during the chill of early spring, in genielike fashion, he loosed a style of play that could not be put back in the bottle. No more hacking at the first pitch as if they had a hot date or twilight golf outing, the Cubs suddenly became baseball's masters of on-base percentage and offensive production just two years after they brought up the rear on OBP and witnessed the fewest pitches in the National League. Combined with 33 home games through the first days of June, they would catapult themselves to the NL's best record, first-place standing, and favorites status for the World Series on the backs of a dominant offense that made Wrigley Field the best home-field advantage in baseball. They would rack up their finest home record in modern times, enabling them to survive a strange Jekyll-Hyde transformation to offensive mediocrity on the road that did not end until a stirring four-game sweep of the Brewers in Milwaukee at the end of July. Piniella mandated a hot start in contrast to the stumblebum efforts of 2007 and would get it thanks to his hitters dominating their own ballyard.

Dubbed the "Friendly Confines," probably by Ernie Banks, Wrigley Field served home cookin' to its team even in the worst seasons prior to the final decade of the 20th century. The Cubs could depend on playing at least .500 baseball at home, their slow-footed sluggers launching home runs on the backs of friendly out-blowing winds. A case study was the dreadful 1956 team, 39–38 at home, 21–56 on the road.

But a perfect storm formed in the early 1990s. Meddling Tribune Company management kept a lid on the payroll while eviscerating the productive farm system of 1985 to 1989. The supposed independent baseball-man solution of 1994, boy-wonder president Andy MacPhail, hardly improved matters: He kept his own strict cost controls. The talent flow of free agents and homegrown prospects thus impinged, the Cubs had the worst of multiple worlds: They were under-powered, impatient, slower than average, and possessed mediocre pitching. They could not hit a lot of home runs, they couldn't manufacture runs, they could not steal runs, they could not wait for walks, and they couldn't stop foes from scoring. From 1992 to 2002, opponents belted 60 more home runs in Wrigley Field than the Cubs. In many seasons the Cubs were outscored at home. Sammy Sosa was the only consistent home run hitter in the lineup during this time. One day in 1996, Sosa, realizing that only teammate Ryne Sandberg would reach the 20-homer mark, remarked that he could not do it all by himself.

Wrigley Field no longer provided a home-field advantage for the Cubs. They had five sub-.500 seasons at home between 1992 and 2002, including a putrid 20–39 walk on the wild side in 1994 that included a 12-game losing streak. In only one season, the surprise wild-card 1998 campaign, did the Cubs have anything close to dominance at home with a 51–31 mark. They were 48–33 in 2001 and in other winning seasons at home were just a few games above .500.

Fewer baserunners and fewer home runs simply meant fewer wins overall, including at home. New-age thinking spearheaded by the likes of Bill James promoted the practical statistic of on-base percentage, of which walks were a central component. The Yankees and Red Sox consistently ranked among the on-base percentage leaders in the American League, which translated into frequent status as contenders and champions. But the concept barely penetrated Wrigley Field, where hitters had a swing-first, ask-questions-later attitude.

"They don't have an offensive philosophy . . . not much attention is paid to on-base percentage," one veteran scout said in 2005.

The closest the Cubs ever came to examining the James technique were conversations between then-manager Jim Riggleman and right-hand man Dan Radison in the late 1990s. In various coaching roles, Radison mentioned one of his favored authors—Bill James—whom he'd read since the sabermetrics guru began writing baseball analysis a generation ago.

"We would have conversations about it," Riggleman said. "Rad was in tune with that thinking, the value of bases on balls." But since Radison was not the Cubs' hitting coach at the time, James's ideas never went beyond the talking stage.

Manager Dusty Baker, who had California-cool, advanced thinking in many aspects of his life, was surprisingly old-school when it came to the value of walks and on-base percentage.

"I've let most guys hit 3–0 [in the count]," he told MLB.com in 2004. "That's one reason . . . I think walks are overrated unless you can run. If you get a walk and put the pitcher in a stretch, that helps, but the guy who walks and can't run, most of the time he's clogging up the bases for somebody who can run."

Baker continued to offer his aggressive-at-all-costs homilies.

"Walks help. They do help. But you aren't going to walk across the plate, you're going to hit across the plate. That's the school I come from. . . . Everyone can't hit with two strikes, everyone can't walk. You're taking away some of the aggressiveness of a kid if you're telling him to go up there and try to work for a walk. It's like when I see kids in Little League and they make the small kids go up there and try to get a walk. That's not any fun."

Thus, when the Cubs finally amassed a lineup of boppers in 2004, they could not get enough men on base to make the home runs count for much. They slugged a team-record 235 homers, pacing the NL by 21 over runner-up St. Louis. However, the '04 Cubs ranked only seventh in runs and RBIs for a good reason—they were 11th in on-base percentage (.328) and a miserable 14th in walks (489). The Cubs had 141 solo homers. Cubs opponents drew 545 walks. In their fatal 1–7 final-week stretch that knocked them out from a previously near-certain wild-card berth, the Cubs scored four or fewer runs five times. Back-to-back 12-inning losses to the Reds at Wrigley Field, in which the Cubs scored just four runs, were particularly excruciating. A combination of poor clutch hitting and a shaky bullpen led to a 19-30 record in one-run games.

Along with his 39 homers and 36 doubles, leftfielder Moises Alou drove in a team-leading 106 runs. Alou was particularly overanxious in clutch situations, such as with a man on third and one out, and would pop up, hit a grounder to the third baseman, or strike out, shaving some 20 to 25 RBIs off what should have been his final total. A declining Sosa drove in just 80 runs on his 35 homers. The best clutch performance was turned in by third base-man Aramis Ramirez, who sported a .373 on-base percent-age, .318 batting average, and 103 RBIs in 145 games. He ranked sixth in the NL in batting average with runners in scoring position (.336).

The numbers again were both outwardly gaudy and realistically hollow in 2005. First baseman Derrek Lee had an all-time season, leading the majors in batting average with .335. He had 199 hits, of which 46 were homers and 50 were doubles. Although his RBI total of 107 was eminently respectable for most players, the count—like Alou's—was probably down 20 to 25 from what logically should have been produced by his other offensive numbers.

Why? Lee did not have as many runners to drive in as he should have. Overall, the Cubs and Cardinals had similar team offensive numbers in most categories in 2005. Both had .270 team averages, with the Cubs actually col-lecting 12 more hits. With 194 homers, the Cubs had 24 more than the Cardinals. The big difference was walk totals. St. Louis had 534; the Cubs had an NL-low 419. The Car-dinals' on-base percentage was .339 compared to the Cubs' .324. The Cubs had 119 solo homers. Thus the Cardinals scored 805 runs to the Cubs' 703.

Lee had a team-leading 85 walks. Rightfielder Jeromy Burnitz racked up 57 bases on balls. No other Cub had more than 40 walks. Cubs' opponents drew 576 walks.

By now Baker came under fire for the team impatience at the plate. He was roasted for his "clogging the bases" comments. No Cub was an on-base maven to serve as a lineup sparkplug or role model for free swingers to moderate their style. The numbers were revealing as the bottom was reached in 2006. A further decline in talent, plus Lee's disablement most of the season due to a broken wrist and Ramirez's slow start, took their toll.

The Cubs' on-base percentage of .319 and walks total of 394 were last in the National League. Only the similarly underwhelming Pittsburgh Pirates saved the Cubs from a cellar ranking in runs scored, the Chicagoans scoring 25 more than the Pirates' 691. The Dodgers led the NL in on-base percentage with .348. There was a correlation between walks and runs scored. The Philadelphia Phillies led the NL with 626 walks and 865 runs scored.

Only one Cub had a .400-plus on-base percentage—second baseman Ryan Theriot in limited play (53 games). Rookie Theriot, the regular at his position in the final month, finished at .412 with 17 walks. Catcher Michael Barrett's .368 OBP paced the season-long regulars, just above leftfielder Matt Murton with .365. Leading run producer Ramirez had a .352 OBP and a team-leading 50 walks. Free-swinging rightfielder Jacque Jones, acquired even though the Cubs already had severe OBP and strikeout problems, had just 35 walks along with 116 strikeouts in 149 games.

These numbers paled in comparison with the NL pacesetters. Barry Bonds had a .454 OBP along with 115 walks. Albert Pujols was .431 with 92 walks. Nick Johnson of the Nationals had a good eye with .428 and 110 walks.

The Cubs trended downward in making pitchers work over the three seasons from 2004 to 2006. They saw 24,597 pitches in 2004, 22,876 in 2005 and 21,615 in 2006.

The patience issue was one of the first addressed in the questions asked of Lou Piniella at his introductory press conference in 2006. He vowed improvement. "Walks score," was his most succinct comment. With only relatively minor changes in personnel, the 2007 Cubs sported an upward tick, though not dramatic, in OBP prowess. They improved to a .333 OBP, ninth in the NL, due to improved overall hitting, but still ranked 15th in walks with 500. They did see a few more pitches at 22,293.

But even after a year of Piniella as an OBP-advocating manager, the Cubs required transfusion of new blood from the Far East and the baseball scrap heap.

Fukudome, of course, imported his trademark discipline that made him one of the Japanese Central League's best all-around offensive stars. Also showing more plate discipline from his first day as a Cub was outfielder Reed Johnson, discarded by the Blue Jays due to a personnel logjam and the perceived aftereffects of back surgery. Johnson was no walking man, yet he typically worked counts to get a hitter's pitch and wear down the pitcher.

The early success of Fukudome and Johnson's heady at-bats were mimicked by a host of teammates. None other than Piniella and Lee, the two most authoritative Cubs, credited the examples set by Fukudome and Johnson in transforming the lineup into a much more patient group— literally into an on-base machine at Wrigley Field that performed a 180-degree turn from 2006.

Fukudome rarely explained his prowess for patience, which resulted in 35 walks the first two months of 2008. The cultural and language gap showed as the outfielder, opting for conservatively phrased, clipped answers through interpreter Ryuji Araki, never adequately explained his talent and was noncommittal when asked if his teammates copied his style.

"I don't know . . . perhaps it just seems that way," Fukudome said, adding that in one April at-bat, his incessant fouling off of pitches resulted from his inability to put the ball into fair territory.

Strange behavior for the formerly swinging Cubs began to surface. In the good ol' days, when Ramirez saw a strike early in the count, he'd usually go full bore with his bat. But in one early-season 2008 at-bat at home, he fell behind 0-and-2, only to work the pitcher for a walk.

After causing momentary panic among always-jittery Cubs fandom by losing their first two games at home against the Brewers, the Cubs won their first game 6–3 against Milwaukee on April 3. Unusual things were afoot. The Cubs drew six walks, and Alfonso Soriano, as aggressive a hacker as exists in the majors, patiently watched four straight pitches go by to force in the lead run in the fourth. That wouldn't be the first time Soriano strategically left the bat on his shoulder in 2008.

Two days later, the Cubs fashioned a victory sparked by a five-run seventh that featured two walks and a pair of two-out run-scoring doubles by Fukudome and Mark DeRosa—the kind of clutch stew scarcely brewed around Clark and Addison. Meanwhile, winning pitcher Zambrano fixed his potassium deficiency thanks to increased consumption of bananas and water, and a decrease in Red Bull chugging.

"I feel like a monkey," a jovial Zambrano said.

"You ever see a weak gorilla?" outfielder Daryle Ward added in a separate interview.

The newfound patience was augmented by fresh blood in the lineup—the first impact run producer out of the Cubs farm system in 20 years. Burying the notion that he was averse to young players playing a prominent role, Piniella handed over the 2008 catching duties to rookie Geovany Soto, no questions asked. The manager had been so impressed with Soto's hitting and demeanor behind the plate when he was called up the previous September that he nudged veteran Jason Kendall out of the job, keeping Soto as the starter in the playoffs against Arizona.

Soto had a rough game against the Brewers, who stole three bases in one inning against him, on April 2. An impatient manager would have second-guessed the kid. But Soto enjoyed a built-in support system with a dash of the same tough love Piniella had doled out to Alex Rodriguez in Seattle in 1994 and '95. Veteran backup catcher Henry Blanco—a savvy handler of pitchers who is deemed a future manager—was informally anointed the Yoda, the all-knowing mentor to Soto's Luke Skywalker. Blanco and Soto lockered next to each other at Wrigley Field and were card-playing partners, constantly together. After the April 2 loss, Blanco and Soto went into the video room to watch tape together. Then, at 10:15 a.m. on April 6, more than three hours before game time, Soto got additional help. He donned all his catcher's gear and stationed himself at home plate. He was joined by Blanco; Matt Sinatro, Piniella's top coach and a former catcher; and coaching assistant Ivan DeJesus. Sinatro figured Soto needed to use his legs more—like a pitcher— when firing to second. He profanely barked instructions as the armored Soto practiced his footwork as he wound up to throw. Other less intense sessions would punctuate the rest of the season in the Cubs' ongoing master-teaches-apprentice system.

Piniella could not get enough of Soto, voted in as the National League's All-Star catcher, first rookie ever to garner that honor, and the eventual NL Rookie of the Year. Blanco, 36, found his potential playing time cut, but as a team elder and leader, he knew it could be no other way on a winning team. He would teach Soto everything he knew and in turn the Cubs' all-around play would be boosted with a productive two-way catcher, a troublesome position for much of 2007.

"If I help him, I help the team," Blanco said. "Whatever we talk about, I'm sure he's going to be good on the field. We know he's going to hit. It's important to help him in dealing with the pitcher, calling the game. The more I can help him, the better player he can be for us. It helps [Sinatro]. We all work together."

The Cubs made their entire lives easier by practicing their new-found patience to rack up walks and hits in bunches on their second homestand. The arrival of cannon-fodder Cincinnati and Pittsburgh helped, but the games and statistics were not discounted or prorated based on strength of opposition. The Cubs went 7–1 in this stretch, scoring 67 runs. Most impressive were back-to-back 7–1 and 8–1 victories over the New York Mets on April 21 and 22.

Piniella got his fast start with a 14-6 record after the final shellacking of the Mets. Some momentary blips followed. The Cubs lost two of three each to the bedraggled Nationals in Washington, D.C.; to the Brewers (with another ninth-inning meltdown) in Wrigley Field; to the Cardinals in St. Louis; and the Reds in Cincinnati, including a four-homer barrage in an inning against veteran Jon Lieber in his only 2008 start.

But more home cooking soon sated the Cubs' appetites. They swept the Diamondbacks, their 2007 playoff tormentors, three straight from May 9 to 11, took three of four against the Padres and two of three against the Pirates through May 18. Their home record stood at 18–6. Wrigley Field at last was a true home-field advantage. No longer would management need to open the rightfield double doors to a billy goat escorted by a group of Wisconsin seminarians, as had occurred on May 4, 1994. The hex-busting animal had circumnavigated the warning track, then turned down the leftfield line and angered starter Steve Trachsel, warming up, as the animal-human entourage sauntered by the Cubs bullpen on its way to home plate. The Cubs had reached the bottom of the barrel in trying to break a 12-game home losing streak. Trachsel's pitching, not the goat lifting yet another curse, had more to do with the 5–2 win over the Reds.

Fourteen years later—and after Piniella had momentarily fallen off the no-superstitions wagon and mentioned the goat after he pulled Carlos Zambrano early in the 2007 Division Series Game 1 against Arizona—there was scant mention anymore of all these traditional Chicago baseball omens and portents. By May 19, 2008, the Cubs' newfound patience was displayed in glorious black-and-white. Their .372 OBP led the NL. Their 201 walks, fully two-fifths of their previous season's total, and their 438 hits ranked second. Along with Fukudome's prodigious walk totals, he flirted with a .300 batting average and an on-base percentage nearly 100 points higher. The math added up correctly: The Cubs led the league in runs scored with 255 while ranking just fifth in homers. The macho-man hitting philosophy of 2004 to 2006 seemed so wrong and out-of-touch with the game's new reality.

There were purveyors of patience much closer to home who could have made a similar difference. But all the transpacific scouting missions, all the careful observations

of Japanese customs that resulted in Fukudome's accep-
tance of a smaller contract with the Cubs compared to
the package offered by the crosstown White Sox, were
worth their weight in gold by the Cubs' position atop the
standings.

Pretty soon the lineup would fully stand on its own
without Fukudome showing the way. There was no turning
back.

THE FONZ

The silver Aston Martin convertible with the pair of tan bucket seats zipped west on Waveland Avenue and quickly made a 90-degree turn into the Cubs players' tiny lot on the northwest fringe of Wrigley Field. James Bond could have been at the wheel, and sometimes the driver dresses as nattily as Agent 007. Silver three-piece suits, matching the color of the car, are his favorite. He's the best-dressed Cub, by far.

"That's my style," said Alfonso Soriano. "I like to be clean. I try to do the best I can. I respect the game, I respect my teammates, so you have to be clean. That's me. I learned that from New York. I saw a lot of major leaguers who are dressed nice. I got some [suits] from 2001 to 2008, it's a lot. You have to be nice and clean, because you never know who's looking at you."

All eyes in Chicago were on Soriano—enjoying his own *Happy Days* with his arrival in Chicago and new nick-name of Fonzie—from the moment he signed the Cubs' biggest-ever contract, worth $136 million over eight years and $14 million in 2008, just before Thanksgiving 2006.

He can now afford to manufacture the suits and run dealer-ships of Aston Martins.

When Soriano pulled up in these special wheels on a late-summer 2008 morning, anybody watching couldn't avoid staring. In one quick move, the convertible pulled to a stop, past the behemoth Hummers and Escalades, veri-table tanks whose owners don't worry about the cost of gas. One of the biggest is Carlos Zambrano's Sequoia with the TORO 38 (Spanish for *bull*) license plate, lent to one of the coaches while Big Z drove a black Mercedes. Soriano has his own Hummer, but his style is more sporty. When the mood suits him, he substitutes a Bentley convertible for the Aston Martin.

Soriano's ebony physique is the Cubs' most chiseled, and it practically ripples out of his polo shirt. No dapper dressing today. He left the convertible in the care of ball-park security man Tony Cooney, whose main duty is to watch over the cramped, fenced-in lot and treat the play-ers' wheels with TLC. Oh, what the legendary 1969 Cubs would have given to have a cordoned-off space for their Cadillacs and Buicks. They used to park across the street past the vintage 1915 Chicago firehouse, and in the frenzy of that aborted first-place run some players had their shirts torn by the adoring masses as they tried to cross Waveland. A throwback to such an era appeared in 2007, when extra man Daryle Ward, a "See the USA in your Chevrolet" dev-otee, parked his mint-condition 1964 black Impala he had trucked in from California in this lot. A muscle car for a muscleman.

Today's Cubs keep their threads safely intact as they turn into the lot past a small group of autograph seekers as they arrive, but must carefully inch their way out postgame while larger crowds press in for a glimpse, greeting and signatures handed out through open car windows. That task was seven hours distant for Alfonso Soriano. So soon after he arrived in the team's most stylish sports car and sat at a table by his locker in the center of the locker room, he pawed at his authentic Dominican breakfast of fried salami, fried eggs, and plantains—faithfully delivered to him and fellow countrymen Aramis Ramirez and Carlos Marmol by a clubhouse man. Between bites, Soriano was asked just how fast the Aston Martin can race if you give it the gas.

"Two hundred," he responded quickly. But Soriano has never gotten it up to speed on the crowded expressways either in Chicago or in Florida, whose license plates the car bears.

The cynics would say Soriano's own legs weren't up to their full pace either, since he signed his $136 million, eight-year contract in 2006. The Cubs paid for not just a sleek, sporty model, but also a unique hybrid baseball creation—a 40–40 man. The 46 homers and 41 stolen bases for the Washington Nationals in 2006 made Soriano the double threat whom the Cubs would not have signed in the Andy MacPhail era. The man driving the premium car was the premium free agent who would restore instant credibility to a tarnished franchise.

Like his car, Soriano could easily get out of fine-tuning, physically and mentally. A year's worth of leg problems that included a partially torn quadriceps muscle and a tweaked hamstring destroyed the second 40 tag. He would run the bases gingerly all the time, using words never heard from another big leaguer, even if deep down they truly felt such fears. Soriano said he was "worried" about his legs even though he said they were physically fine. He also used the word "scared" in describing his fears about pushing his legs too hard. Typical was a comment on September 15, 2007, in St. Louis, three weeks after he returned from the torn quad.

"I think my leg is fine," Soriano said. "The [bigger] problem is in my mind. Anytime I want to try to run, I don't feel nothing, but I worry in my mind. [I want to] be comfortable. Sometimes I make a move, but I feel nothing. When I think I have a problem in my leg, I run like 80 percent, 75 percent."

Such comments fueled the grist for the Cubs Universe and many media pundits, to move Soriano from his professed comfort zone—at leadoff—down in the lineup, where his only duties would be whacking the ball over the fence with men on base. Manager Lou Piniella had done his research on Soriano, and concluded he risked "losing" him if he was removed from leadoff without justification, such as the acquisition of a more classic No. 1 hitter like Brian Roberts, target of long but unsuccessful trade talks by the Cubs in the winter of 2007–08.

A litany of other peculiarities enveloped Soriano and attracted attention, the majority of it unwanted, to a player who insisted he signed with the Cubs to win a World Series. First and foremost were those leg muscles and tendons he believed were balky. By his nature as an aggressive hitter, he endured his alternating hot-cold spells at the plate. He stopped and stared at the flight of several baseballs he had whacked that fell short of home-run distance, putting a target on his back, especially from the Atlanta Braves. His one-of-a-kind "hop" as he caught fly balls preceded one leg injury and two misplayed fly balls in Pittsburgh, while other outfield moves ranged from the clumsy to the eccentric.

Between his mercurial performance and his monster contract, Soriano became the top lightning rod for Cubs fans, who would have enthusiastically welcomed his presence in more penurious management days five years previous, but now harp over every flaw, every strikeout, and every leftfield misplay. After a breather in the summer of 2008, the controversy fired up hotter than ever the following October, after Soriano's inability to switch to a small-man's offensive game was a huge contributor to his 1-for-14 nosedive against the Dodgers in the division series, on top of a 2-for-14 snoozefest against the Diamondbacks the year before, on top of generally poor postseason forays going back to the Yankees in 2001.

Most of the burdens of the Cubs Universe rested upon a man who professed simple goals that did not suggest grandstanding, flightiness, or egotistical behavior.

"I just want to stay healthy and play 162 games," Soriano said when he had a month of good health under his belt in August 2008, after he missed the equivalent of two months with a strained calf and a broken hand. "When I play healthy, I can do a lot of things to help the team win. I played 159 [games] twice, 161 with the Yankees. I never ask for a day off. I like to play, I don't need a day off. Not 159, I want to play 162. When the season is over, I'll have a lot of days off. Sometimes the manager says I want to give you a day off. I say, 'I'm fine, I don't need it.' I understand—sometimes the manager thinks I need a day off. I have to take it."

Soriano incurred all the brickbats without ever stating that Wrigley Field was "my house," a longtime proclamation of Sammy Sosa. The superstar who did not mind chatting about his game, who often was first by his locker after the last pitch, who did not seem to acquire Sosa's ego that might as well have been inflated by steroids. Like Sosa, Soriano got caught up in a title-starved city's penchant for consuming its own, like a beast eating its young.

Soriano quiets this Chicago phenomenon when he goes on one of his patented tears with the Cubs happily riding his back. But let him go into a strikeout spree, screw up a fly ball, or run at less than a gallop around the bases, and he's an albatross around the Cubs' neck, according to popular baseball culture. To be sure, Soriano continually courts the leftfield fans, tossing baseballs to good-looking women or kids between innings, jabbering back and forth with the bleacher bums, and holding up two fingers if a fan yells in mid-inning, "How many outs, Alfonso?" He even stopped to sign autographs in the players' parking lot as he cleared out his locker three days after the downbeat ending of the 2008 NLDS. But away from this two-way relationship of superstar and $45-per-ticket rooters, the issue of Soriano was the most heated amid the mounting success of 2007 and 2008.

Manager Lou Piniella, who estimated he fielded more questions about Soriano than any other combination of players and was sick of it, remarked that it's fortunate Soriano probably couldn't read the English-language jibes thrust his way. Soriano reads English, all right, but not stories about himself. Opening up a *Chicago Sun-Times* on the clubhouse table by his locker on September 1, 2008, he quickly flipped past the baseball stories straight to an entire page of box scores. "I've got to check on my friends on the Yankees, Rangers, and Nationals," he said.

Piniella's biggest blowup at the media in 2008—during which he huffed, "You think I'm stupid or something?"—was prompted by a question about his failure to substitute Reed Johnson for a gimpy Soriano for defense in the ninth inning, when the outfielder misplayed a Gabe Kapler drive to left in a blown game against the Milwaukee Brewers. Criticism is as close as the Cubs' broadcast booth, where

TV analyst Bob Brenly, who as Diamondbacks manager devised an effective defense against Soriano in the 2001 World Series, has ripped his shaky outfielding. At one point Brenly said you could aim a dart into the Cubs dugout and hit a better defensive player than Soriano.

"That's part of my job," Soriano said when asked point-blank about his unwanted centerpiece in controversy. "I have to do what I have to do. I work very hard to try to do the best I can. I'm very strong mentally and try to get over my injury to get my leg strong and help team win.

"Sometimes this game's very hard to play, especially if it's sore. I try to not think about it if I have something sore in my body. Every day I come to the ballpark and play 100 percent for nine innings.

"I'm very confident in myself. I have a very strong heart and mental [state]. I have a backbone."

Soriano's fundamental mistakes can be more than canceled out by seven-homers-in-seven-games streaks. More important, he has not set himself apart from all other teammates, low-keying it in the clubhouse and blending in to the Cubs' hard-won team chemistry. He doesn't infuriate all ends of Wrigley Field, as Sosa did with his preening and selfishness, angering teammates so much that they called him the "biggest asshole in baseball" and the "game's worst teammate." The clubby's breakfast delivery from a nearby Hispanic restaurant is Soriano's only visible outstanding privilege, compared to the team's employment of Julian Martinez as Sosa's manservant. Ask for Soriano's time and he'll more often than not talk at a low-decibel level for a few minutes. Sure, the "scared" and "worried" slip through, but the emphasis is on what Soriano can do for the Cubs, not the other way around.

Other prominent teammates will rush to his defense in a manner unthinkable for Sosa.

"He can hit," said ace Carlos Zambrano. "He knows what he's doing at home plate. Some people think he's a dumb hitter. But he's not. He's a smart hitter. At the beginning, some people were booing him and he was doing no good. Look, everybody in baseball can go through slumps and bad times, and superstars do what Soriano's doing now. Good for him. I feel good for him. I feel good he's doing a lot of work with his hitting coach. You can see the result."

The proof that Soriano is not a Sosa relation came in his recovery times. When he ripped the quadriceps running from first to third on August 5, 2007, against the Mets, it was projected that recovery time would be up to six weeks. Soriano was back in the lineup for a crucial series against the Milwaukee Brewers on August 28. Within a week he was on a September spree that produced a team-record 14 homers. He could not advance the recovery timetable of six weeks when he returned from a broken hand on July 23, but he only required a handful of minor-league rehab at-bats to get ready.

Soriano is in his element as a leadoff man because he knows he'll get a healthy diet of fastballs. Frank Robinson, his Washington manager, crooked his finger and pointed to his own temple during the National League Division Series at Chase Field in 2007 when asked why batting No. 1 was so important to Soriano.

"That's my job," Soriano said. "I bat leadoff because of the manager. I'm not the guy who makes the lineup. I'm not a guy who makes the lineup. I'm the wrong guy to ask that question. I think this team is different, they don't want me to steal a lot of bases, we have a lot of power hitters.

"In Washington, I was the only power [hitter]. If I get on base, I wait till D-Lee, Ramirez, Fukudome, somebody drive me home. So I don't have to steal a base like I used to. If the team needs me to steal a base, I can do it, but not like in Washington. It's different. We have to play more careful. It's more important to be in the lineup every day and not try to steal [more bases] and go to the DL. It's more important to me to be in the lineup, more important for the team."

But if Soriano is sated mentally at leadoff, the Cubs draw comfort that the critics of his lineup positioning could not refute. When they revived in the final two-thirds of 2007, the Cubs were 24–5 when Soriano had two or more hits in a game. Amid two injury absences in 2008, the Cubs weren't as good without Soriano as with him. As August 2008 drew to a close, they were 54–23 when Soriano was the leadoff hitter. Problem was, if he endured one of his cold spells, as in his back-to-back play-off appearances as a Cub, the lineup followed suit and shut down.

Frustration about the situation mounted with the realization that Soriano at his best is a one-man wrecking crew who gives his team instant offense at leadoff, then is even more dangerous with men on base later in games. Take the homestand of May 9 to 17, 2008.

He batted just .191 coming into the May 9 game against the Diamondbacks. Soriano just is not comfortable with Chicago's cold springs. "It's not easy to deal with the cold weather," he said. But with increasingly sunny days and the mercury creeping up, he capped off a four-hit afternoon with a two-run double that put the Cubs ahead for good in the eventual 3–1 victory. Minutes later, he scored the fourth run of the inning with a head-first slide into home plate, beating a throw from centerfielder Chris Young on Ryan Theriot's single despite admitting later he was "a little scared" to use his legs so assertively.

He was only warming up. He doubled in the two key runs the next day in a 7–2 win against Arizona on the way to a three-game sweep of their 2007 playoff tormentors. Two days later, against the Padres on May 12, Soriano launched a power spree with a two-run homer against the Padres' Randy Wolf in a 12–3 victory.

"I feel very comfortable at home plate," he said afterward. "I'm swinging at strikes and being more patient at home plate. That's what I want to do to help the team win. I'm being more aggressive, but at the same time being selective at home plate. When I swing at strikes, I know I hit the ball very hard."

On May 13, Soriano's first leadoff homer of 2008—and 45th of his career—wasn't enough to prevent former Cub Shawn Estes from beating his old team 4–3. But on May 14, he staked Ted Lilly to a 1–0 lead with another leadoff homer, then collected a two-run single two innings later to help fuel an 8–5 victory. Both hits came on 2-and-1 pitches, displaying Soriano's perceptible increase in patience.

"He's seeing more pitches than [2007]," Cardinals pitcher Todd Wellemeyer confirmed later in the summer. While Soriano claimed working the count to 3-and-0 in the manner of the early-season Kosuke Fukudome was "not my game," he desired to be more selective in pitches in the strike zone. Just the mere fact that he'd take a couple of pitches invited more fastballs in hitters' counts, and then he could really go to work. And he did not appear an automatic sucker to flail at curves off the outside corner.

"I'm not saying they're wrong," Soriano said of the pitching strategy to fool him with curveballs. "Breaking balls are harder to hit, but when it's a strike, I can hit anyone's breaking ball. When they throw it for a strike, I can hit it hard. I think I'm a very good breaking-ball hitter. I have to be more selective at home plate when I hit breaking balls. Not swing at pitches they throw away at home plate."

Soriano collected two hits in each of the four Padres games. Now he'd raise the ante with two more homers on May 16 to boost Sean Gallagher to his first big-league win in a 7–4 victory over the Pirates.

Just as a reminder that one man versus 25 often doesn't compute, Soriano's two homers among his five hits could not prevent a 7–6 loss to the Pirates on May 17.

"I feel very hot right now," he said after totaling seven homers in six games while raising his average more than 100 points to .295. "Oh, man, I want to have the most at-bats I can and swing at strikes. If they don't throw strikes, I don't want to swing." But Nate McLouth had the best swing of them all with a two-run ninth-inning game-winning homer off ace setup man Carlos Marmol.

By now, the periodic boos had faded and Soriano basked in frequent standing ovations at Wrigley Field.

"That's good," he said. "It makes me feel great. The fans love the players doing well here. That's a very special moment for me."

But unlike 2007, Soriano's merry month of May proved to be his only trademark hot spell of the season. To be sure, he was set back by his broken hand. When he returned in mid-July, he did not enjoy another huge outburst, save for a three-homer night in Cincinnati on September 6. He batted just .244 in September, a harbinger of things to come and a factor in a slowdown of the Cubs lineup in the final month, finishing at .280 compared to .299 after his 14-homer September 2007.

Throughout 2008, Soriano offered up subtle improvements in his trademark lack of patience at the plate. He drew 43 walks—his second-highest total ever—in 109 games compared to 31 in 135 games in 2007. Within individual bats, he insisted he tried to be more selective in the pitches at which he swung. On average, he saw one more pitch per game—almost 17—than he did in 2007. His most patient eye came during the power-mad final month of 2007, when Soriano witnessed almost 18 pitches per game. As another modest uptick in an otherwise undisciplined approach, he said he could identify when he had a poor approach. In his NLDS postmortem, he insisted he tried to make an adjustment after a poor Game 1 and tried to go after strikes in the next two contests, to little effect. He simply could not downshift his game to slapping 20-bouncers through the infield or slicing the ball to right-field when his power was taken away. The calls for Soriano to be dropped in the lineup and replaced by a classic leadoff man loudly revived.

Associated with his wildly fluctuating production at bat was the stark fact that his days as a prime base-stealer were likely over. Soriano swiped just 19 bases in each of his first two Cubs seasons after his 41 total with the Nationals in 2006, four years after the same total captured the American League stolen-base crown as a Yankee.

"It depends, if I'm healthy, I steal bases," he said later in 2008. "I did 40 or more three times. It's combination of the right time, like the [July 28 to 31, 2008] series in Milwaukee, you do anything you can to win games. More important, my legs feel good. I don't think about what happened in the past. I'm very comfortable and very happy about how I feel. I don't think about my hands. I just play."

Soriano bursting out like the May foliage established the 2008 season's bottom line. When he led off—and hit—the Cubs usually hummed like a well-oiled machine. Few other leadoff hitters in the game can set the positive tone that the instant karma his leadoff homers provide. The Cubs climbed to 10 games over .500 for the first time in 2008 during the mid-May Soriano spree, on their way to their 97-win season.

The issue was settled. There would be no more controversy over Soriano batting leadoff. Lou Piniella's media sessions just got less stressful.

But one question about Soriano at No. 1 still begged an answer. How did batting No. 1 become so addictive to Soriano that Piniella practiced his greatest mind-game job as Cubs manager?

Only Joe Torre could shed light. As Yankees manager in 2001, he tabbed Soriano to succeed Chuck Knoblauch as the Yankees' leadoff man. Then, as now, Soriano had great natural gifts, yet was almost the antithesis of a classic No. 1 hitter. He had awesome power that seemed better suited for the middle of the lineup. And Soriano struck out far too much as a leadoff man, hardly walked, and had only a fair on-base percentage. And finally, in 2008 he did not run as much—his redeeming quality at the top of the lineup.

Torre hit Chicago a week after Soriano's rampage against the Padres and Pirates. Now the Dodgers manager, he fielded almost as many questions about Soriano as his own team. Eventually Torre would use his insider's knowledge of Soriano against him in the NLDS.

"Not really," Torre said when asked if Soriano was an ideal leadoff man. "But what he could give us [was positive]. The home runs and the speed. He's not a burner. He has base-stealing ability. He runs hard, plays hard. Of all of our options, he was our best bet up at the top of the batting order.

"You never noticed any change in him. I always encourage all my players to be who you are. I know how aggressive [Derek] Jeter is and I put him in the leadoff spot. I didn't want him to take strike one. Just go up there and be who you are. But Sori, he was a true baseball player. He was going up there to be aggressive.

"Plus he was dangerous," Torre continued. "One pitch, one run. It's so easy. The only time I ever saw him struggle was when he was trying to be that 40–40 guy. When you try to hit home runs, it becomes damn near impossible. He liked playing. There were times in the World Series in '03 when he was struggling. I batted him seventh because he was struggling. I couldn't put him eighth in a National League park because of his lack of selectivity. He was such a free swinger."

So just what is Soriano's mental comfort zone at leadoff?

"It means you know you're going to get pitches to hit," Torre said. "You're at the top of the batting order and you're a guy who possesses some speed, [the pitcher] is not likely to want to put him on base. All of a sudden your best hitters are coming up. To me, the security of a hitter going up there knowing he's going to get a strike to hit certainly helps a guy's personality."

Torre only had to worry about Soriano's stiff moves around second base, having moved him over from his original amateur/minor-league position at shortstop. He was even tried briefly at third base as a Yankee. But Torre never had the headache of dealing with then-second baseman Soriano's one-of-a-kind flycatcher with a "hop" in which he leaps forward as he catches a ball.

Soriano started out as a reluctant, if not recalcitrant, outfielder when he was shifted to leftfield when the Nationals acquired him in a deal from the Rangers for outfielders Brad Wilkerson and Termell Sledge on December 13, 2005. Almost immediately, he put his foot down that he would not switch to leftfield from second base, where he had been a shaky defensive performer much of his career. All-Star Jose Vidro was encamped at second then for the Nationals.

"I have the same position [on moving] as I always had when I was with Texas," Soriano said. "I said that I'm not going to change from second base. Obviously, I have the control. Of course I'm not going to play the outfield."

In spring training 2006, Soriano refused to take his position in leftfield in a March 20 game against the Los Angeles Dodgers. Only eight Nationals came out of the dugout. Ryan Church hurriedly took Soriano's place in left while Brandon Watson played center. The Nationals threatened to put Soriano on the disqualified list. Soriano changed his mind in time for the March 22 game against the St. Louis Cardinals.

"I love this game," Soriano said after playing all nine innings in left. "That's why I changed my mind." A third-day story by Soriano and agent Diego Bentz suggested a miscommunication about whether the Nationals intended to keep Soriano's name in the lineup when the March 20 game started, prompting the ghost outfielder in left.

"I say, 'If you put me in leftfield, I'm not sure,'" Soriano added. "I'm not ready to go there. . . . I didn't know that situation when I left the ballpark on Monday." Nationals manager Frank Robison had met privately with Soriano before the March 20 game. Soriano told Robinson he would take grounders at second instead of fly balls in left during batting practice.

Even when he accepted his position change, Soriano expressed doubts. "I'm not comfortable," he said.

Once Soriano accepted his fate as a leftfielder, he developed the hop as a way of moving toward the ball, in the manner of an infielder in forward gear, and not allowing the ball to play him. The move was totally unorthodox, never seen with any other outfielder, and it generated constant questions and head scratching directed at both Soriano and Piniella.

The queries taxed Piniella almost beyond his limit on the Internal Revenue Service deadline day of April 15, 2008, when the Cubs hosted the Reds at Wrigley Field. As Soriano performed the trademark hop catching Ken Griffey Jr.'s easy fly ball to end the top of the first, he strained his left calf. An MRI test confirmed the injury, and Soriano— already feeling slightly hobbled by past leg maladies— would go on to miss two weeks.

Recognizing Soriano's delicate psyche weighed against his otherworldly run production when hot, Piniella refused to delegitimize the hop even though he knew it was fundamentally unsound.

"He catches the ball that way," he said. "It seems like a natural move for him. I can't remember [anyone else catching the ball that way]. It's his unique style."

Piniella was asked if this was yet another Cubby Occurrence, his own description for the litany of strange events in team annals that he picked up on after one year on the job. But he backed off from branding the injury as such.

"Don't put words in my mouth," Piniella said. "It was a freak thing."

When Soriano returned from the injury, he misplayed a fly ball in the late-afternoon sun on May 25 in Pittsburgh to allow the Pirates to escape a near-certain defeat and win 6–5 in 11 innings. Taking Soriano off the hook the next day was centerfielder Reed Johnson, who conferred with him prior to the inning about the severe sun problem that had also baffled such longtime Pirates as Jason Bay. "The ball went up in the one spot in the field where he couldn't see it," Johnson explained.

"I have not seen him hop and drop a ball," Cubs outfield coach Mike Quade said on May 28, leaning against the leftfield wall near the Cubs bullpen just before batting practice. "It's unusual and it's unorthodox. When they moved him to the outfield, he was not as comfortable just standing and waiting for the ball. He wanted some movement. He felt better going to get it. I am not concerned about his catching routine fly balls, when he hops. At spring training, I wanted to deal with the warning track and wall, and he did not do as well as he'd liked. The hop is what it is and what it will be. Routine plays using the hop are working out just fine."

Until the night of August 26, 2008, at that same cursed leftfield at PNC Park. Soriano went to hop for a routine fly near the leftfield line. The ball deflected off his glove for a double. Doug Mientkiewicz soon followed with a two-run triple, but the stripped-down Pirates could not hold down the Cubs in an eventual 14–9 loss.

Soriano periodically would goof up in leftfield, drawing Bob Brenly's on-air criticism and no doubt privately infuriating Piniella. Meanwhile, Quade kept trying to instill fundamentals one at a time with Soriano.

"It's trusting his legs," Quade said of his mobility in the outfield. "It was a challenge coming off two leg injuries. It affected the amount of time you can work on it. When you combine all these little things from all these angles with a guy who's not very experienced, you can find why it hasn't been as consistent as you'd like. He works for a good 20 minutes a day in the outfield.

"The only thing left [to work on] is understanding different situations, and how to get out of tough situations.

We kind of protect the leftfield well [the curve in the outfield wall in Wrigley Field]. There's no better time than in batting practice. He can watch caroms and learn a great deal, and then have some anticipation during the game of what will happen. My job with Sori is as an inexperienced guy and a guy who's still learning, if you want to avoid this problem, here's a couple of things to try, and then try them."

Through all the controversies and misplays, Soriano had a singular premium talent as a leftfielder—his arm. He led the NL in assists with 22 in 2006 for the Nationals, then the next season tied the all-time Cubs season assists record for outfielders with 19 originally set by Hank Sauer in 1951.

Soriano lets loose his line-drive throws to the plate or the infield with a compact, almost fliplike motion instead of the over-the-head, windup form of most outfielders. Maybe that technique lulls runners to sleep when they continue to test him.

"I don't know," he said when asked why runners still challenge his arm. "I'm happy what I do in leftfield. I played infield before. Don't try to do too much. I have a very strong arm. But try like an 80 percent [of total strength] throw. I think I have a chance to make a lot of outs at home plate. Throw the ball on one bounce to home plate."

Soriano said that the best throwing outfielder he's witnessed plays in Seattle.

"I think Ichiro [Suzuki]," he said. "If you want to score [on a hit to right] field, he's made me out at home plate."

Quade's list is longer.

"For me the big arms in the league that are stronger than Alfonso's are [Shane] Victorino, [Jeff] Francoeur, [Rick] Ankiel when he's healthy, and [Carlos] Beltran."

Such a rating is part of the strange dichotomy of Alfonso Soriano: the best at what he does when he's hot, the ingrained flaws in his game, an ability to admit his mistakes and recognize what corrective action must be taken, and a personal flashiness that's enough under control.

The Cubs got a lot, good and bad, for $136 million. Fonzie is who he is. Typecast, perhaps he can add one little wrinkle to his part in the remaining six years of his dream deal: any kind of smoothing out of an individual game as jumpy as the stock market.

THE RIOT

Good thing that Ryan Theriot kind of creeps up on you, slips in through the side door, and before you know it, he's in the starting lineup, batting second and serving as that little pest who takes two and hits to right.

If Theriot tried simply to walk through the Cubs' front door, by now he might be at some godforsaken, far-flung baseball outpost clear out of the organization, or back in his native Baton Rouge, Louisiana. Modest-size middle infielders signed, sealed, and delivered by the Cubs farm system are supposed to make an indifferent, cameo appearance, then slip back into the obscurity from whence they came and never be heard from again.

Theriot was different. Somehow he curried the favor of Lou Piniella when the manager first saw him work out in spring training 2007. A year later he's hitting .300, flirting with a .400 on-base percentage that had been his goal, playing shortstop every day, and ranking as one of the Cubs' resident matinee idols, a longtime franchise tradition. As a rookie, he was branded with his nickname The Riot, a double meaning for the last four letters of his surname and his style of play. The spunky infielder, cagey and politically savvy as befitting his roots in politics-rich Louisiana, was the first middle infielder to spring from the farm system to snare a regular's job with the Cubs since Shawon Dunston in 1985. And just in time. Piniella needed a modest-size bat handler to break up all his right-handed power that started with leadoff man Alfonso Soriano and continued with Derrek Lee and Aramis Ramirez batting behind Theriot.

What's so difficult about developing a slap-hitting player who could bat, say, .250 and pick up a ground ball? Well, even those modest qualifications escaped the scouts, roving instructors, and farm directors. The sheer dearth of good position-player prospects since the late 1980s, let alone skilled middle infielders, would have ensnared the rare legitimate top prospect in suffocating hype had he come along, so much so that he'd flop under the pressure once he reached Wrigley Field. Theriot's good fortune was that no one in the big city paid attention to him, even though he was a No. 3 draft pick in 2001 and a mainstay of Louisiana State's national championship baseball team. An aborted attempt to transform Theriot into a switch hitter kept his minor-league numbers artificially low, and he was thus able to develop out of the spotlight once he righted his offensive game. By the time he got a month-plus trial at second base to finish up the 2006 season, hitting an impressive .328 with a .412 on-base percentage, hardly anyone was paying attention to the Cubs as that last-place campaign wound down.

Even as he established himself as a regular in 2007 and going into 2008, Theriot was easily to overlook, or even dismiss as a less-than-first-rate middle infielder. He did not possess a missile-launcher of an arm. He did not hit for power or even a lot of extra-base oomph. He could run a bit, but his percentage of successful steals to attempts was below average. Theriot also harked back to Dwight Smith with some overaggressive baserunning.

Nevertheless, here he was as the regular shortstop for two successive Cubs postseason teams. He stays in his position and thrives most of the time simply because he doesn't dare look back. Nothing ever was assured in pro ball. He knows all too well his good fortune could slip away if he lets up.

"I wasn't able to really get comfortable in my position, my spot," he said of his debut as a regular in '07 and his subsequent growth. "I was constantly fighting for a chance to get out there on an everyday basis. Once I did, I still felt like I had something to prove, because you go out of your game a little bit to try to open eyes.

"I'm still getting to know a lot of the pitchers. Out of a seven-day week, I wouldn't have seen four or five of them. Being comfortable in my skin, knowing my job, and knowing what I'm asked to do every day has a huge bearing on my performance. Knowing if I don't get any hits, I'll be out there the next day."

Theriot's plucky play and hustle first attracted the attention of Piniella in spring training 2007. The manager, casting his net far and wide for those he felt could play coming off the 2006 disaster, assured Theriot early on in camp he'd go north with the Cubs. Dutiful play as a utility infielder in the first two months of the season positioned Theriot to take over at shortstop when Piniella found veteran Cesar Izturis wanting. Even looking over his shoulder constantly at Piniella, wondering about his job security, Theriot was good enough to stay in the lineup, and even hit .300 at the leadoff spot during Alfonso Soriano's three-week absence due to a torn quadriceps muscle in August. Piniella could have panicked when a tiring Theriot's offensive game nose-dived in September, but he stayed in the lineup.

Having passed all the trials by fire, a more natural Theriot emerged in 2008. He followed the description of a No. 2 hitter almost to a T, consistently hitting the ball to right and right center to keep the busy line of Cubs base-runners moving. If Soriano was involved in more hit-and-run plays, Theriot would have earned a savvy bat-handler's reputation.

"It's something I've done my whole life—that's where I've hit the ball," he said of going to the opposite field—with the exception of some stilted 2007 performances. He also can be a bit self-deprecating, mimicking locker-mate Mark DeRosa: "Maybe it's because I don't have any bat speed.

"The key to it is being able to hit inside pitches the other way," he said. "When you do that, they really don't know where to pitch you. It's easier said than done. When you're going good, that's what you see, pitches down the middle and even inside a little bit, and you're going to rightfield.

"I always get that question about hitting the ball to rightfield. One of [the] reasons it turned out as it is, is because I can stay on the ball longer. There's certain times you look for a certain pitch and pull it. But a lot more good things happen if you hit the ball up the middle or the other way rather than pulling it. You advance the runners, hit, and run. There's never really a good outcome on a fly ball to leftfield. It's a tough sacrifice fly most of the time. You hit a good hard line drive to the third baseman, who cares? It's not a high percentage play for me."

Theriot developed the technique to inside-out his swing in his own backyard, back in Baton Rouge, between ages 8 and 15 in one of the most unusual youth hitting drills ever conceived, in this case by his father, Randy Theriot.

"I had a pine tree and went out there to hit with a slow-motion swing at point of contact where I wanted to hit it," he said. "My hands would be in front of the barrel and the barrel on the tree. My father made me push for 10 seconds . . . push, push, push, push. While I'm pushing, my hands are going forward while the barrel is staying back. I would finish and follow through. The point of the drill wasn't to hit to rightfield, it was to strengthen my hands and forearms. You're practicing exactly what you do when you hit, keeping the barrel behind your hands. Still, to this day, there's a huge indention in the pine tree. Sap would drip out."

Good enough to get a college ride to LSU's national-power baseball program and squire the captain of the cheer-leading squad, now his wife, the 5-foot-11, 175-pound Theriot looked like a prototypical "little man's" candidate to switch hit. Dutifully following the program, he did not take to the move. His average peaked in the .250s in the lower runs of the Cubs farm system in his first two full sea-sons. Finally, he gave up switch-hitting, batted right-handed full-time, and began soaking up hitting techniques.

As a Cubs rookie in 2006, he had a good idea of what to do with the bat—and a stream of consciousness actually forecast the offensive formula that became the Cubs' basis for success two years later.

"I want to be .400 [on-base percentage]," Theriot said at the time. He finished 2006 with a team-leading .412 in 53 games. "Not too many are there. If you got two or three guys at top of order doing that, you're going to be winning some ball games. If they can run a little bit, they can score on doubles. That's what you can hope for, but realistically that won't happen.

"If I don't get on at .350 [OBP] or more, I'm not going to be in the lineup. If I'm not scoring 100 runs, I'm not valuable to a team. Players do have to buy into it. It's the players' responsibility. How do you win games? You either save runs or score them."

Theriot did not miss his longtime OBP goal by much in 2008. He finished at .387, based on a .307 average—sixth in the National League—along with a career-high 73 walks. His 154 singles ranked first in the NL and second in the majors behind master batsman Ichiro Suzuki. He fell short of 100 runs scored, but 85 is still a respectable total.

Somewhere, Bobby Dickerson is smiling. Working in 2008 as the Cubs organization's infield/bunting coordinator, Dickerson had been Theriot's Double-A manager in Jackson, Tennessee, in 2005. He advocated an on-base philosophy of hit-first, but with a specific plan.

"Play hard pepper," Theriot said of the Dickerson lessons. "Put the barrel on the ball. Don't try to force the pitch somewhere. It's not easily definable. Wherever that pitch shows up, put the barrel on it. If you do that on a consistent basis, more times than not you're going to have a positive outcome."

Take a walk, if necessary, but strive for hitting your pitch. And do not be afraid to hit deep in the count.

"You hit the nail on the head," he said. "Hit with two strikes. If a hitter has confidence to do that, if you simplify it with me, the pitch shows up that you're going to hit, put the barrel on it.

"If the guy's pitch count is up, take a few pitches. If he's got dominating stuff and you know he can strike you out, hit the first straight one you see. It's real easy, but as a hitter you have to think along with it a little bit and buy into it. If you don't buy into it, it's not going to work.

"It's not like the *Moneyball* [philosophy]," he continued. "It's not take till you get a strike. If there's a dominating pitcher on the mound and I feel he can strike me out, if there's a ball up there I can hit and it's the first pitch, I'm going to hit it. I don't want to fall behind in the count against [the game's best control pitchers]."

Theriot showed early on that he could adjust and take pitches if necessary. In the ninth inning of a September 2, 2006, game against the Giants at Wrigley Field, he took a close 2-and-2 pitch from closer Armando Benitez for ball three. Eventually he used up 10 pitches in drawing a walk, forcing Benitez from the game. Theriot showed similar patience at other junctures. He slipped from his desired goal in 2007 as he felt under the gun to prove himself to Piniella, a .202 September knocking down his final on-base percentage number to .326 on a .266 batting average.

"Maybe it's experience," Theriot said of his coming-of-age season in 2008. "I had some tough series and tough at-bats. I felt I was hitting the ball well and not getting hits. All that stuff starts to pile up. When you're not getting hits, you start to think there's something wrong when there's really not. Although you hit balls, they're going to people. This year, I'm starting to understand that. I'm not going to get two hits every day, I'm not going to get one hit every day. It doesn't mean anything's wrong, it's just the way the game is set up.

"I definitely pay attention to who's pitching. I don't feel overwhelmed at all. I've never been in awe, never been scared. I think it's understanding hitting, understanding the major leagues. You're not going to get hits every day.

"Right now, if it's over the plate and I can hit it, I go after it," he continued. "I'm seeing the ball pretty well. A lot has to do with guys hitting in front and in back of me. I'll get pitches to hit because they don't want to walk me.

When I'm really feeling good at the plate, if it's a good first pitch, I'm going to go after it. You're not going to get too many [hittable] pitches in an at-bat. You may get one pitch to hit. If it's the first pitch, you've got to take advantage of it. But if you have a starter out there who's dominating and want to get him out of the game, try to work the count and get the pitch count up. It's a very unselfish way of playing the game."

Although Theriot's preference is swing-first, his walk count dramatically increased in keeping with the astounding turnaround of the entire lineup. He agreed with Piniella and Derrek Lee that the new faces in the lineup helped transform the hitting styles from the laggard on-base percentage style of 2004 to 2006.

"I think it could be looked at two different ways," he said. "On one hand, because of the increased number of pitches everyone is seeing, you tend to see higher on-base percentages. We've thrown three players in the mix who weren't here last year. It's an increased number of pitches seen by Kosuke [Fukudome, earlier in the season] and Reed [Johnson]—obviously it's their games. The style is contagious, guys throughout the lineup tend to do the same thing. It takes pressure off the big guys. They don't have to sit there and wait and see pitches. Alfonso takes more first-pitch fastballs than I saw all of last year. His batting practice has changed. He hits the other way, more line drives."

Theriot welcomed almost all interview requests in his rookie season. In 2008, he was a bit more distant, obviously busy with pregame workouts or batting practice. Yet he isn't likely to fall prey to the egotism that has resulted in bad media relations and the resulting poor image for many big-name athletes.

"I know where I come from and know what it took to get here," Theriot said. "I wasn't a first-round draft pick and never made an All-Star team in my life that I can remember. I've always been on winning teams, but never been *the* guy on the team that's been the focal point.

"I've been undersized and told I couldn't do it. It will keep you grounded. I have the luxury of having great support at home. My older brother and my wife don't let you forget it. I don't take a day of this for granted. Being able to play ball for the Cubs, playing in the majors is a dream for millions of people. Every day I put a uniform on, I feel lucky and fortunate to have the chance to do this. I don't think about the fame and fortune."

With his boyish good looks, charming Louisiana accent and hustling style, Theriot in 2007 quickly became one of the most popular Cubs, even before he established himself as a regular. An appearance in north suburban Wheeling in June 2007 drew about 400 fans, gathered on a park district baseball field to hear Theriot handle a question-and-answer session. Theriot asked to run the Q & A himself and seemed an old pro at the process. He was at ease in other Chicago-area personal appearances, which attracted as many as 1,000 fans. And why not? Theriot said he was instructed in media training while an LSU baseball star and had to handle the public's demands at an early age.

But fans who write to Theriot at Wrigley Field are cautioned to be patient for a response.

"You can get four to five letters a day or 10 to 15 a day sometimes," he said. "I put 'em in a box, take 'em home in the off-season, open 'em up, and send 'em back. Mostly cards [to sign]." He has helpers to screen out more negative mail.

Amid the increasing fan attention, Theriot is protective of his growing family. He and wife Johnnah are parents to a son, Houston, and two daughters, Macey and Georgia

Grace. Houston made his first public appearance one 2008 morning in the Cubs clubhouse, when he sang "Take Me Out To the Ball game" for an entertained horde of media gathered around Theriot's locker.

Houston's serenading session was just one of many light clubhouse moments involving Theriot. Smack-dab in the middle of the locker room, he has developed a great rapport with double-play partner and locker neighbor Mark DeRosa.

Earlier in the 2008 season, Theriot placed a photo of himself batting above DeRosa's locker. The picture was captioned, "Keep your eye on the ball," as a bit of friendly advice.

"The photo wasn't working, we had to take it down," Theriot said. "We wanted to remind him to keep his eye on the ball. We've grown to be pretty good friends. It's a pleasure to have him as a lockermate and teammate."

DeRosa devalued himself while he mockingly built up Theriot.

"I still say Ryan Theriot has the distinction as the media darling on the team," he said. "There's no way I can be a darling. I'm a grinder, man. The way you realize you've arrived is when you're sandwiched between Ryan Theriot and Jeff Samardzija. He's already proven to be one of the best rookies I've ever been around."

But DeRosa, tongue always in cheek, reminded Theriot to stay humble. "He's got to be knocked down and put back in his place," he said. "I'm not going to lie to you, the guy doesn't hurt for looks. At the same time, you can't tell him that."

Theriot does not disagree, even after he got a buzz cut late in the 2008 season that discarded his boyish shock of hair as a typical baseball superstition to lift the Cubs out of a short slump.

"Now I'm only the second most handsome guy in the league," Theriot said. "Before I was No. 1. I won't tell you who is No. 1 now."

DeRosa always tried to get in the last word.

"Fame is fleeting—as Ryan Theriot will find out 10 to 15 years from now when he's back in Baton Rouge, running a hitting school with his son," he said. "He'll long for the days seeing himself on a billboard near O'Hare Airport."

That's all frosting on Theriot's cake now that he's established himself in the majors. Most of his goals are already achieved, but an important one was unfulfilled after his two-plus Cubs seasons.

"I want nothing more than to win a World Series here in Chicago," he said. "Millions of people who watched me every day, and when games are over they smile because the Cubs won. Kids write you letters, saying you are their role model. That's why you play that game, that's what keeps you grounded and you understand why you're doing this. I'm here to affect as many lives in a positive manner as I can. That's the bottom line."

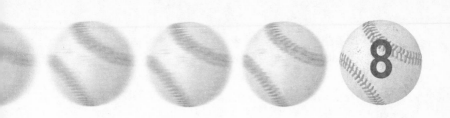

SWEET LOU AND HIS INQUISITORS

On Thursday, May 1, 2008, at Wrigley Field, the Cubs HAD JUST blown the game against the Milwaukee Brewers in so many different ways in the ninth inning that media interrogators would not soon run out of questions. And if Lou Piniella was going to cool down to answer them, it would not be soon enough for his entry into the crowded interview room some 15 minutes after the last out.

A well-played contest by the Cubs for eight innings washed down the drain as closer Kerry Wood dramatically coughed up a 3–1 lead. A gimpy Alfonso Soriano, fresh off the disabled list, misplayed a long drive to left by Gabe Kapler with no outs and a man on first for the central play in the collapse. The loss was the most shocking of the early season, and it of course did not sit well with Piniella. The brevity of his answers foretold an impending eruption.

Your humble narrator asked the first question: Did Wood not have his good command?

Piniella: "I don't know if he had his command or not. What else?"

Bruce Levine of WMVP-ESPN 1000 radio queried if Kosuke Fukudome broke the wrong way on Ryan Braun's game-winning double to right.

Piniella: "I don't know. The ball was hit well. It short-hopped the wall."

Carrie Muskat of MLB.com wondered about Soriano's handling of Kapler's drive over his head.

Piniella: "I asked [coach Mike] Quade. I didn't get a chance to see it. It was hit in the air. I don't know what happened. It short-hopped the wall, too."

Ryan Mendenhall of WLUP-Radio questioned how tough a loss was this?

Piniella: "You got a two-run lead going into the ninth. You let one get away. It's a tough loss."

Then Jesse Rogers of WSCR-The Score really lit the boiler of Mount Lou again, albeit with a reasonable question: Did he consider putting Reed Johnson in leftfield for defense in place of Soriano?

Piniella, his voice and anger rising quickly: "You're damn right I thought about it. You think I'm stupid or something? God darn it."

Piniella then exited and muttered several profanities as he walked down the dank corridor to the clubhouse.

"I don't think that question was out of line," said the *Chicago Sun-Times'* Gordon Wittenmyer, who witnessed the event. "It wasn't necessarily a tough question. Because Lou snapped, any of a half-dozen other questions would have gotten the same response out of him because of the circumstances of that day."

The main circumstance, a disastrous loss, was the type Piniella never could stomach, going back to the very first game of baseball he ever played. The timing was perfect for the kind of volcanic response coveted by TV and radio producers, along with the YouTube crowd. They had been

waiting for more than a year, when I inadvertently provoked Piniella's famed Tampa temper after another Cubs
in-game collapse.

The public witnesses Piniella's different emotions
largely through his two regularly scheduled daily media
briefings before and after games. Sweet Lou provides the
standard game rehash, some serious analysis, homespun
philosophy, humor, misdirection, and obfustication on
purpose, a nice dash of malaprops and unfortunately, not
enough of the man's rich baseball history. But most in
demand by baseball buffs and the sexy sound-bite crowd is
a Piniella explosion, the kind that historically occurs on the
field via a dislodged and thrown base, and invectives hurled
at umpires.

With Piniella vowing a calmer on-field demeanor as
he neared social security age and Major League Baseball's
lords of discipline watching like avenging angels, an out-
break of his legendary temper would have to be largely confined to his reaction to questions in moments of crisis that
were always lurking near the center of the Cubs Universe.

On Friday the 13th in April 2007, Cubs ace Carlos
Zambrano and lefty reliever Will Ohman quickly gave back
a 5–0 lead over the Cincinnati Reds in the fifth inning at
Wrigley Field. Zambrano's performance was unpredictable
from game to game that season due to suddenly stalled talks
over a new long-term contract. The first nine Reds reached
in the inning as Zambrano gave up four singles, a double,
a walk, and a bases-loaded hit batsman, good for four runs,
before being pulled. He yielded to Ohman, who issued two
successive bases-loaded walks to force in the inning's final
two runs.

The Cubs could not recover from the pitching collapse and lost, part of their 22–31 start to a 2007 season
that Piniella—proverbially patching gum, spit, and wire

together—melded into a National League Central Division title. Afterward, Piniella—dragging his somber disposition into the expanded but still cramped interview room—did not care whose feelings he'd bruise as the battery of questions spewed forth.

"This guy's your ace," Piniella said of Zambrano. "You've got a 5–0 lead with the eighth and ninth hitters coming up. You feel pretty good about that inning. And all of a sudden it turns into a six-run inning. What do I do? I just pitch him when it's his turn again. What else can I do? Then I bring in a reliever [Ohman] that's throwing 30- and 40-foot curveballs to boot.

"Now I can start to see some of the ways that this team has lost ball games. We've got to correct it, obviously."

Several more questions were posed to the angry Piniella. Yours truly decided to ask a kind of wrap-up, or summary, question about the latest Cubs pratfall: "What do you think isn't working?"

Mt. Lou blew, and the entire sports world witnessed the rumbling via lead-highlights video.

"What the hell do you think isn't working? You see the damn game," Piniella yelled, his decibel range reaching near three figures.

No matter that he answered five more questions before stalking out, back to his office to stew over the loss. The Piniella anger-mongers had hit the jackpot, lifting the bite and making it the most famous managerial postgame reaction of the still-young 21st century. "You see the damn game" was flashed around the world, rerun for more than a year to come—and I had the inadvertent reputation of being the top Piniella-baiter. I couldn't get away from such a tag. "What are you doing to our manager?" Cubs president John McDonough asked me, not at all complimentary, as he shook his head over lunch in the Wrigley

Field media dining room a month later. And when Piniella blew up at Jesse Rogers's question nearly 13 months later, the first reaction of a former Cubs official upon hearing of the volcanic activity was whether I, not Rogers, had set off Piniella.

The fallout from that first blowup would follow both Piniella and me through the next couple of seasons. His reaction on that unlucky day was one to which all other Piniella public statements about the Cubs would be compared. Neither of us wanted such notoriety. My questions weren't printed or broadcast; the object was to obtain honest, informative answers. And Piniella, desiring to cool his traditional temperamental image, said he studiously desired to avoid such outbursts.

"I understand the importance of the media and I respect the jobs they have to do," he said months after the blowup in a quiet moment in his office. "I don't get offended by things. I say to myself, 'Don't be huffy when you go in there, whatever you do. Be as kind, cooperative and patient as you can be.'"

Any chance to listen to and parry with Piniella was must-attend theater. And it has never been only the inquiring media minds that hunger for every Piniella syllable. The man's fiery reactions, homespun delivery, and voice that begged for imitation attracted the attention of opposing players in a manner not seen for any other big-league manager. After a victory in the second game of the 2008 season on April 2, a whole gaggle of Milwaukee Brewers hung on every word of Piniella's postgame talk, piped into their cramped Wrigley Field visitors clubhouse via the in-house video feed. An echo resounded in the steamy quarters; several Brewers mimicked Piniella's nasally, half-Tampa, half–East Coast delivery. One of the faux Piniellas seemed to emanate from slugger Prince Fielder. Earlier in 2007 pitcher Dontrelle Willis and a bunch of Florida Marlins formed their chairs in a semicircle around the clubhouse TVs to listen—and sometimes laugh—along with Lou. But mimicking Piniella, his distinctive accent and his catchphrases became a cottage industry that picked up momentum. Media types turned into faux Sweet Lou's to comment not only on baseball but also other current events. Cubs infielder Ronny Cedeno reportedly performed the best impression within the clubhouse. But the mercurial Carlos "Big Z" Zambrano went two steps further—he mimicked Lou congratulating him in Spanish for his no-hitter in an interview with Comcast SportsNet's Josh Mora the day after the September 14, 2008, feat.

Piniella made the biggest media-relations impression—positively and otherwise—of any Cubs manager in history during his first two seasons on the job. Deftly handling the ink-stained wretches and microphone jockeys—and through them reaching out to the fan base—is a job requirement for the 21st-century manager. Even an admitted nonpeople person like former Cubs general manager Larry Himes said good media relations was one of the three main job requirements he had for a managerial candidate. He's the daily face of the ball club, generating the most quotes about his team, previewing the contest via a scheduled pregame group gabfest, then performing a postmortem to the pen-and-mike crowd minutes after the final pitch.

Decreased access to managers and players throughout baseball has cut down on the more informal cracker barrel–style office chats and behind-the-batting-cage one-on-one gabfests of past decades. Only team and network broadcasters, along with assorted celebrities, are freely allowed to hang around the cage with the managers, although intrepid reporters sometimes can get close enough for a quickie conversation before they're shooed away. It was in this keep-away environment that Piniella followed a variety of interesting acts in the Cubs manager's chair, going back a decade.

In the late 1990s, Jim Riggleman became a kind of saint among a sport of sinners in understanding the media's role in publicizing baseball. Never granted talent-laden Cubs rosters by a conservative front office, Riggleman drew praise as a highly prepared manager, and he'd take time to explain the game in one-on-one chats in his Wrigley Field office. I had several occasions where the chats lasted until 25 minutes before game time for a 1:20 p.m. contest, forcing me to sneak out the back door into the concourse, hoping media relations director Sharon Pannozzo wouldn't catch me. During this era, a writer could also chew the fat in the coaches' dressing room, a few feet away from Riggleman's offices. In group settings, Riggleman was more than accommodating, greeting the writers with the salutation of "Hello, scribes." One momentary bit of irritation at my postgame question was turned around into an immediate apology. Riggleman was so well-liked that he spent 90 minutes greeting Chicago-area media when he came back into town at the White Sox's U.S. Cellular Field as a Cleveland Indians coach in 2000, the year after he was fired from the Cubs.

Don Baylor succeeded Riggleman at Wrigley Field, and while friendly enough in short spurts Baylor seemed media-averse. Remembering how his old Angels manager Dave Garcia spent too much time schmoozing with the media while short-changing his players, Baylor did not allow interlopers into his office, and reporters were no longer welcome in the manager's inner sanctum and the coaches' room. Baylor tried to keep his pregame and postgame media sessions as short as possible. One day I asked all three pregame questions, and then Baylor moved quickly toward the batting cage. But in the end, Baylor did not discriminate just against the media. Many of his players complained that Baylor was a poor communicator who sometimes would inform reporters of a change in a Cub's status before he actually talked to the player.

Following an interim managerial period by Bruce Kimm after Baylor was fired in midseason 2002, Dusty Baker flitted into town full of California-cool homilies that eventually did not play well in the Midwest. A players' manager, Baker almost never lit up his charges and repeatedly assured that the team "still had action" when it was all but mathematically out of a game or the divisional race. In group settings Baker could be evasive. But, over time, if you tried to establish a one-on-one relationship with him, you could be rewarded. Despite several confrontations, I managed to get Baker to take me aside near the batting cage in 2004 and 2005 to reveal information about the troubled Sammy Sosa and his own future contract status.

Cubs expectations had been raised sky-high by the near-miss World Series team of 2003. Eyebrows collectively then were raised by the sudden collapse of the franchise, starting in August 2005 and carrying all the way through the 96-loss season of 2006. Baker's cool-man slang and platitudes only made things tougher for whomever would follow.

Piniella's initial irritation with the media overall and several of my questions did not make a lot of sense. After all, he had played smack-dab in the middle of the Yankees' Bronx Zoo during the mid-1970s; we're talking about white-hot competitive reporters for the screaming New York tabloids. A decade later, Piniella was baptized as a big-league manager for the same team working under the microscope of the same media, under orders from their sports editors to scoop the competition—or else. So one day later in the spring of 2007, after his "You saw the damn game" eruption and a couple of other bits of snippiness, I approached him near the batting cage at Wrigley Field with one simple question. If he could break in as a younger, even more emotional manager and survive the most bloodthirsty media market in the country, why was he aggravated by less confrontational Chicago media?

"You guys are getting inquisitive," he responded, and walked past me to the dugout. Had we tapped into his secret scouting reports? Were we reading his mind?

More so than the tabloid crowd in Piniella's Bronx Zoo Yankees days in New York? Maybe not, but as Piniella explained to me later in 2007, there are simply more inquiring minds.

"When I was in New York playing and managing— it's a bigger media market," he said in a calm, thoughtful session in his Wrigley Field office in July. "You had the beat writers, you might have had a columnist here or there, but you didn't have all these talk shows, you didn't have all these television shows. There were less people to deal with. It's changed a heck of a lot."

Piniella told his old beat writers from Seattle during a June 12–14, 2007, interleague series at Wrigley Field that he was enduring an entirely new media experience than he had encountered in decades.

"He said the media was different," said Larry LaRue of the *Tacoma News-Tribune*. "They had good questions and bad questions. The Cubs of course got more coverage than the Mariners. He wasn't really complaining."

Piniella connected the Cubs' near century-long championship drought to the harder edge of questioning.

"I guess it's the fact this team hasn't won in a long, long time," Piniella said. "They want their answers and they're a little more impatient. They're more inquisitive after ball games."

But Piniella should have developed a tough-enough skin from his 15 years in New York to handle anything a much more folksier Midwest metropolis could throw at him.

"After playing in New York? He couldn't have deluded himself too much," said Dave Brown, formerly baseball beat writer at the suburban *Northwest Herald* newspaper, who turned into a sometime Piniella antagonist late in the 2007 season.

"I might describe the collective media as more annoying than ferocious, and I'm not trying to put us all down," Brown added. "We're just kind of 'there' and in the way sometimes, and it gets annoying. I think we could all ask tougher questions more consistently, myself included."

Perhaps the formerly genteel Chicago newshounds were fortunate that only a watered-down and controlled Piniella temper was on display by the time he hit town. They might have run for cover had Piniella been his early 1990s self as a Reds manager wearing his heart on his sleeves in front of a more limited—and tolerant—audience.

"Cincinnati, the market is smaller than Chicago, but people enjoy their baseball," he said. "They praise you and they criticize you."

My first encounter with a hyperpassionate Piniella as manager came on August 31, 1990, at Wrigley Field. Leading off the ninth inning, Reds rightfielder Paul O'Neill lost an Andre Dawson fly ball in the late-afternoon sun with the Reds leading 3–2. The double opened the door for a two-run rally against closer Randy Myers that temporarily detoured the Reds from their destiny as world champions. Afterward, Piniella exploded in the tiny visiting manager's office. I thought the diatribe was directed at the small group of writers in attendance. A veteran like Hal McCoy of the

Dayton Daily News, a member of the writers' wing of the Hall of Fame, could have explained that it was just Sweet Lou expressing himself—nothing personal.

McCoy also remembered Piniella reacting—for effect—to Myers's desire to be traded.

"Myers dressed outside Lou's office," said McCoy, still the majors' senior beat writer in 2008 with 35 years covering the Reds. "He went off on Myers, so Myers could hear him. He hollered that if Myers wanted to be traded, has he ever figured no one wants him, and that he could take his paycheck and go home!"

McCoy also triggered the most famous Piniella off-the-field outburst, one with Rob Dibble on September 17, 1992, at Cincinnati's Riverfront Stadium. He had asked closer Dibble why he hadn't worked in a save situation. Dibble responded, "Ask the manager." McCoy did just that, with Piniella revealing that the fireballer had tenderness in his arm. Going back to Dibble with that analysis, McCoy heard back that Piniella was branded a liar. As soon as McCoy told Piniella of Dibble's accusation, "He practically flattened me charging out of his office. He jumped Dibble—they were pushing and shoving and wrestling." Recorded by a TV camera, Piniella was overheard hollering at Dibble, "I'd treat you like a man, but you don't wanna be treated like a man." Pitcher Tim Belcher was the first to pull the combatants apart, and seconds later other players acted as peacemakers as Piniella, his hair disheveled and clothes nearly torn, got up. The next day Piniella apologized to Dibble, then continued using him as closer. They remain friends to this day.

Piniella never held any ill will toward the messenger either. And McCoy certainly could have aggravated Piniella with his questioning, as he was light years ahead of any other Reds reporter in garnering insider-baseball stories.

"He never ever once got mad at me," he said. "He would answer questions, and answered them honestly, didn't try to evade. Lou's my all-time favorite Reds manager [over media-friendly Sparky Anderson and Jack McKeon]. I just like the way he was always honest with me. He was a good manager."

But there were limits—particularly after a tough loss or controversy surrounding a player.

"I don't think he likes to be pushed," McCoy said. "He'll give his answer, and if you push him, he'll react [loudly]."

Piniella largely confined his high-decibel blowups to the field when he moved on to the Seattle Mariners in 1993. Like Cincinnati, his media crowd comprised a handful of traveling beat writers and a few more radio and TV types working home games only. The laid-back Pacific Northwest market was still getting used to the idea they that were major league, as least in name, as the Mariners were 16-year losers when Piniella took over.

"Seattle, when I first got there in 1993," Piniella recalled, "myself and a few of the coaches were eating breakfast one day, and a guy says, 'You're the manager of the Mariners, aren't you?' I said yeah. He said, 'when does your season start?' We had played 11 games already. It changed dramatically over the 10 years I was there."

On a few occasions Piniella would get irritated at questions from a regular group of writers that included Larry LaRue of the *Tacoma News-Tribune* and John Hickey of the *Seattle Post-Intelligencer.* But he enjoyed generally cordial relations with the media in his decade-long tenure in the Pacific Northwest.

"His patience goes up and down," LaRue said. "If the team is doing well, his patience is up. But if he got a question he didn't like, that would be the end of the media thing [for that day].

"A lot of times he would surprise us. If there was a tough [losing] clubhouse, he was at his best. Or when they were winning, he was at his worst."

Writers could catch the manager one-on-one quite frequently during Piniella's 10-year Seattle run. Gordon Wittenmyer, who came to Chicago to cover the Cubs at the *Sun-Times* at the same time Piniella was hired, said Sweet Lou was much more casual during the two years he covered the Mariners for a now-defunct suburban Seattle newspaper in 1997 and 1998.

"He was much more forthcoming then," Wittenmyer said. "Every manager in baseball now has a set time when they meet with the media. Even with four beat writers [in Seattle], there was no set time. If you had a question for Lou, you popped your head into his office. Maybe somebody already was sitting there, maybe two guys. The PR guy definitely was not the manager's caddy.

"It's definitely a lot different here. It's pretty clear he doesn't like [press-conference settings]. He's so much better if it's just a few writers around. The microphones and cameras formalize everything. All of a sudden everything is an on-the-record, watch-what-you-say thing. He's not even close to his best then."

When LaRue had a heart attack in early in 2008, Piniella called him to wish him well.

One common thread that ran through Piniella's time in Cincinnati, Seattle, and Tampa Bay was small-market size, which means modest local media coverage and little national media attention. Seattle was the most distant big-league franchise from the other 29 teams, and, operating in the Pacific Time Zone, its night home games rarely made the Eastern and Midwest papers or earlier editions of ESPN's *SportsCenter*. Tampa Bay was considered the majors' worst-run franchise and might as well have played 3,000 miles distant for all the coverage it was getting outside the market.

"Tampa Bay, it was a small market," Piniella said. "The writers there were fine. They understood the situation; they were very tolerant of that and I thank them for that."

Wittenmyer said Piniella indeed adopted a softer overall personality in between his Seattle and Chicago days, which included a year working as Fox Saturday Game of the Week analyst.

"From what I can tell, his time in Tampa Bay made a big difference in how his temperament changed," Wittenmyer said. "The time off helped. He still has the fire and he's still obsessed about winning. But he's not as apt to fly off the handle. He's a lot more patient with media compared to how I remember him. The fans would like to see him go off more."

Piniella faced a radical change in his working conditions upon arrival in Chicago. He always conducted his media talks either in his manager's office or on the bench. But his Wrigley Field office was little better than closet-size. The space could not accommodate a full load of local TV cameras, almost always present before night games to snare sound bites and live reports on the early evening news. The Cubs' home dugout also was cramped with hardly room for more than a dozen media to get within earshot.

"I've never done a media room like we have here in Chicago," he said. "I've always done it in my office. This office is too small. It's a daunting task to be taken out of your comfortable environment and be put in a media room, especially if you're a little hot losing a ball game and get hit from all sides on this, that, and the other. I'm learning to deal with it; I'm doing the best I can. Hopefully I'll get better at it."

Baseball writer Dave Brown absolutely understood.

"It's probably both old-school and controlling," he said of Piniella's desire to stay in his office. "He should have control over his environment. I'd want a certain amount if I were Lou. The interview room is more like a stage. I would be uncomfortable up there. I think we get better answers away from the interview room, no matter where it is."

Piniella was not alone in his discomfort. Fellow old-school managers like the Braves' Bobby Cox and Jack McKeon, who led the Marlins to a World Series title in 2003, disliked the choreographed mass session. Cox loved to chew the fat on the bench for half an hour or more before games. McKeon dutifully did his group interviews, but then was fair game for most one-on-one gabbers.

Piniella timed his arrival in the Wrigley Field media room just right, if that can be believed. Had he come in 2005 or 2006, he would have squeezed into the formerly tiny interview room. That miserable cubbyhole, every pun intended, heated up to 90 both in degrees and percent humidity, on sultry days when too many people and TV cameras were packed in and that noisy 1970s vintage wall air conditioner had to be turned off, so everyone could hear.

The contrast between Piniella's sessions in the expanded interview room and the less-frequent visits to his office and the bench were striking as late 2007 transitioned to 2008. The interview-room Piniella was polite, often greeting all with "good morning" as he entered. "What've we got?"

was his signal to begin questioning. After an escape-act 11-inning Wrigley Field victory on July 12, 2008, when setup man Carlos Marmol blew a 7–2 lead in the ninth inning, Piniella was delayed arriving for his postgame talk. "Sorry I'm late, I had a nice, cold beer before I came down here," he explained.

But he was still more stilted than when he could lean back in his office chair, just dressed in a T-shirt, and hold court. He was totally conversational and relaxed then. He could find humor, too. "Your questions are confusing, but I see the reason behind the madness—just joking," he told me one morning in April 2008.

When he was brought to the bench before day games as 2007 proceeded, he was almost as relaxed and lingered after the game-oriented questions died out to make more casual conversation for 10 to 15 minutes more. He was more candid and opinionated away from the interview room, where obviously he felt an interrogation factor was at work. And sessions on the bench permitted short one-on-one interviews that yielded nuggets of insight about both the game in general and Piniella's strategy.

Piniella had his distinctive collection of catch-phrases, such as "Look . . ." to begin his answers. When he couldn't pin down a definitive answer or simply didn't know, he'd conclude with "What can I say?" Or a confident, final-word answer would end with "That's the end of the story." A true hitter for his entire career, Sweet Lou knows more about pitching than he'd ever let on. Piniella would often defer a specific question about a pitcher with the admonition to "talk to the pitching coach."

The sharpest edges of Piniella's personality—professions that he did not have the answers to questions and outright refusals to answer queries—still took place in the

Lou Piniella promised he would turn the Cubs around when he was hired. He had more to smile about than not in his first two seasons as manager.

After constantly experimenting with lineups in his first Wrigley Field season, Lou Piniella was able to settle down the order when he guided the Cubs to 97 wins in his second season, the most victories in franchise history since 1945.

Lou Piniella may have calmed his traditionally fiery temper as Cubs manager—most of the time. However, a number of his pitchers have heard him speak his mind—often profanely—during trips to the mound.

Mark DeRosa became Lou Piniella's man for all positions. Piniella could plug in DeRosa at second, third, right, and even left while getting clutch hits from the former Atlanta Braves utility player.

Geovany Soto plugged up a hole behind the plate while becoming a run producer in his rookie season in 2008. Soto was a rare position player who came through as a product of the Cubs farm system.

Aramis Ramirez became an all-around steady player both at third base and as the Cubs cleanup hitter. Ramirez showed both more patience at the plate and leadership in the clubhouse in 2008.

Lou Piniella greets Kosuke Fukudome after a victory at Wrigley Field. Fukudome's patience at the plate helped transform the lineup early in 2008, but the Japanese import slumped badly in the second half.

Alfonso Soriano follows through on his swing. Lou Piniella, who helped recruit the left fielder as a free agent, did not get Soriano at his peak in his first two Cubs seasons due to injuries.

Ryan Theriot slaps a ball to right field. The Cubs shortstop won over Lou Piniella as a rookie, then improved in his second season as a No. 2 hitter.

Ryan Theriot watches a play unfold while running the bases. Theriot joined Geovany Soto as one of two home-grown regulars in the Cubs lineup.

Infielder Ronny Cedeno follows through on his swing. Cedeno contributed to the Cubs as a utility player.

First baseman Derrek Lee is fired up over team success. Lee became a team leader quickly in his Cubs tenure while trying to get back to his former power-production levels.

As is his custom, Carlos Zambrano thanks higher powers after another positive achievement on the mound. Zambrano blew hot and cold in his performance for Lou Piniella.

Rich Harden loves to work in cool weather, and he is especially prepared to pitch in the snow outside his parents' home in Victoria, B.C. *Courtesy of Russ Harden*

Off-duty in the off-season, Cubs outfielder Reed Johnson plays in the snow with a trusted friend, his dog Shooter. Johnson was as nimble as a retriever with his hustle in the outfield. *Courtesy of Reed Johnson*

Reed Johnson makes the catch of 2008 at Nationals Park in Washington, D.C. He outran the ball near the Cubs bullpen, crashed into the fence, and came up with the bill of his cap upturned. *Photos courtesy of Comcast SportsNet Chicago*

Aramis Ramirez (center) gets a welcoming committee of Ryan Theriot (left) and Derrek Lee after another home run at Wrigley Field. Ramirez has become the Cubs' best regular-season clutch hitter, but the playoffs have been another story.

Billy Goat Tavern proprietor Sam Sianis (left) and his latest mascot appear outside Wrigley Field before the fateful Game 6 of the National League Championship Series in 2003. Sianis and his late uncle, William, have fostered the legend of the latter's supposed curse on the Cubs. Periodically, the goats have been admitted to the ballpark. *Photograph by Tammy Lechner ©2003*

interview rooms. After two long night games in 2007, Piniella simply refused to come into the room, claiming to be tired or more accurately, feeling disgusted over negative turns of games that he did not want to share with the media pack. He also passed up the June 29, 2008, postgame session after a depressing loss against the White Sox in which Piniella was ejected for arguing over strike three on a questionable Joe Crede checked swing. Piniella dispatched bench coach Alan Trammell, who took over the club following his heave-ho, to do his talking. Still other postgame sessions lasted as little as one minute when a fuming Piniella was in no mood for reflection after tough losses, thus nipping those famed eruptions in the bud. And by the second half of the 2008 season, Piniella typically passed up talking to the media before day games that followed night games, or before 12:05 p.m. Saturday starts.

Throughout 2007, the man whom *New York Times* baseball bard Murray Chass called 'the man who knows as much about hitting as any man alive or dead," claimed puzzlement concerning why the Cubs sluggers weren't belting homers—they hit just 32 homers combined in June and July of that season. Flustered with the repeated questions, one day he played amateur weatherman, suggesting the wind blew in different directions inside and above Wrigley Field. A year later he admitted he was an expert on hitting, but whatever he analyzed about the power shortage of '07 he kept to himself.

Too many times to remember, Piniella might not directly answer a question, veering off the topic and perhaps returning to the original idea after the steam had been taken out of the inquiry. Stammering was another tactic to either gather his thoughts or throw off the original question. Piniella sometimes came off as a befuddled uncle, but reporters quickly figured it was the managerial equivalent of a running back's juke. He could be the master of misdirection.

Piniella also used the politician's tried-and-true device of throwing the question back to the interviewer and injecting his own humorous comments, breaking up the moment's momentum by getting the entire interview room to crack up with laughter. I've been on the receiving end a number of times.

"He can tease pretty well," said Larry LaRue.

One time in 2007, I asked whether outfielder Cliff Floyd, having used up his time on the bereavement list due to the death of his father, Cornelius Floyd, would be put on the restricted list.

"Yes, and you should be on it, too," he answered with a grin.

"Did you rehearse that all afternoon?" I snapped back.

"No, it just came to me," Piniella concluded.

Passing by near the Cubs dugout, he twice called me "Simon," as in *American Idol* provocateur Simon Cowell, obviously equating the acerbic Brit to my direct-questions style. I reminded Piniella that "Simon" was the star of the show.

After that wild blown lead–turned–extra-inning victory on July 12, 2008, *Chicago Tribune* beat writer Paul Sullivan asked if Piniella might bring up any pitchers with Carlos Marmol and Kerry Wood unavailable for the next day. "No, we don't need any pitchers," the manager said. "If we can't get by tomorrow with what we got, we'll pitch you, Sullivan." Two weeks later, I asked a similar question, and Piniella scraped the bottom of the barrel by suggesting that I should pitch.

Showing that the long season did not dull his wit, Piniella nailed Sullivan on September 18, 2008, when he turned to the scribe in his postgame talk to confirm whether Rich Harden had thrown the most number of pitches in a start to that date. "What do you think, Sullivan, or are you falling asleep on me?" he said to raucous laughter from Sullivan's colleagues. "You had a bad night last night. No, I'm fine. I'm going to have a bad night tonight." And when I asked Piniella the next day if he still admired rookie pitcher Jeff Samardzija's poise and composure, he shot back, "I like your composure better," prompting The Score's David Schuster to suggest, "Your nose just grew."

Piniella did not limit his zingers to his Chicago pests. Old friends got nailed. When confidant Marty Brennaman—the Reds' Hall of Fame announcer—along with *Cincinnati Enquirer* beat writer John Erardi walked into the pregame interview room on August 20, 2008, both wore shirts in various shades of pink. Piniella immediately took notice. "Hot pink from Cincinnati," he exclaimed as the room went up for grabs. "Is it Sadie Hawkins Day or what?"

If any of his managerial foibles were pointed out by the inquisitors, then Piniella delighted in some mishaps by the same. Just after I broke in my new digital tape recorder later in the 2007 season, I accidentally hit the Play instead of the Record button as I placed it near Piniella on the interview-room table. As an interview began playing, Piniella laughed uproariously, with the assembled media joining in. "Oh, Lord," he exclaimed, as I rushed to stifle the awry recorder.

The same device was silent on May 13, 2008, when I put it before Piniella as he arrived for his pregame chat. "I was hoping you'd take the day off," he said to me with an ear-to-ear grin. I issued a half-hearted apology, but should have told him I'd take off when he'd take off.

After I inquired four days later if he could tell when a team was "emotionally" ready to win, Piniella asked why I asked so many "profound" questions. And 24 hours later, he said I was asking too many "cerebral" questions, offering to buy me "two steak dinners" to ask those questions of the players rather than him. My response this time was that I couldn't be bought off so cheaply, plus that was too much red meat for one week.

Indeed, Piniella prefers meat-and-potato questions, the shorter the better, dealing with the "what" and not the "why" or "how." On August 10, 2008, he again used the "cerebral question" qualifier to avoid answering whether the slumping Kosuke Fukudome's sudden lack of patience at the plate the previous month had a ripple effect on the lineup before it revived.

On other occasions, though, Piniella found not a slice of humor in his media encounters—and said nothing about them. Famed for his voluble responses, Piniella could say just as much with dead silence. Dave Brown got a zero decibel level on the Lou-O-Meter on September 1, 2007, in the interview room. The Cubs had just acquired veteran starter Steve Trachsel from the Orioles, and Piniella suggested the Cubs could go with a six-man rotation. But Brown suspected that was not the real motivation with second-year lefty Sean Marshall having endurance problems pitching past the fifth inning. As the media briefing started wrapping up, Brown asked Piniella whether Trachsel would replace anyone presently in the rotation.

Piniella stared straight ahead, not looking at Brown, off to his left. He did not answer for 10 seconds. Then he slowly turned his head to his right, Jack Benny/Johnny Carson–style. Again he kept his silence. After another six or seven seconds, Piniella got up and exited stage right. The following week, Trachsel replaced Marshall in the rotation.

"Nothing that comes or doesn't come from Lou's mouth surprises me," Brown said. "It was an awkward moment for sure. I hate to be a guy to kill a press conference. I just didn't buy the Cubs' whole 'We're going with six starters' thing."

Piniella was not so silent for some subsequent Brown questions. He sometimes expressed irritation in his answers and concluded the thought by addressing Brown and others as "Sir." That was in contrast with Dusty Baker's super-cool salutation of "Dude" to someone he didn't know who asked a tough question, as *Chicago Sun-Times* columnist Rick Telander did in 2003 when Sammy Sosa was caught red-handed with a corked bat.

And in conferring upper-echelon British status on an inquisitor, Piniella changed his own greeting from his Cincinnati days.

"It used to be, 'Listen, friend,' or 'My good man,' " said Hal McCoy. Piniella used "My good man" a few times in Chicago.

"'Sir' usually means he is annoyed by the question/questioner and is probably a reverse-psychological ploy to act polite while burning a hole through you with his eyes," Brown theorized. "Sure, I believe he doesn't know some names, but he knows many regulars. He's called the *Daily Herald*'s Bruce Miles 'Bruce,' the *Sun-Times*' Gordon Wittenmyer 'Gordon,' and you 'George'. I was excited because in 2007, I got through most of the season without being called 'Sir.' Then he got me two or three times in the last month and playoffs. Damn."

But first the media got Piniella—when he pulled ace Carlos Zambrano after six innings in a 1–1 tie in Game 1 of the National League Division Series against the

Diamondbacks in Phoenix on October 3, 2007. Piniella's logic was to save Zambrano's arm for an expected start on three days' rest in Game 4. The strategy backfired when crack setup man Carlos Marmol gave up a leadoff homer to Mark Reynolds to open a two-run seventh.

Afterward, Brown asked Piniella if he could be accused of looking ahead to manage Game 4 when Game 1 had yet to be won.

"I'm not accused of anything, sir!" Piniella shot back to Brown. "I've got a good bullpen here, OK, and I trust my bullpen. I'm bringing back a pitcher with three days' rest Sunday, and I took a shot with my bullpen.

"It didn't work. They've done it all year. I've got confidence in them, period, end of story."

Possessed of a wit that can more than match Piniella's, Brown tried to explain the manager's response.

"Lou either didn't understand my question or didn't listen to it or didn't give a shit anymore," he said. "Or all three. The question was, 'Do you think you could be accused of looking ahead in the series when you haven't even assured yourself it will go that long?' That got the 'I'm not accused of anything, sir!' response that's so funny, to me, anyway. It's like they were expecting to lose a game and planned that way, which I didn't get. I don't know for sure if Lou was right or wrong, but it was worth questioning him over it."

The pesky media did not stop with Piniella's putdown of Brown. The early Zambrano hook was chewed over again the next day in Piniella's pregame chat. Exasperated, he continued defending the move.

And when he moved over to the Chase Field dugout a few minutes later, another mob led by Rick Telander descended on Piniella to goad him again.

Previously sloughing off all the bad omens, portents, and screw-ups folks associated with the Cubs' quirky history, Piniella finally caved and made reference to two of the most prominent.

"I bring in Marmol, it's like the goat left his grave, right? Like Leo Durocher turned in his grave?" he said in hands-up frustration. "For God's sake, it's only Game 1. We got a five-game series here. It [taking Zambrano out after six innings] was planned. There's no sense talking about this anymore. This is yesterday's news."

But yesterday's news from 2007—as in the state of Alfonso Soriano and Piniella's constant fiddling with line-ups—would span the old season and hit him smack in the face to the point of aggravation as 2008 began. His handling of Soriano would lead to a blowup just as sound-bite-friendly as his Friday the 13th, "You saw the damn game" rumbling.

Questions about the ability of superstar Soriano, whom Piniella helped recruit at the 2006 general manager's meetings in Orlando, to lead off with his high-strikeout, low on-base percentage began to pepper the manager late in the 2007 season. The queries were twinned with requests to analyze when Soriano would be able to run freely on the basepaths after he partially tore a right quad muscle going from first to third on August 5, 2007. Late in September 2007 Soriano claimed the leg was physically fine, but he hesitated mentally to run all out.

Curiously, in spring training 2008, Soriano's leg was still not deemed 100 percent by the slugger. He said it felt fine, but that he mentally held himself back. Piniella was no babe in the woods—he knew Soriano was sensitive and was locked in for seven more years in his $136 million contract. He had to handle him carefully or risk losing him.

No wonder I got a combination misdirection play and a miffed response when I asked Piniella early in the 2008 season whether Soriano had a mental block about running. And after Piniella proclaimed Soriano was fit to do all baseball activities coming back from a two-week disabled-list stint in April 2008 due to a strained right calf, I followed up with a question about whether he'd start stealing bases again. Piniella turned the interview room upside down with laughter, bellowing that he had just answered the question. Still, he had not specifically said Soriano had the green light to run.

Continued Soriano-related questions hammered Piniella daily. He threw them back at reporters, claiming they fantasized about his lineups in their off-hours. One day, he vowed to call the reporters at home at night to talk over the lineups. But Soriano's physical and mental condition was serious business, and it came home to roost on May 1, 2008, provoking Piniella's explosion in response to Jesse Rogers's question on replacing Soriano with Reed Johnson for defense. This Louism had legs, too, provided by Piniella himself.

The next day in St. Louis, he was asked to explain why he blew up at Rogers's query.

"The guy that asked it knew the answer before I had to answer," Piniella said. "Why ask it? Why can't he just report the news instead of try to create news? That's why I told him, obviously I knew. I'm not going to take Soriano out for defense. [Rogers] knows it, you know it, and unless it's a double switch—that's the only way he's going to come out of a ball game. Everybody knows that. You don't take superstar players out of the lineup. You don't do it.

"It's a long, long season. I have confidence in Soriano, and yesterday when I was asked a question, I probably should have answered it a little different, but I was a little hot under the collar. And if you can't get hot under the collar as a major-league manager losing a two-run lead against a division rival that you're competing with for a championship, well, then you shouldn't be managing."

Piniella then proved that he reads the two top Chicago dailies, defying the stereotype that baseball figures don't read their own city's sports pages when he used then *Sun-Times* columnist Jay Mariotti and *Tribune* national baseball writer Phil Rogers as analogies to Soriano.

"It's like me asking, 'On Sunday, with the *Sun-Times,* take Mariotti out. He's not writing a column today,' " he said. "Or, 'Put the third subordinate behind him. Or doing it with Rogers, [telling the sports editor] 'Don't use Rogers on Sunday. Use the third guy.' You'd look at me like I'm stupid, you know what I'm saying?"

Cooler heads soon prevailed. But by now, if anyone continued ignoring the flashing yellow light in dealing with Piniella after a tough loss, then they were more than color blind.

Even though the manager knew the Chicago media had a job to do, at times the perceived inquisitions would become wearying. Again, a more controlled Piniella expressed his frustration with incessant probing of his decisions after a disastrous 8–3 loss to the Rays in St. Petersburg on June 19, 2008, after his bullpen had spectacularly coughed up a 3–1 lead amid a seven-run Rays seventh.

"The whole road trip, we have had trouble scoring runs," he said. "And I don't want to hear any more when I get back to Chicago . . . when we get Soriano back, about [the leadoff spot], or anything else. I mean, I really don't know. I'm not going to put up with it anymore. I think we know what we're doing here."

But after the Cubs turned around with a four-game sweep of the Milwaukee Brewers from July 28 through 31, 2008, Piniella's media life was a lot less stressful. With his roster intact and healthy and without daily Soriano questions, he was in a fine mood.

Yet working inside the Cubs cauldron could cut both ways. The Cubs played so well in August 2008, reaching heights above the break-even part not experienced since the last pennant season in 1945, that fans and some media expected them to win just by throwing their gloves on the field and to run away with the NL Central. The concept of "spoiled with success" was first used by a Cubs manager.

After the Cubs lost the final two at home to split a four-game weekend series with Phillies from August 28 to 31, 2008, their NL Central lead over the Milwaukee Brewers decreased to 4½ games. Cubs hitters scored just seven runs against the Phillies starters in the quartet of contests while not getting an extra-base hit in the final two games.

Having been through countless pennant races with their ups and downs, Piniella was hardly perturbed by the setbacks. But after the August 31 game, the line of questioning prompted some agitation, about a grade below his two best Chicago eruptions.

Piniella was asked whether the lack of offense was frustrating.

"Why is it frustrating?" he said. "Why should it be? We're supposed to win every day? I don't think so. We went out and played hard and got beat. Give them credit.

"Listen, if we could get guys in every time we got men on base, we'd be 162–0. That's not going to happen."

So was Piniella fine with his team's effort?

"What the hell am I supposed to be? Not OK?" he said.

"It's not that easy. I think we've spoiled people and we've gotten people used to it. How many games did we win [in August]? Twenty games? Not bad."

Not bad, indeed, when the Cubs' final 97-victory total for the regular season was tabulated. Piniella was in a good mood at the turn of events he fully expected when he signed up for the job. There would be no more classic Piniella performances amid the tight control of postseason press conferences. But, true to form, he chose not to appear in the interview room at Dodger Stadium after the shockingly downbeat finish to Game 3 of the division series on October 5, 2008. Mobbed by reporters outside his tiny office, he provided a brutally frank assessment—if the Cubs couldn't score more than a half-dozen runs in a three-game playoff series, another 100 years would pass before they'd win a World Series.

Minutes later, a small group of writers gathered around Piniella in the office to shake hands and offer best wishes for an off-season during which he was named National League Manager of the Year. The greetings were cordially returned as Piniella, truly at a loss for words, could not sum up why his formerly efficient, motivated club had accomplished a massive pratfall for the second postseason in a row.

For all his occasional explosions, post-losing-game snippiness, malaprops, verbal misdirections, and zingers tossed at his inquisitors, the public Piniella was far more good than otherwise. When he was re-upped through 2010 just as the 2008 postseason began, he assured a long run for the best manager/coach's entertainment this size of Ozzie Guillen.

The sequel is revving up. . . .

THE TRIALS OF D-LEE

A TEAM LEADER DOESN'T NECESSARILY CUT A WIDE SWATH EVERYWHERE HE GOES, nor do you hear him before you see him. Just his mere presence and personality does the job. Respect precedes him and it doesn't have to be confirmed with body English and verbosity.

So when Derrek Lee went about his daily rounds at Wrigley Field, he never overpowered you despite his 6-foot-5 frame. The first baseman almost silently appeared at his locker or at the main clubhouse table, to which he would tote his favorite breakfast, ham and eggs, and where he joined teammates or read the papers. There was little or no displacement of whatever flow of vibes coursed through the locker room. If anything, Lee could put you at ease. A big man with such a quiet, easy-going conversational style is the antithesis of the egotistical baseball star and makes himself welcome in any environment.

Lee must've done something right to gain his teammates' universal acclaim as a leader after barely one season as a Cub. He had started as the fourth wheel in the middle of the lineup after Sammy Sosa, Moises Alou, and

Aramis Ramirez, Lee being a fortunate acquisition by the Cubs in the off-season of 2003–04 after a trade from the Florida Marlins—his team of the previous six seasons—to the Baltimore Orioles fell through. A 2005 season total of 46 homers, 107 RBIs, and a .335 average, the latter pacing the major leagues, will grab anyone's attention, but Lee's persona outlasted that career-best performance. Everyone from Lee to the most frustrated fan desired a reprise of that dream season or even a prorated version of the same. That wasn't forthcoming in the three years to come, but Lee the leader was evergreen and important in its own right.

Does he like the team leadership role?

"I do," Lee said. "That's the beauty of the game. You evolve and it's my time to take that responsibility."

No matter what numbers Lee is fated to put up in his remaining Cubs days, he made his team classier by his mere presence, not by his decibel level or thirst for confrontation or controversy.

"That's the type of leader where I want to be," he said. "Not a leader where I tell people I'm the leader. But I don't take it lightly that people are putting that on me. I appreciate that. That comes from the way I carry myself and the way I treat people. I'm not going to be yelling and screaming. I pull people aside. The biggest thing a leader can be is be there for your team every day. If the team can't rely on you on the field, what do your words mean off the field? I'm going to be there, I'll play hurt, I'll play sick. It makes it easier to pull someone aside.

"I'm the one who has to answer the questions after the game. I'm completely accepting of that. Later on in your career there's times you have to accept more responsibilities. I feel right now it's my time. The only way you command respect is backing up what you say. If you're going to get on someone, you better be doing it yourself. I just try to go out and play the game the right way. Lead by example."

With Lee doing more watching and listening than talking, the Cubs developed a cohesive clubhouse after too many upheavals from 2004 to 2006.

"There's no tension in the clubhouse," he said. No feuds. Everyone's comfortable going up to someone else speaking their mind."

Lee moves easily among the United Nations' worth of players on the roster.

"Mostly I'm friends with most on the team," he said. "There are very few times I'll scream. The best way is stay positive to get players to respond the best."

So do people respond to sugar instead of vinegar if you back it up with substance?

"You couldn't say it any better," Lee replied. "Practice what you preach. Your words are empty if you're not doing things the right way."

Lee's leadership ability was put to the test on the late afternoon of May 30, 2007, at Wrigley Field. The Cubs had lost seven of their last nine games, and both players and manager Lou Piniella seemed to be losing their grip on their situation. The downward trend was so severe that some critics claimed Piniella, after just two months as manager, was going senile. Lee decided to call a team meeting before a night game against the Florida Marlins.

"But so what?" he recalled more than a year later. "There was time something could be said. Anybody could have done that."

The players hashed out their frustrations with some wondering about their roles as Piniella, desperate to find a winning combination, tinkered with the lineup daily. Reports filtered out that the meeting ended up a complaint session against Piniella.

"Some misinformation came out," Lee said. "Someone in the media went to Lou and said it was about him, and it wasn't. It was about us. We weren't performing, we talked among ourselves and wanted to get better."

Afterward, Piniella called Lee into his office to ask him about the meeting.

"I think he wanted to make sure what was going on and how the team was feeling about things," Lee said.

Just to prove team meetings don't solve a team's ills, the Cubs lost 9–0 after the get-together. They went on to lose their next two games with ace Carlos Zambrano brawling with catcher Michael Barrett and Piniella intentionally getting himself kicked out of a game to place the attention on himself. But immediately after that third loss, the Cubs turned it around and played consistently—with the exception of the playoffs—for the next 1⅔ seasons.

All along, Lee's burdens grew more than he ever expected. Piniella has said baseball is a cruel game. And it was especially nasty to a man who otherwise was one of the game's most upstanding citizens. Lee's an old-school player who on one spring afternoon in 2008 played as usual a 1:20 p.m. home game after being up until 5:30 a.m. that morning tending to wife Christina. She was released just before dawn from a hospital emergency room. In Lee's value system, illness or lack of sleep is no excuse for not playing. He wants to play every day with the recognition that at some point he might have to take a game or two off. Piniella picked up on this mind-set and allowed Lee a wide swath in playing time, gingerly approaching him about taking a day off in the heat of summer.

"He's such a presence in our lineup and he does such a good job defensively at first base," Piniella said one day in 2008 when asked about a Lee offensive downslide. "Look, we need for him to hit, obviously." And if Piniella did decide to rest him: "I'm sure he won't like it."

Lee has insisted that he's no maniac on the bench during an infrequent game off.

"I cheer, stay loose a little bit," he said. "I just hope they'd take care of business and I wouldn't have to go in. I'd rather be playing, but I understand. Sometimes you have to sit down."

But just three weeks into 2006, Lee broke his right wrist when the Dodgers' Rafael Furcal collided with him at first base. He never fully recovered the rest of the season. And that dominant power production that produced 78 homers in his first two Cubs seasons only returned in fits and spurts. Lee was dogged by questions about his lack of power for much of 2007 and 2008. There was no uptick. As the dog days of 2008 proceeded, the strongman who could joke the previous season that he was hitting "like a second baseman" was reduced to slapping harmless grounders to the left side of the infield and ranking second to Miguel Tejada in the National League in hitting into double plays.

Not fulfilling his potential as a No. 3 hitter in a productive lineup paled to Lee's personal travails. In 2006, then four-year-old daughter Jada's vision in one eye had been impaired, prompting a diagnosis of Lebers Congential Amaurosis (LCA), afflicting some 3,000 people in the United States. After shedding tears in a September 2006 press conference announcing his daughter's illness and his temporary absence from the Cubs, Lee quickly picked himself up to spearhead a fund-raising effort for research into LCA.

Compared to trying to keep Jada's life as close to normal as possible, baseball wasn't nearly as challenging. Even after more moist Lee eyes were observed in mea culpas for the Cubs' shocking playoff exits in both 2007 and 2008, his words rang true about another at-bat, another game, another season.

"You know it's a long season and you go into it with an understanding you're going to have your peaks and valleys," Lee said. "Try to do other things to help your team. It sticks with you. Anytime you have a chance to win a game, it sticks with you. You're not always going to come through, that's not how it works. Experience helps you deal with it.

"You take it day by day. Sometimes you're hot, sometimes you're not. You're not going to win seven of eight all the time. The more even keel you have, the quicker you come out of your bad spells."

Lee is so even-keeled—with the exception of rare emotional bouts—that he dares read the newspapers, a contrarian admission compared to most big leaguers who admit that they don't digest what is written about them on a daily basis. Good thing, because Lee's frequent power droughts and other offensive shortcomings could not be gussied up in a positive manner no matter how much media types could try.

"I know some players who don't read the paper," Lee said. "But I think most guys do read it. I love to read the paper. If it's in the paper, I'll probably see it. Negative writing on me doesn't bother me. If someone wrote something untrue or fabricated it, it would bother me. If it's about the game, I don't worry about it. Every morning on the road, I read the whole paper. I look at the box scores, see what guys are doing. I eat breakfast, read the paper. I get on the Internet, check e-mail and read other papers there. The newspaper is part of my morning. You get the information you need and go on with your day.

"There are writers who know what they're talking about and there are those who don't. I don't take it as life or death. I just want information. I read it at least six days a week.

In the same breath, Lee professes not to be bothered by sports-talk radio, which self-advertises itself as entertainment anyway.

"I listen only to [music on] FM," he said. "I don't put a lot of weight on it [sports-talk]. That's just their opinion. It's their job to go on the air and stir things up."

Lee would never call a talk show to defend himself in the manner of the late closer Rod Beck, who one day in 1998 called Mike Murphy's show on WSCR-AM The Score in Chicago to refute a statement that he was too fat to cover first base on a grounder to Mark Grace.

"Unless they said something about my family that's untrue [he would not call back]," Lee said. "I know what I do on the field, so I don't put any weight on what they say. I know when I'm slumping, I know when I'm hitting good. I know what's going on."

The ebb and flow of 2007 and 2008 might suggest otherwise, at least in explaining how Lee's power and run production declined. Perhaps he spoiled the Cubs Universe with the 2005 campaign, obviously a once-in-a-career season. But classic baseball wisdom suggests players usually will end up around their career norms. Take away 2005, and Lee up to that date was about a 30-homer, 90-RBI producer who probably lost some homers playing six seasons with the Marlins in cavernous Dolphin Stadium in Miami.

After coming back too quickly from the broken wrist in 2006, Lee insisted he was completely healed the following season. Yet his power numbers—just seven homers—were paltry the first half of 2007. Then, he mysteriously picked up the pace with 15 homers in the second half, including a key two-run shot in Cincinnati on September 27 to help clinch the NL Central that night. With a .317 average and 180 hits that included 43 doubles, he had a good year by other statistical measurements. But one other crucial number that lagged was RBIs with 82, a modest number for a No. 3 hitter with 66 extra-base hits. This coming from the man who put the dagger in the Cubs' hearts with a game-tying two-run double in the Florida Marlins' fateful eight-run eighth inning on October 14, 2003—the "Bartman Game" at Wrigley Field.

Lee's power dilemma seemed solved in April 2008. He had eight homers, nine doubles, one triple, and 23 RBIs in 27 games in the season's first month. But his momentum immediately broke with a .234 May. He stopped hitting homers altogether in June, with just two each in that month and in July, one in August, and two in September. In one stretch he went 21 games without a homer. Lee finished 2008 with just 20 homers. His 90 RBIs would have seemed somewhat respectable, but the hitters in front of him were more efficient overall than in 2007.

Power fluctuations visited other big-name Cubs in the past, giving Lee a historical track that proves he could muscle up again. Hall of Famer Billy Williams dropped from 30 homers—about his career norm—in 1968 to 21 in 1969, then exploded with his best overall season with 42 in 1970. Williams dipped to 28 in 1971, then rebounded with 37 along with the NL batting title (.333) in 1972 before beginning a career-concluding slide. Andre Dawson, the NL MVP for slugging 49 homers for a last-place Cubs team in 1987, dropped to 24 the following season, when suspicions abounded that the baseball was "de-juiced." Dawson dipped even more to 21 in an injury-plagued 1989, then rebounded with 27 and 31 the following two seasons before finishing with 22 in his final Cubs campaign in 1992.

"That's kind of what I've been saying," Lee said early in 2008. "I think I've already known that [fluctuations]. You generally come within a certain range, but it's not rare to take a dip or have a spike with no explanation. [In 2007] they just didn't happen. For some reason I didn't hit in the air. I'm not trying [to hit home runs]. The main thing is when I step in the box, am I a productive hitter? Am I creating a presence in that three-hole? I was a good hitter [in 2007], I just didn't hit a lot of home runs."

Lee always gauged success with team achievements anyway. He said he had far more satisfaction with lesser numbers in a playoff season in 2007.

"I hit .335 with 46 homers, but we didn't come close to winning," he said. "I went home disappointed after that off-season. I hit .317 with 22 [homers] and we made the playoffs [in 2007]; I was happier after that season. Whatever helps the team win is success [by a player]."

But Lee's fall into the pit offensively as never before later in 2008 did impact the Cubs when he failed to drive in key runs. With the exception of his hot start, he often couldn't even buy a fly ball with a man on third and less than two out. Of 107 outs he made between August 1 and September 18, 2008, 31 were left-side infield grounders (28.9 percent of his total outs). In the same time period, Aramis Ramirez, batting right behind Lee, had 16 left-side grounders among his 101 outs (15.84 percent). Lee personally seemed so down about his hitting that he had no explanations anymore—worse yet, he flat-out refused to talk about it.

That stance proved Lee was frustrated and getting out of his game as a person. As a hitter, he apparently developed mechanical flaws. A good rightfield hitter, Lee had stopped hitting the ball in the air to the opposite field. As

an example, a game-deciding grand-slam homer against the
White Sox in 2007 at Wrigley Field landed in the right centerfield bleachers. Yet at the bottom of the trough in late-
summer 2008, Lee kept lunging over the plate and topping
the ball toward third and short. He had just five extra-base
hits in August.

Word got around the fraternity of pitchers that Lee
could be pitched inside. Several scouts said he appeared out
of balance at the plate. Another theory suggested his hands
were not far back enough.

Lee started to come out of the funk in mid-September
by resuming to a small extent his opposite-field style. He
actually led the Cubs in RBIs with 13 in the season's final
month. Although his uncommon error in Game 2 of the
NLDS against the Dodgers symbolized the Cubs' playoffs
skittishness, Lee continued his hitting revival with six hits,
including three doubles, in 11 at-bats, after going 4-for-12
against the Diamondbacks the previous October. Problem
was, with Alfonso Soriano and Ryan Theriot ice-cold, he
had no one getting on from the No. 1 and No. 2 lineup
spots to drive in.

Lee's mounting frustration over the playoff failures
obviously had to be tempered when he went home to Sac-
ramento in the off-season to be a full-time father for Jada,
whose eye condition had stabilized. He did not spend a
moment wallowing in depression over his daughter's vision
problems. Instead, he became proactive in directing attention and funds to research in fighting LCA. He immediately set up the Project 3000 foundation, named after the
number of Americans afflicted with the disease.

"Without question, I'm determined to do what I can,
do my part, to find the treatment and cure for the 3,000
people afflicted with the disease," Lee said. "I feel it's part

of my responsibility. I'll give it everything I have to knock this thing out."

"Everything" at the moment is backing the Project 3000 effort, an umbrella organization to direct fund-raising efforts to battle LCA. Lee is working with researchers at the University of Iowa.

"We're setting up dinners, receptions, fund-raisers all over the country," Lee said. "We're working with optometrists all over the country and working with Vision Service Providers, the largest health care company for eye care."

Lee said donations can be made through www.firsttouch.org and www.Carverlab.org.

"Medical technology from 10 years ago to now is like night and day," Lee said. "The things they can do are unbelievable. The importance is in getting the others [not tested already] for their genes tested. It's very important to get their genetic testing done.

"Researchers and doctors are very encouraged with the progress they made in the last couple of years and they feel there's [eventually] a treatment for LCA."

Most of all, Lee wants to ensure that Jada has as normal a life as possible despite her vision impairment. So far, she has adjusted well emotionally.

"She does a good job describing her symptoms," he said. "For the most part it's something she's had since birth. We really didn't know it. She's adapted well to it. She never seems to get frustrated or down-spirited. She's always in a great mood and happy."

Jada could not have gotten down going around Chicago with her parents. Her father is a little less guarded about his privacy than former Cubs reliever Kerry Wood and does not mind going out in public. Although he bought a condo in a doorman-fronted building for basic security, he has not encountered the kind of overzealous, near-stalker fans that teammates have reported as the Cubs' popularity soars to the top rung in the majors.

"It's really not bad," Lee said. "My family, we just continue to do things we want to do. People are generally great, they say hello, every once in a while they want to take a picture. They really respect your space with your family. That's why I like Chicago. They recognize you and say hello, but don't smother you. When you're with your family, you don't want to sit there and sign autographs.

"We walk around all the time. When it gets to that point [stalking], it's not right. Maybe I've been lucky, but my experience is good. Ninety-eight percent of time it's not a problem at all."

Lee wasn't around Chicago in the sour fall of 2008, when the twin bummers of the Cubs' latest playoff pratfall and the lousy economy made for a witches' brew of depression, cynicism, and sarcasm. It was best for any Cub to keep a low profile, or stay away, until passions cooled. But come another baseball season, when Lee walks around town, he'll likely see smiles again.

No matter what his line score, no matter if he has not conquered the fence with a batted ball, the tallest man in the regular lineup gives off good vibes with his heart and soul, not his mouth. And that quality will make him stronger than the considerable challenges tossed his way.

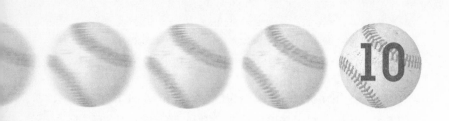

THE BIG Z

On a nice spring day in 2008, Carlos Zambrano lounged around the Cubs dugout at Wrigley Field, as relaxed as ever. In forthcoming months Zambrano often would shoo away pesky media before a game when he wasn't pitching. Too bad, as the native Venezuelan has long been comfortable with his English, knows far more about the nuances of baseball than he lets on, and can be engaging when in the right frame of mind. Clamming up pregame all but a minority of days during the 162-game season is not only the public's loss but also Zambrano's, as his education about joining the mainstream of baseball etiquette has proven to be ongoing by necessity.

But on this mid-morning jaw fest on the bench, Zambrano, the man who would be the Cubs' ace right-hander but could not lock down that tag, let himself dream big dreams, far bigger than his strapping, 6-foot-5, 255-pound persona. The subject was his switch-hitting prowess, most impressive for any pitcher in the majors, which at age 27 already had netted him the Cubs' career record for home runs by a pitcher. Zambrano, by now called Big Z more than his surname, gestured toward the legendary centerfield scoreboard. He broke into a grin, like a mountaineer knowing he'd complete a long-sought upward conquest.

"I'd like to hit the scoreboard in batting practice," Zambrano said. That stopped verbal traffic in its tracks and attracted the attention of several nearby teammates. A Wrigley Field historian present reminded Zambrano that a batted ball has never struck the scoreboard—only a golf ball hammered by Sam Snead from home plate in a 1951 exhibition of long driving. Roberto Clemente launched a homer to the left of the scoreboard that landed in a gas station in 1959, while Bill "Swish" Nicholson, a favorite Cubs strongman of yore, hit it out to the right of the green landmark in 1948. Of all people, the Mets' John Milner mashed it halfway up the centerfield bleachers under the scoreboard in 1973. Zambrano also was told that Jim Thome, possessed of the best centerfield power in baseball during his prime, proclaimed the edifice beyond his maximum range back in 2002. Thome belted several homers into the centerfield section at U.S. Cellular Field in recent years. They were measured at 451 feet, but Wrigley's target had to be 100 feet further.

Obstacles, though, meant little to an effusive Zambrano. "Sammy [Sosa] and Glenallen [Hill] used to hit the beer sign in BP," he said of the distinctive ad atop a building across Waveland Avenue. Other baseball types shook their heads and smiled when informed of Big Z's goal. "You sure could screw up your swing doing that," one said of trying to mash a ball specifically to dead center. When informed of Zambrano's goal, manager Lou Piniella jokingly suggested that the pitcher with the desire to hit like a first baseman should "aim for the [scoreboard] clock."

This charming little episode was one more hint into Zambrano's complex, sometimes unfathomable mind-set. He's not scared of anything in baseball, to be sure. Imagine the mental and physical power generated if Z could practice Zen, finding both inner peace and laser-focus concentration. He was not able to attain such baseball nirvana in the first two years of Lou Piniella's Cubs' tenure, frustrating both pitcher and manager. Even with the security of a $91.5 million contract in his pocket and his first career no-hitter that displayed all his best attributes, Zambrano could not achieve an even-keeled level, busting up dugout Gatorade coolers and frequently melting down on the mound. Throw in two episodes of shoulder discomfort and his first-ever disabled-list stint, and 2008 was a season of discontent. He did not draw the Game 1 starting assignment in the Division series against the Dodgers, as you'd expect a rested, ranking senior ace to garner.

And to think the latest woes came on top of even more combative Zambrano episodes of previous seasons that included a two-round punchout of battery mate Michael Barrett, the showing up of teammates that required rebukes from pitching coach Larry Rothschild and former manager Dusty Baker, and throwing and gesturing at future teammate Jim Edmonds while he was a St. Louis Cardinal. He also had three seasons' worth of mid-game arm cramps caused by low potassium levels that had him eating bananas as a cure. He was admittedly distracted in 2007 by on-again, off-again talks that eventually resulted in his $91 million dream deal in August of that season.

After the playoff failures of the Piniella Era, Zambrano remains the Cubs' top riddle wrapped in an enigma. Early in his career, he was said to possess even better stuff than rotation mates Kerry Wood and Mark Prior. Sheer mastery of baseball, where he could stride across the game like a colossus, seems so close. But with plenty of good seasons left, it remains just out of Zambrano's reach. He can say it, he can believe it, he can understand it, yet he cannot yet harness it game by game. That's the last, and biggest, hurdle in his career.

"Every time I pitch, I think I go with the same mentality," Zambrano said "Some days it's just not working the way you plan it. I try to do it same way as in Milwaukee [no-hitter]. Be able to control myself, be able to do the things you supposed to do. There are things you can't control. I go every time with the same focus and same mentality."

Piniella knows that, too. Right behind getting the Cubs out of the division series all the way to the Fall Classic, harnessing Zambrano's inner self and temperament remains his biggest challenge.

"I wish he would just quit fighting himself out there and just relax and pitch and have some fun," said Piniella. "He gets angry when he doesn't do what he expects to do, and it detracts from his ability."

Though Zambrano may not hold the harder-edged Piniella in the same regard as predecessor Dusty Baker, he is in total agreement.

"That's the one thing that I have to correct in me," Big Z said of his emotional roller coaster. "Yeah, it's [hard]. But it's all up here. You put it in your mind that nothing will bother you, and then nothing will bother you.

"Believe me, I go out there and try to give everything I have. Nothing else I can do. My confidence has always been there. Never lost my confidence. My head can be down, but I never give up.

"I thought I was able to do more than you can. Sometimes you can't do more than you can. You know you can be in the next step. One thing I always have in my mind is you can be on any floor and you see the ceiling, you want to be in the next floor. You have another ceiling to [step up to]. Every time I go out there, there's another ceiling to see, another step to take, and make adjustments [to get there]."

Hearing such philosophical bents, Zambrano has proved to be the most teeth-gnashing ace in the majors. Burdened from even greater success by high pitch counts and walks-allowed figures in his first five full seasons in the Cubs rotation, he appeared to start mastering control starting out the 2008 season. He issued just nine walks in his first 40⅔ innings spread over his first six starts. But as the season wore on, he fell into his old bad habits, his heavy, sinking fastball betrayed by poor control in the strike zone, leading to more outbursts on the mound and in the dugout.

"Every time I go out there, I just try to not walk anybody," he said. "I don't like walks. I don't want to throw a ball. But I'm human. I have to throw strikes. It's [lower pitch counts] very important, especially when our bullpen is tired on the day before I pitch. When I can throw 105, 110 pitches in eight innings, it would be good for the team."

Actually, in those moments when he collects all his thoughts and is emotionally settled, Zambrano gives the impression that he knows his role in the locker room and the proper way to conduct himself in relation to the greater concept of a team.

"Everyone wants to be happy," he said. "If you take [2007] out of the years I've been in the big leagues, I've always been like this. I like to have fun in the clubhouse and the dugout, I like to have fun with my teammates."

At his best, Zambrano is almost outrageously funny. He keeps a collection of Wrigley Field giveaway bobble-head dolls, including one of vanquished pugilist Barrett, by his locker. In 2005, he offered a clubhouse man some money if he'd pretend to throw diminutive *Northwest Herald* sportswriter Nick Pietruszkiewicz out of the locker room. Three years later, the soccer devotee kept trying to kick a red ball through the imaginary goal formed by the handle of a locker-room laundry cart. Zambrano gestured to Kosuke Fukudome, four lockers away, to "look lively," evoking a smile from the usually stoic Fukudome. Frequently working on his laptop at his locker, he'll break into song every minute or so, singing a line while a salsa tune plays along with a video on the computer.

Taking a page from Piniella, he'd give it back to the media after several starts. After an April 21, 2008, win over the Mets in which he walked only two in seven innings, I asked him if he was pleased he kept his pitch count low.

"No, I'm not happy," he said mockingly as the interview room erupted in laughter.

Then, the *Chicago Tribune*'s Paul Sullivan asked if this was his best April since 2004.

"What do you think?" Zambrano asked back.

"I think so," Sullivan said.

"I think so, too," Zambrano replied, a grin from ear to ear.

Moments later, ESPN-1000's Bruce Levine, standing behind a group of Japanese writers so his tape recorder could be plugged into a "mult box" to receive the interviewee's sound, began to ask, "Carlos, did you feel any extra energy—"

Zambrano interrupted: "What are you doing over there? You Japanese, too? You surprise me." More laughter filled the room.

Almost a year earlier, when asked if anything was wrong with his arm in the wake of a poor series of starts and his fight with Barrett, Zambrano looked straight at his interrogator and vowed he'd throw up to 98 miles per hour to prove he was healthy. He did not hit that speed goal in his next start, but made 98 on the radar gun in the following outing.

Zambrano's starts have been interrupted by shoulder soreness and arm cramps, but the delay in the fifth inning of his August 21, 2008, outing against the Reds at Wrigley Field was the most unique. He suffered a cracked molar.

"I'm not a dentist; I'm a pitcher," Zambrano said. "I had too much gum and the gum had a lot of sugar. I keep telling my daughters not to eat a lot of gum. I'm not a good example. My daughters will be all over me."

After a Zambrano start in which he allowed just one run in seven innings and slugged his 16th career homer, Piniella could find humor—unlike too many other Big Z games.

"I've been out to the mound many times to check pitchers' injuries, but never for a cracked molar," he said. "That's just a little Cubby Occurrence. That was a first for me, and a first for the umpire."

Obviously, the Cubs got more than they bargained for when they signed Zambrano as a 16-year-old out of hometown Puerto Cabello, Venezuela, in 1997.

He briefly was converted to relief in 2000 when the Cubs felt a need for a short-term closer replacement for an aging Rick Aguilera. He fell behind the string-bean-statured Juan Cruz as the organization's top pitching prospect in 2001, but passed Cruz the following year when he claimed a starting rotation spot while Cruz encountered problems.

By 2003, at 22, Zambrano was a lock in the rotation, finishing 13–11 and taking a no-hitter into the eighth inning in one start in Phoenix. He was entrusted with three postseason starts in which he was not successful due to fatigue and inexperience. But he obviously knew enough about his pitching makeup and recent baseball history to offer up a goal for himself. He professed an admiration for right-hander Kevin Brown, who at the turn of the millennium possessed the hardest sinking fastball in the game.

"I like how he throws the ball," he said in 2003. "I enjoy every time Kevin Brown throws the ball. I like his reaction, how the ball moves. I want to pitch like him when I'm older. Right now I have my own style. I try to be Carlos Zambrano."

Constant injuries to Wood and Mark Prior over the next three seasons enabled healthy-as-a-horse Zambrano to shine even as Cubs' fortunes plummeted. He was a composite 46–21 from 2004 to 2006. Two major factors held him back from even greater achievement: lapses in control that inflated his pitch count frequently into the 120-range by the seventh inning, and a temper that often crossed the baseball etiquette line, infuriating teammates, coaches, and manager Dusty Baker, who was otherwise a tolerant, enabling "players' manager."

In 2003, as in later years, Zambrano recognized the drawback, but was not able to check himself in the heat of battle.

"Many people say I'm cocky," he said. "The first time in rookie ball, I pitched like that. My style is to pitch like that. If I'm mad, I'm not mad at the hitter. I'm mad at myself because I don't throw a strike. I don't try to be cocky with anybody. I respect the hitters, everybody, because they have a bat. They can hit a home run against me."

Zambrano's lack of anger management proved a bigger problem than the high pitch counts. Allowing errors or other setbacks to bother him, he'd stomp around the mound and even gesture at teammates responsible for the miscues. Baker had to pull him into the clubhouse one day in spring training 2005 to rebuke him.

Similarly, pitching coach Larry Rothschild, who to this day finds some difficulty in discussing his longest-running aggravation, had to air him out about his misbehavior in the tunnel leading to the clubhouse on July 19, 2004, in a heated Cubs-Cardinals night game at Wrigley Field.

Then ranking as a top Cubs killer as Cardinals centerfielder, Jim Edmonds praised Zambrano's fiery temperament before the game. But after Edmonds clobbered a two-run homer in the fourth, Zambrano said something that appeared profane to Edmonds as he rounded third. Cardinals manager Tony La Russa then shouted back, and Cubs catcher Michael Barrett took exception, gesturing at the St. Louis players. The benches began to empty, but no melee ensued as both managers were warned.

"He didn't say nothing," Zambrano, who earlier had served up an Edgar Renteria homer, said. "I just told him to run the bases, don't be cocky." But when Zambrano struck out Edmonds in the sixth, he appeared to shake his finger in the batter's direction. He still was not finished. After Zambrano served up Scott Rolen's two-run shot that gave the Cardinals a 5–3 lead in the top of the eighth, he swiped at the air in frustration. Then he plunked Edmonds again, on the hip, earning an ejection, due to a previous warning, from plate umpire Joe Brinkman.

"I didn't try to hit him," Zambrano claimed. Nobody ever admits immediately after the fact they put a bulls-eye on a hitter. "I tried to make my pitches."

Four years later, when Edmonds joined the Cubs six weeks into the 2008 season, Zambrano insisted there were no hard feelings lingering. The two got along well. And once again, Zambrano conceded the error of his ways.

"That's in the past," he said. "Whatever happens in the past is already in the past. Let's move on. I don't have anything against him. I believe he has nothing against me. We shook hands yesterday. If anyone has to apologize with somebody, it's me. That was part of an immature guy. There's some things I know I can't do. Let's move on.

"What happened [in 2004], I was immature. He hit a home run off me. I was frustrated after Scott Rolen hit a home run. I didn't try to hit him. I was trying to pitch in and the ball cut too much. That was a good pitch. I was immature. I saw him two years ago. His head was down. I tried to say something, then he went away."

By the end of an otherwise lost 2006 season for the Cubs in which he went a sparkling 16–7, Zambrano appeared to put his most tempestuous self behind him. He suggested he was truly in keeping with the faith that has him pointing to the sky coming off the mound after every inning.

"I'm in the process of learning [to be calm]," Zambrano said at the time. "I appreciated Dusty every time he called me in the office, show me how to be a leader. I'm still learning how to take care of some situations, like if someone makes an error, don't show him up.

"Back in those days, I was younger, make a mistake like any other player," he said. "I try to do too much. My relationship with the Lord wasn't that good. The Lord likes the way I've been playing. It's a process. I was talking to Woody [Kerry Wood] about how Brandon Phillips showed me up with a home run. I told them, 'Thanks to God, I'm a new man, I have Jesus Christ in my heart.' [In past years] I would have hit him. Now, I strike him out the next two at-bats. I'm happy because I have Jesus in my heart."

Zambrano's recognition of the better side of himself would have been an important first step if he were able to bottle it. He was unsuccessful too many times in 2007 and 2008. Zambrano allowed the 2007 Opening Day cutoff of contract negotiations, mandated by the unsettled Cubs ownership situation, to creep into his mind for the first two months of the season. The talks were very near to a wrapping up of his dream deal at that point. Zambrano's performances were uneven at best, with the worst dip in a game against the Braves resulting in his brawl with Barrett. Issuing an apology on June 2, 2007, Zambrano then dedicated himself to starting a new season. He then went 9–2 over the next two months in the best stretch of his career.

But when Cubs general manger Jim Hendry got the OK to resume talks in early August to conclude the deal, the positive turn of events still played with Zambrano's mind. He endured a big drop-off that did not stop when the five-year, $91.5 million payout was announced on August 17, 2007. Zambrano gave up 30 earned runs on 43 hits and 15 walks in 33⅔ innings over five starts, dashing his dreams of winning the Cy Young award. When the Dodgers knocked him out amid a four-run fifth, the last of eight runs he gave up on Labor Day, September 2, 2007, at Wrigley Field, he looked at jeering fans sitting behind third base, crooked a finger, and pointed to his head as he headed to the dugout. Aggravating the usual capacity crowd further was the sight of Zambrano, charging through third-base coach Mike Quade's stop sign like a crazed water buffalo, after Alfonso Soriano's none-out double to left in the third. Zambrano was easily thrown out at the plate. Of course, the next batter, Ryan Theriot, followed with a single that would have scored two instead of one.

"I don't accept the fans booing me. I can't understand that. I think these were the greatest fans," Zambrano said. "I think they showed that they just care about them. That's not fair. When you're struggling, that's when you want to feel the support of the fans.

"I know the great moments of my career will come."

Once again, Cubs management had to practice damage control with their emotion-wracked ace. The next day, Zambrano uttered another mea culpa he insisted was self-motivated after he met with Hendry and then-team president John McDonough.

"The first thing I want to do is apologize to the Cubs fans," he said. "When a human being's angry, they say a lot of things he shouldn't say. I am human. I made a mistake. This comes from my heart. I love these fans. They have the right to boo people . . . because they've been waiting for 98 years."

Zambrano didn't aim anger at the fans throughout 2008. Nevertheless, the season was filled with dugout explosions, vituperation on the mound, and even a couple of bats Zambrano broke over his tree-trunk-size thigh after failures at the plate.

For most of the way, Piniella—the original red-ass player himself—soft-pedaled Zambrano's outbursts. He suggested that his competitiveness was a naturally good quality that only needed to be applied properly. Takes one to know one. The talking-to's from the manager centered around his awry pitching. The only exception was the broken bats, the acts of which the manager considered semidangerous.

However, as 2008 drew to a close, Zambrano's histrionics appeared to be wearing thin on Piniella, and never more than on September 19. In his first start after his no-hitter in Milwaukee, the St. Louis Cardinals wracked up Zambrano at Wrigley Field. He'd be charged with eight runs. With two out in the second, after Zambrano had given up a double, two walks, and a single, while casting a wild pitch as two more runs scored, Piniella came to the mound to pull him. Zambrano walked off the mound, in yet another violation of baseball etiquette, before Piniella reached him. Piniella pointed to the mound, Zambrano backtracked, and gave him the ball.

"All I expect when I take a pitcher out of the ball game is wait, stay on the mound, and give me the baseball," Piniella said. "No more, no less."

By now, Zambrano chroniclers had lost count of his apologies, this time to Piniella. He called his action "stupid."

A bit of sniping soon ensued. Zambrano hinted that Piniella wasn't his favorite, that he rationed his words to him compared to Dusty Baker's players' manager treatment of him.

At one point Zambrano denied he needed the assistance of a sports psychologist, who could improve focus and help control wayward emotions. But it's doubtful that Piniella would push such cutting-edge counsel on Big Z after he considered thoughtful, intellectual questions from media "too cerebral" for him. The job of linking up Zambrano and a sports psychologist would logically fall to Hendry and pitching coach Rothschild.

Interestingly, both Hendry and Rothschild had past connections with Harvey Dorfman, probably the best-known sports psychologist in baseball. Although he had worked with other Cubs players, he had not been approached about Zambrano.

The ace's frequent admissions that he goes over the top emotionally are "a great first step," Dorfman said.

"That's good. A lot of guys are in denial. The second step to solving a problem is strategy. The third is to integrate that strategy into behavior. I don't know if he [Zambrano] has a strategy. He needs someone to help him.

"The final [step] is always up to the athlete. When I was with Oakland, one player said he ran away from me for two years, that he had something to hide. Then when it hit the fan, he came running to you. That doesn't impress me at all. When he says he does not need it, he's embarrassed, stigmatized. They don't want the public to know."

But focusing Zambrano's psyche might have to take a back seat to keeping the wing in good repair.

In his first five seasons, Zambrano's durability was his trademark. Fine-tuning his approach and repertoire, along with his improving his control and high pitch counts, was the main project of Rothschild.

"With left-handers, he has to be able to throw inside," Rothschild said in 2006. "He's got a very good cut fastball, but he doesn't use it a lot. He had a lot of problems with left-handed hitters. He had something like 75 walks to left-handed hitters. This year was worse than last year. The trick will be to use his sinker to get quick first-pitch outs. He's got to trust his stuff more."

Something changed in 2007, though. The first questions about a mysterious drop in Zambrano's velocity began being directed toward the pitcher, Piniella, and Rothschild. In his August downslide, the sight of Zambrano dropping his arm much lower than usual, a cut above a side-arm delivery, became noticeable. Piniella left an ineffective Zambrano in an August 14 start against the Reds an inning or two longer than was logical in order to correct the low arm slot under game conditions. His strikeout totals began plummeting. Rothschild theorized that when Zambrano felt he could not attain top velocity with his fastball, he'd drop down in his arm slot to compensate with more movement on his pitches.

Zambrano seemed to recover in September 2007, then dominated the Diamondbacks in Game 1 of the 2007 division series with a four-hit, one-run yield with eight strikeouts in six innings in Phoenix. All the heat was on Piniella for pulling him early, ostensibly to save him for a projected Game 4 start that never took place. And with only the blip of a couple of typical Zambrano-an outbursts to his credit, he enjoyed an 8–1 record and 2.54 ERA in his first 13 starts going into mid-June 2008.

Perhaps all the high pitch counts started taking their toll when he complained of shoulder soreness in a June 19 start against Tampa Bay. He was put on the disabled list for the first time in his career. After the rest, he recovered to post a 4–1 record with a 1.78 ERA in July before slumping again in August, by now his most troublesome month, with a 7.43 ERA. He was skipped nearly the equivalent of two rotation turns after a September 2 start, already pushed back two days because of what was termed a "dead arm," ended after five because he felt more shoulder twinges. The astounding September 14 no-hitter only punctuated a bad two-month spell for Zambrano, who finished the 2008 season giving up 13 earned runs in six innings over his final two regular-season starts before his competitive, but error-plagued, loss in Game 2 of the division series against the Dodgers.

Obviously, a new Zambrano, mentally and physically, must emerge as he enters his late 20s. How he does it— whether he conditions himself more rigorously, learns to repeat his mechanics à la Greg Maddux, achieves the special inner peace that his abiding faith logically should evoke— isn't the final bottom line. His enormous talent and base-ball savvy is not being employed to its fullest. If it's ever harnessed, he can achieve a goal he verbalized the day he signed a contract that provided him lifetime security.

"I have a mission to complete—lead this team to the promised land," he said of the World Series.

He thinks about taking the mound amid bunting and the eyes of the world upon him, an image deferred in startling fashion in the three postseasons in which he's pitched.

"Two things can happen, I lose or I win," Big Z said. "But I want to be there to win. I can dream about it, but I can't be too excited about it. Yeah, no doubt, I want to see myself and my teammates in the World Series."

MILWAUKEE MASSACRE

EMOTIONS WERE RATCHETED UP. THE COMPETITIVE ENERGY WAS AT FEVER PITCH. On July 28, 2008, the Chicago Cubs and literally tens of thousands of their fans visited Miller Park in Milwaukee to begin a four-game series.

On the visitors' side, one sensed confidence tinged with a bit of nervousness. How would they rev up a laggard offense on the road against the toughest of opponents—the Brewers' prize midseason acquisition, gargantuan lefty C. C. Sabathia—in Game 1 on a warm Monday night? No doubt there were private gabfests among the Cubbies about the Brewers' cockiness that had rankled other opponents, such as the Cardinals, with their raucous postgame celebrations that included untucking their jerseys, with the blessing of manager Ned Yost.

Projecting ahead, the Cubs rationalized that anything from a series split to a sweep would be positive. "A push [split] isn't bad, we win the series [three games to one] it's great, and a sweep is awesome," said Kerry Wood.

In contrast to the businesslike Cubs' goals, the upstart, often brash Brewers coveted everything about their visitors, from their first-place standing to their worldwide appeal. To the perennially doormat franchise, in a turnaround mode for three seasons, the Chicagoans were the best team money could buy, a contrast to the predominantly home-grown lineup on their own roster.

"They're the National League's version of the Red Sox and Yankees," Brewers general manager Doug Melvin said as he leaned against his dugout's railing 90 minutes before the first pitch. "Just because they haven't won a World Series, people hold that against them. They're a very competitive team. Jim Hendry has done a good job."

Melvin's star hitter, Ryan Braun, further confirmed a state of envy as he thought about the question by his locker.

"They're certainly more than just another team," Braun said. "We enjoy the atmosphere and intensity of the games we play against them more than any other opponent. We're going to know year-in and year-out we're going to have to compete with them for the postseason. We look forward to the challenge."

Brewers catcher Jason Kendall had the best peek inside the Cubs' mind-set, having been their regular catcher for two months in the second half of the 2007 season.

"There's definitely mutual respect," he said. "I enjoyed playing over there. They are great guys, they play the game the right way. Obviously the Cubs are the Cubs. The three teams people talk about are the Yankees, Red Sox, and Cubs. But anything can happen in baseball."

The small-market Brewers always will be caught short in the battle of the exchequer with the Cubs, hailing from a world-class city. Their challenge is to prevent the natural inferiority complex from spreading onto the field while having to smartly manage their talent evaluations.

"They have financial power more than some teams do, but you still have to make the right decisions," Melvin said. "We are never going to be in the top six, seven payrolls. When you see an opportunity, you try to capitalize on it. You don't know how many times that opportunity will come around. Teams that don't have that $100 million payroll, you're only an injury or two away from not being the team you hope."

A personable, open Canadian, and a veteran front-office man, Melvin inherited a core of good homegrown talent, but then had to shift strategy to better position the Brewers long-term.

"Before I got here, [Prince] Fielder, [Corey] Hart, and [J. J.] Hardy were drafted," he said. "We had a strategic meeting that our next draft should be college players. If you draft just high school players, they're never going to catch up to Fielder, Hart, and Hardy. Rickie Weeks was that guy, Ryan Braun was that guy, Matt LaPorta also, and Matt's presence allowed us to trade for C. C. If you're just going to draft high school players, it's difficult because they'll never catch up [with the original core of talent]."

Of more pressing concern to the Cubs was how to catch up with Sabathia's heavy fastball and yeoman endurance. Having slipped away from their trademark patience-at-the-plate strategy during a middling July, pregame talk centered on whether the Cubs should wait out Sabathia to run up his pitch count and possibly get him out of the game earlier than he desired.

To be sure, the Cubs appeared to be calculatingly working the count when they used Alfonso Soriano's double and stolen base to score in the first inning on Derrek Lee's single as 45,311 people, the season's largest crowd and third-largest all-time at Miller Park, continued to file in.

Traffic was so heavy that many later-arriving fans could not find nearby parking despite lots that totally surrounded the ballpark, and pedestrian bridges were still jammed by arriving fans in the third inning, just as Soriano reached Sabathia for a home run.

Cubs starter Ted Lilly held off the Brewers on just two hits through five innings. The Cubs missed a chance to boost the lead to 3–0 when Lee was thrown out at the plate by centerfielder Mike Cameron on Mark DeRosa's sixth-inning single as third-base coach Mike Quade made a questionable call to send Lee. The play then appeared costly when Lilly, often prone to the gopher ball, served up back-to-back homers in the bottom of the sixth to Hardy and Braun. Fielder then singled and rumbled home on Hart's double as the Brewers took the lead.

But the Cubs' patience soon paid off. Singles by Ronny Cedeno and Kosuke Fukudome led off the seventh. With one out Reed Johnson walked to load the bases. Derrek Lee then grounded to short for a potential double play, but Johnson barreled into second baseman Rickie Weeks, who threw the ball away for an error. Two runs scored, the Cubs grabbed a 4–3 lead and Sabathia was forced from the game after 6⅔ innings and 124 pitches.

"In that situation, the first baseman's not holding you on, so you want to get as big of a lead as you can," said Johnson, a heady player who had a hand in so many crucial 2008 moments. "When I'm in that situation, I tell myself to follow the ball. I was able to get in there and get a good piece of him."

Although pinch-hitter Russell Branyan nailed long ball–prone Bobby Howry for a game-tying homer in the bottom of the seventh, the Cubs were undeterred. The newly selective Soriano drew a one-out walk in the ninth, then pinch-hitter Mike Fontenot also worked a free pass. Derrek Lee doubled in the lead run. Three batters later Mark DeRosa singled in an insurance run. The Brewers were retired in the ninth with the Cubs locking in their hard-earned 6–4 victory. They had battled Sabathia, otherwise unbeatable, to a standstill long enough to work on the Brewers always-shaky bullpen.

Twenty-four hours later, amid a "playoff atmosphere" in Lou Piniella's words, some Brewers fans began to grumble. Witnessing upward of one-half the crowd garbed in Cubs blue, callers to local radio talk shows accused some Brewers season-ticket holders of making a fast buck with the visiting Chicagoans, selling their prime seats even though that would turn the Miller Park decibel level decidedly in favor of the Cubs. The visiting fans also took over the vast parking lots to engage in the popular local custom of tailgating as trademark white-and-blue *W* flags proliferated to mark their territory for all four games.

"The tailgating that was going on was all blue. We saw [Cubs] flags flying high," said Roger Vogie of Valparaiso, Indiana.

Cubs fans felt liberated in stoking their barbecue with burgers and brats to go along with the local beer; there is no place to tailgate around Wrigley Field.

The disaffected Brewers fans should have talked to their star slugger, who was jacked up by the loud crowd, no matter what its allegiance. "They bring a lot of fans here, and it's loud and rowdy," said Braun. "It's awesome. It makes it more fun. You can feel the energy, you can feel the excitement. I enjoy that."

Problem was, ace Carlos Zambrano took the Milwaukee rooters out of the game with his most dominant performance to date in 2008 on Tuesday, July 29. Big Z had six strikeouts in the first four innings while not allowing the Brewers to even sniff home plate. He had to be that good as Brewers right-handed ace Ben Sheets allowed just one run in the fourth. Sheets finally cracked in the sixth, when the first seven Cubs collected hits—single by Lee, double by Aramis Ramirez, two-run triple by the previously snoozing Kosuke Fukudome, RBI single by DeRosa, singles by Fontenot and Geovany Soto, and finally a run-scoring single by the hit-hungry Zambrano. A Soriano sacrifice fly finally finished Sheets as the Cubs took a 6–0 lead on the way to an eventual 7–1 triumph.

Sabathia and Sheets were hyped incessantly coming into the series, mildly irritating Piniella.

"Our two guys, [Ted] Lilly and Zambrano, aren't exactly chopped liver," he said. "They're two pretty good pitchers. We respect the two guys we beat."

The biggest distraction before Game 3 for the Cubs was not the specter of the Brewers, but the spectacle of ESPN reporter Erin Andrews sashaying into the spacious visitors' clubhouse 2½ hours before the first pitch. Andrews already had turned heads and forced jaws to drop weeks before prior to a Wednesday night game at Wrigley Field when she wore a canary-yellow mini-dress with a frilly hem that would have been great at cocktail hour or at midnight at the club. On this afternoon, Andrews appeared in a low-neckline, zebra stripe-patterned black-and-white minidress that caused eyes to roll, tongues to cluck, and instant analysis to be whispered out of her earshot by both players and astonished media. Now, Andrews's getup would have been fine for strolling Michigan Avenue in Chicago or Wisconsin Avenue in Milwaukee on a summer day, or watching the game in a luxury suite. But female journalists long have largely obeyed an unwritten rule to err on the side of conservatism in attire while working the testosterone-fueled boys club of a big-league locker room. She began boosterish conversations with Alfonso Soriano and Aramis Ramirez. Andrews even followed pitcher Ryan Dempster around, a strict taboo on the day of a start. Dempster later said he knew Andrews from her days working on the Tampa Bay Lightning's broadcasts; his wife, Jenny, had worked in Tampa then, too. Andrews's choice of apparel and body English was duly reported by GateHouse sports columnist Mike Nadel, who set off a storm of controversy on whether he should have even written about the Worldwide Leader's prime eye-candy's actions.

Finally, as Andrews hovered near Ramirez's locker, Piniella passed by to walk to his pregame press talk in the visitors' dugout. He spotted her and was quick with the quip as always.

"Hey, hey, hey! Look at this!" Piniella said. "Are you doing a baseball game today or a modeling assignment?"

"It's hot out there," Andrews replied, citing the low-80s climate.

Despite the elevated clubhouse mercury reading caused by Andrews, the Cubs lost not one click of focus once the game started. The Cubs scored two in the first on a Manny Parra wild pitch and DeRosa's single. Dempster allowed a run on a wild pitch in the bottom of the inning, then went into lockdown mode. He'd permit just four hits in the next six innings as the Cubs widened the lead with a three-run sixth, including a two-run Ryan Theriot triple that knocked out Parra.

The Cubs scored 19 runs in the first three games on just one homer, as they put on their finest hitting clinic of the season.

An even bigger percentage of Cubs fans turned out for the matinee finale on Thursday, July 31. Many were caught in expressway construction zipping north from the Chicago area and were late in occupying seats, given the parking snarls. The gate was 45,346, largest of the series. Somewhere in Miller Park Bud Selig smiled, but had to restrain his total joy. On one hand, the franchise he had midwifed in 1970, having obtained the bankrupt Seattle Pilots–turned–Brewers on the cheap, had now established itself for the long run in Milwaukee after too many years as a financial basket case. The strategy of switching the Brewers from the American to National League Central to take advantage of the pilgrimage of Cubs fans had been a smashing success with consistent capacity crowds over the past decade. But the partisan Brewers rooter still present under the politicking outer skin of baseball's commissioner had to cringe at the beatings the Cubs administered to the talent-rich young Brewers. Selig, who always loved hob-nobbing around the press box going back to old County Stadium, made only one cameo appearance in the series to chat briefly with a *Milwaukee Journal-Sentinel* writer. Anyone trying to flag down Selig in the public way was better off showing up at lunchtime at his longtime neighborhood hangout Gilles Frozen Custard, several miles northwest of Miller Park on Blue Mound Road, where he'd lunch on a grilled cheese sandwich and a diet soda.

The first three wins buoyed many of the road-tripping Cubs fans, who felt at home. "It's at least 80 percent Cubs fans," Munster, Indiana, resident Jan Poledziewski said of the "Uecker Seats" high in the upper deck just to the left of home plate. Poledziewski was used to traveling far and wide to root for the Cubs. As a child in the 1960s, she accompanied her father John to Wrigley Field, where she ate Ron Santo's Pro's Pizza, where the box often tasted as good as the cheese and dough. "Those were the worst," Poledziewski said. She and her husband, Wayne, had better reviews of the Miller Park brats and beer, much better than the disgusted Brewers fans. By the fourth inning, the Cubs had zoomed to a 5–0 lead on two Jim Edmonds homers, including a grand slam to left off Dave Bush. Brewers fans mocked their Cubs counterparts and warned them to wait till September.

In the end, all the Brewers could do was lash out in frustration. Much-battered former closer Eric Gagne threw behind Edmonds' head leading off the ninth inning, and was promptly ejected by plate umpire Doug Eddings.

"I can bet a lot of money that didn't come from the pitcher," Edmonds said, obviously meaning an easily frustrated Ned Yost, the Howard Beale "mad as hell, not going to take it anymore" of big-league managers.

Rich Harden's nine-strikeout performance sealed the deal. The Brewers scored just six runs off Cubs starters in the four games. Overall, the Cubs outscored the Brewers 31–11 as they boosted their lead to five games. They would feed off the fruits of this series for much of the rest of the season.

After an inevitable letdown on August 1 via a 3–0 loss to the punching-bag Pirates at Wrigley Field, the Cubs regained their momentum with two wins against the Bucs. Now the Astros, another team wallowing—for now—in the lower reaches of the NL Central—hit town for a night game on August 4. Almost 20 years to the day after an epic rain stopped the first scheduled night game in Wrigley Field history, an even more violent storm ripped through the old ballpark 35 minutes after the first pitch. The civil defense siren behind the leftfield bleachers wailed twice—for the first time during a game in anyone's memory—to sound the alert for a citywide tornado warning. The storm, marked by winds clocked at 68 miles per hour at the nearby Latin School, forced Cubs security personnel to usher many of the 40,000-plus fans out of the stands and into the lower-deck concourse. One women's washroom was locked because it was flooded and water seeped into the leftfield concourse from the bathroom. Near-tornadic winds caused the rain to swirl around 8:15 p.m. in a sight rarely glimpsed at Clark and Addison. The winds were so strong that the open-air press box tucked under Wrigley Field's roof became unusable with rain pounding the first two rows and was half-evacuated.

Vivid lightning continued to crackle around Wrigley Field even as the rain lessened in intensity around 9 p.m. The game, already official after five innings, eventually resumed after a two-hour, 45-minute delay, but a second round from Mother Nature crept closer. The lightning flashed more brilliantly with accompanying thunder growing ever louder as another storm moved in from the northwest. The frequency and power of the lightning was reminiscent of the alien-transporting bolts in *War of the Worlds* with Tom Cruise. The Wally Bell–headed umpiring crew in charge of the game was assured by the Cubs that the storm was still miles away and that they had time to play. A few press-box cynics suggested that the home team had lobbied hard for a continuation of play after the initial storm with the score just 2–0 in the Astros' favor. Some 5,000 Cubs diehards, all potential living lightning rods, stuck it out in their seats.

The game continued until lighting struck right next to Wrigley Field. The explosion-level thunder literally scared the Astros off the field and an ESPN employee away from his centerfield camera. With one out in the eighth, Bell finally stopped the game with Houston the victor.

With such danger lurking, golf tournaments are halted and the course is cleared, football games are stopped with players and spectators taking cover, and any amateur sports event is suspended. The Cubs and Bell either were oblivious or decided to ignore all the anecdotes about faraway lightning striking people. They had one such story at hand available in the Astros clubhouse. All-time Houston star Craig Biggio was knocked off his feet playing second base as an American Legion player in New Jersey in the 1980s. The storm was on the horizon, but nowhere near overhead. When Biggio came to his senses, he saw his shortstop teammate prone on the ground, his sock on fire, dying from a direct lightning hit from the faraway storm.

Two days later, the sheer ferocity of the Cubs-Astros storm was analyzed. The *Chicago Tribune* reported that a half-year's worth of lightning bolts—some 90,000—struck northern Illinois. At the storm's peak, some 800 bolts per minute were estimated to have hit the ground in the region.

"There was no precedent for this," WGN-TV weather guru Tom Skilling said. "In every way imaginable, that storm last night was in its own league."

So is baseball, often ignoring both weather and civil laws as if it operates on an impregnable island. The sport, played in prime thunderstorm season in spring and summer, had no rule governing lightning. But it lives by the fiat of the show must go on, get the game in. The Cubs and Bell really dodged the bullet, a possible baseball-shaking tragedy in the stands or on the field avoided only by a stroke of luck.

"My whole concern was the lightning, but also the fact that it wasn't on top of us," Bell said the next morning, without comment about overall lightning danger. "The whole crew knew what was going on. I told several players when they asked me about it if one [bolt] gets close, I'm going to take them off the field."

Astros first baseman Lance Berkman and leftfielder Carlos Lee were scared out of their wits as the storm bore down on them. Berkman made a beeline for the dugout after the final bolt hit. Strangely, the Astros pitcher on duty, the tallest player on the field, was undeterred.

"It didn't make any difference," said former Cub LaTroy Hawkins, always prone to the unusual statement. "I looked around and started laughing because the guys were running from the thunder and lightning. I didn't even flinch. I just looked at my guys running off the field, everybody jumping.

"It's only thunder and lightning. If it doesn't hit you, you're fine."

Sunny, calm skies greeted the next morning. The nitric acid left behind by the rain and lightning not only promoted the growth of flora and fauna, but also left a charge in Cubs bats not displayed during the storm-ravaged game. They were back to their old selves with back-to-back 11-run outbursts in wins over the Astros. Mark DeRosa drove in eight runs in the two games, including four on a grand-slam homer on August 6, putting behind him a forgettable July in which he hit just .195.

"July was a rough month," said DeRosa, the most quotable 2008 Cub. "Even though the team was successful, you still want to be productive and take some of the pressure off some of the big guys.

"You never doubt yourself, you never lose confidence. You wonder sometimes when you're going to get going. I've always been a streaky hitter my whole career. I've had a lot of ups and downs. I never doubted the fact I'd get hot again. You don't want to be that guy moping in the corner. A lot of flaws are hidden when the team's had so much success."

After an off day in which Piniella took his grandchildren for a boat ride on Lake Michigan and marveled at Chicago's skyline framed against the water, the Cardinals hit town.

For weeks, Cubs fans and pundits had been gnashing their teeth, demanding to know when the Cards—perceived to be playing way over their heads keeping within reach of the Cubs in the standings—would finally play up to their true level and simply pack it in. Or simply "go away," as one radio talk-show host framed it.

"No, haven't heard that," Cardinals pitcher [and ex-Cub] Todd Wellemeyer said of the attempts to wish the Cards away. "I think it's just they're so freakin' eager, the [Cubs] fans and media want it to happen so much, to go to the playoffs, they're scared of one team that has a chance, and every year has a chance to knock them out. If you [the Cubs] want to win the NL Central, we'll take any way we can get in and we'll face you in the NLCS."

As long as three-decade managerial veteran Tony La Russa and chief aide Dave Duncan remain on the job, they will be a Cubs competitor to be reckoned with no matter their level of talent.

Duncan may be the more valuable of that duo. The pitching coach is a wizard with the Wellemeyers of the world, who either have not gotten a chance in several organizations or have underperformed. The 2008 Cardinals staff was chock-full of such pitchers.

"It's not one specific thing I can come up with," Wellemeyer said of the Duncan style. "It's got to be a cross between the fact he can see talent and know he wants those guys on his team. He can tailor a game to each individual pitcher. He's not one of the guys who sits there and does the rinky-dink [mechanical] stuff. He's not so much into that. It's more the intangible stuff [mental approach].

"He's seen me pitch before. He knew what I had. Same thing with these other guys. That's why it's so hard to explain—I can't give a direct answer. It's him and Tony, absolutely.

"It's not that he reworked anything. I'm still throwing the same mechanical delivery. We've talked a lot about pitch selection. He just knows the game, he's way beyond [understanding the game] than what I got."

So how could Wellemeyer define the La Russa style?

"He's kind of like a general out there," he said. "He's not a player's manager. He's a super nice guy. But when it comes to game time, he's as serious as it gets. It's serious business. Up till that final out, he's a little different than any manager I've ever had. I won't say superintense, you can still talk to him. It's like he's in the middle of a chess match, but you know he's thinking about the next move."

The Cubs outlasted the Cardinals in a 3–2, 11-inning victory opening the series on August 8 as Jim Edmonds greeted his old teammates with two homers. Then, in a harbinger of his own mounting troubles, Carlos Zambrano served up a career-high four homers while Wellemeyer pitched acceptably for the win in a 12–3 Cardinals triumph. And in another Cubs subtext to overall success, Piniella put Fukudome on notice before the ESPN Sunday night telecast on August 10, a 6–2 Chicago win that boosted the Wrigley Field record to 45–17.

Despite a brief revival in the Milwaukee series, Fukudome hit just .236 overall in July. He had gone 30-for-138 in the 39 games through the Cards finale. He was just 3-for-28 on the early August homestand, his average dipping to .269. He had a paltry 8 homers and 42 RBIs.

"We need him to start hitting," Piniella said. "Otherwise, we'll look for other options." Second baseman Mike Fontenot, batting .291 with 8 homers as a part-timer, "needs to play," the manager said. But making such a decision a quandary were Fukudome's defensive gifts. Piniella earlier had branded him the best rightfielder in the NL. Sure enough, despite going 0-for-4 in the August 10 game, he made a nice diving catch in the ninth, prompting loud chants of "Fukudome."

"He does such a good job in rightfield that we hate to take him out of the lineup because of that," Piniella said.

Fukudome wasn't the only Cub on which the heat was turned up. The entire roster was about to take a Humidity Tour through Atlanta and Miami.

"This is a tough little trip," Piniella said. "[Starting in] Atlanta, where it's going to be nice and hot. And Florida, where it's going to be a little hotter than Atlanta."

But Piniella also wanted to ration the sizzling after-hours times, particularly on South Beach. He recalled how the Cubs, trying to clinch the NL Central, were swept three in a row at Dolphin Stadium the previous September by a last-place Marlins club.

"I don't like to talk to the team, but I will say a couple of words to them about being ready to play and getting your rest," he said.

The Cubs played like they were sport's best-rested team, sweeping through Atlanta like General Sherman, outscoring the Braves 29–9 in three games. The Marlins, as expected, were tougher, as Daryle Ward—struggling much of the season to date—slugged a pinch-hit three-run homer in the ninth on August 15 to beat the Fish 6–5. A loss and a resounding win in Florida rounded out the road trip and finally boosted the Cubs to a .500 mark away from Wrigley Field at 31–31. The six-game trip might as well have been at home anyway—the majority of the crowds, particularly in Miami, were pro-Cubs.

A 4–2 homestand against Cincinnati and Washington brought the Cubs to 30 games over .500 at 80–50 on August 24. A three-game sweep at Pittsburgh put the Cubs further over the break-even mark than at any time since the last pennant-winning season in 1945. Two more wins at home against the contending Phillies on August 28 and 29, fueled by late-inning clutch homers by Aramis Ramirez (a grand slammer) and Alfonso Soriano, boosted the Cubs to 85–50, a 6½-game lead and a 20–6 record so far in August.

The giddiness was spreading far and wide through Cubs Universe, unwarranted in the grizzled eyes of Lou Piniella. He had seen too much in 40 years in the majors. He also saw the underpublicized storylines of Carlos Zambrano's 1–1, 7.43 ERA of August, the need to rest Rich Harden with his sometimes balky shoulder, zero production from Fukudome with Edmonds joining him in the dumper, and Derrek Lee's lack of strength at the plate.

Almost immediately, the hoopla turned to consternation, even panic. Nobody had listened to Piniella, who had long forecast anything but a cakewalk.

THE RETRIEVER MAN

Ever play ball with a retriever—be it a golden or lab?

Spiritually higher forms of life than most humans, these are canines who tap into a wellspring of joy and share it with all. They like nothing better than to outrun a thrown ball. Try it. Whip the ball along the ground, the golden or lab will tear off after it and when the ball finally starts to slow down, the dog will inevitably overtake it, snatch it up, cradle it softly in its jaws, and gleefully return it to you. They'll eye the ball in your hand as if it was a prime porterhouse. Keep throwing the ball and the retriever always will corral it, the land-based version of their swims—bolstered by double coats of fur—through water to fetch fallen fowl.

So during the bottom of the fifth inning on April 25, 2008, Shooter the yellow lab must've been proud of his human pop, a Cubs outfielder named Reed Johnson. Playing centerfield in spanking-new Nationals Park, Johnson took off after a Felipe Lopez drive sliced into left-center like a retriever knowing a steak reward awaits a successful catch. Muscles and sinew pumping at 110 percent, Johnson was not going to be beaten by this baseball. A former grade-school gymnast, he began a dive through the air, spearing the ball as he stretched his 5-foot-10 frame to the max and flew over the warning track. He finally came to earth scrunched against the outfield fence as amazed relievers in the Cubs bullpen gaped at the spectacle as the bill of Johnson's cap turned upward by the contact with the fence. Johnson sprang up as if he had landed from the parallel bars, his bill still upturned in a new fashion statement, proudly cradling the ball. Neither the umpires nor a manager named Lou Piniella would have looked askance if Johnson had run in with the ball softly in his mouth, à la Shooter.

"You're not going to get a great jump on every ball," Johnson said. "As an outfielder, it's [a dive] more of a desperation thing. The only way to make the play is to lay out and that's where I was.

"I was thinking that day when I got to the park, I never had made a great play, diving. I had done it over-the-shoulder, but nothing full out. I was kind of thinking of that before the game and it came true."

In his first season with the Cubs, Johnson could outperform Shooter, who was hobbled by a leg injury most of the summer. The human retriever would probably give some goldens and labs a run for their money—or meat.

"With Shooter I throw the ball in the air," Johnson said. "He has his moments where he drops the ball. On *Baseball Tonight*, he dropped the ball. He looked bad."

Johnson had pulled off probably the majors' catch of the year, a Web Gems to end 'em all, and certainly one of the best snares in the history of the Cubs, a team with a strange tradition of placing slew-footed first basemen in center.

No worries about Johnson, though. Whatever small aspects of athleticism he might lack, he more than makes up for with hustle, grit, and intellect. He put all those qualities to the test with the catch.

"The wall was padded pretty good, fortunately," Johnson said. "I took off a few feet [from the warning track] and I didn't really feel the track until my last plant foot took off from there. I knew that once I landed I was going to have to curl up and turn away from the ball.

"I just knew I had a good jump on the ball. When I first took off I said, 'I don't know if I really have a chance to catch it,' but I knew I was closing in on it pretty fast. That's one of the nicer plays I've made."

Such an understatement.

"At Wrigley Field they might have had to call a time-out to find his head in the vines," said Piniella. "The way he not only caught the ball but slid almost headfirst into the wall and then the cap came up. . . . You're not going to see a nicer catch than that."

Johnson simply played up to his personal standards snaring the Lopez drive, with the little additional motivation of paying the Cubs back for their confidence in him. Unceremoniously released in spring training by the Blue Jays, a team for which he provided yeoman's service for five years, he quickly signed with the Cubs on March 25 and high-tailed it to the team's Mesa, Arizona, camp. The Blue Jays had to clear roster space for recent pickup Shannon Stewart and did not want to take a chance with Johnson having recovered from back surgery in 2007.

"Everything happens for a reason," Johnson said. "If I didn't have back surgery in Toronto, I'd probably still be playing there now. I'm starting to figure out the reason I had that surgery was to come here and play."

The move may have been the best scrap-heap pickup in the majors as Johnson dove all over big-league outfields to retrieve balls while serving as one of the Cubs' best clutch hitters with a .303 average and 50 RBIs in 103 games. He'd personally win games with grand-slam homers, pinch-hit shots, and even a walk-off hit-by-pitch, serving as a platoon centerfielder, defensive replacement for a corner outfielder and pinch hitter.

Johnson was prized for his ability to work the count, both waiting for a hitter's pitch and wearing down the pitcher. Piniella credited Johnson along with Kosuke Fukudome with injecting the concept of patience at the plate into many of their teammates, who totally turned around their poor on-base percentage performance from 2004 to 2006.

Better yet, he is a consummate good man around the clubhouse. Johnson usually arrives before most of his teammates, works hard, and has not a shred of pretense about him. He can get along with anyone and talks authoritatively about any aspect of baseball.

The consummate team player who earned the loyalty and gratitude of Cubs fans with his style after too many laggard players over too many decades, Johnson said nothing about playing time and waited for his moment. He knew no other way. Simply be prepared when called upon. Fetch the ball, like Shooter, and expect nothing more than perfunctory praise. Do it often enough and there's plenty of reward.

"It might just be work ethic from my parents," the shaven-headed Johnson said. "It's seemed that's the only way I've known how to play the game. When we take infield or outfielder, take it in spring training with the big-league club, you see guys go over to the ball and lobbing it in. For me, if I try to do that, the ball's going to be all over the place, I'll be misplaying it. It's just the one speed that I know. If you ask guys that are similar like one of my good buddies, Aaron Rowand, he's the same way. He doesn't do it for show. That's the only way he knows how to have success."

Figures that Johnson would go practically sideways through thin air to beat the feats of Rowand, his old teammate and roommate at Cal State-Fullerton. He can't play a game of "can you top this?" with Rowand doing vertical leaps to swipe home runs, or just plain planting his face in outfield fences at the cost of a broken nose.

"I've never robbed anyone of a home run," he said. "Even with a good vertical leap, it doesn't assure me that I'd get over the fence because I'm not that tall enough. Aaron runs into it. He doesn't go over it, he goes through it. I just knew he liked to play hard, that's why we've always gotten along."

That wasn't the first time Johnson's path intersected with another future big leaguer. Growing up in Temecula, a city south of Riverside, California, Johnson dueled eventual Blue Jays teammate Troy Glaus in Little League.

"It's attitude," now-Cardinals third baseman Glaus said. "He's been one of those guys in the minor leagues who had to play well at every level to move up. He's done that. He wasn't the guy who moved up just because [he was a top prospect]. He had to play hard at every level and be successful at every level. He was little then [in Little League].

"In college he started to flourish. I played two years with him in Toronto and [he] played well for us. I'm not surprised [at the Lopez catch]. I would expect him to find some way to do the job because that's what he's always done. He's going to put a good at-bat together every single time, he's going to play hard, he's going to play good defense. He's going to be a good player nobody ever hears about. He sees a lot of pitches, and that's key. He helps get [pitch] counts up, maybe wears a starter down, fouls balls off."

Perhaps Johnson learned mental toughness and discipline, along with physical agility, not from youth baseball, but from gymnastics. Although he started throwing a ball around at age four, his parents enrolled him in a local gymnastics programs in Temecula at the same age.

"It helped me out with balance," he said. "I did it till 14. The high bar and rings were probably my two favorite events. I think it helped me early in my career. I was further advanced and a little stronger than some guys at my age. I broke an arm and had small kinds of nicks. A lot of athletes can do a lot of same things I do but haven't had a gymnastics background. It might have helped [make the Lopez catch].

"I wouldn't trade it [gymnastics] in, because it makes you tougher, that's for sure. Every trick you learn in that sport, you pay for physically. It gives you an awareness of your body and makes you a tougher person in general. There's a lot of visualization in gymnastics where you visualize a routine before it happens. There's a lot of that every day in this dugout, guys taking at-bats before they're actually standing in the box."

And that quality separates Johnson from many of his peers. He has greater mental discipline and preparation techniques than those more talented who can rely on physicality and instinct. Johnson does not need to get heavy into high-tech aides as his mental acuity enables him to adjust as he goes along.

"I don't like to get too involved with video for my own swing," he said. "You can look at a good swing or bad swing, resultwise, whether you get a hit or not, and see if split images is like splitting hairs. You can't tell the difference mechanicswise. As a hitter you're searching for things, trying to make things up. I know I'm going good if I'm going off a feel, how things felt. I'll look at video to watch a replay to see where a pitch was. If I'm not going to change my approach in my next at-bat, there's no reason to look at video. Mechanically, my swing hasn't really changed much. It's the mental approach I've had success with.

"For instance, I'll take a swing and roll the ball down the third-base line, and I'll feel my hands tighten at contact. So I step back in and make the adjustment, hopefully in that at-bat. Concentrate on keeping hands loose at the start and hopefully the whole swing. You make that in-at-bat adjustment or in-game adjustment, and a lot of times it works if you know what you're doing.

"If I was a hitting coach, my whole philosophy would be on timing. Dip your back shoulder, swing at bad pitches—a lot of bad things go wrong with the swing are the result of timing. If you get timing correct, you can get everything started slow and early and be on time. A lot of those mechanical things will fall in place, problems will go away if you have good timing."

And what happens when Johnson is on a hot streak?

"I feel I'm getting in rhythm with the pitcher," he said. "It's almost like you're dancing, rocking back and forth, getting that fastball rhythm."

Although Johnson draws few walks—only 19 in 109 games in 2008 with a season high of just 33—he developed plate discipline from batting No. 1 in the order.

"Look at on-base percentage through our lineup, just taking good at-bats in general is contagious," he said. "It's not necessarily getting walks. Your first at-bat off a guy is really important because you want to gain as much information as you can. If you can see four, five, six pitches—the slider, curve, change, fastball—you feel you can go up there in the second and third at-bat with runners in scoring position, you're seen all the pitches. I'm up there to swing for sure. With J. P. [Ricciardi] in Toronto, it was all about drawing walks.

"I had a .390 OBP in 2006, leading all leadoff men in the American League, but the knock on me was because I didn't walk enough. There's a right way and a wrong way to walk. You don't stand up there and walk. When you're batting leadoff in front of [Alex] Rios, [Vernon] Wells, [Frank] Thomas, chances are they're not going to put me on base [with walks]. They're going to come after me. I'd have to swing at strikes and hit my way on. If a guy makes a pitcher's pitch and paints a couple of fastballs away, you tip your hat. You want to be aggressive in a small area."

Although the scouting report on Johnson slotted him in as a potential everyday player—he appeared in at least 134 games each season for the Blue Jays from 2004 to 2006—he buried his ego to accept a platoon role with Jim Edmonds in center in 2008. Johnson regarded the part-time status as an attitude-tester, that players should be hungry for more if they're restricted in playing time.

"Jim Hendry's got the right type of guys in this clubhouse—guys who want to play every day," he said. "If you didn't want to play every day, you shouldn't be here. We prepare ourselves on an everyday basis to where we're ready to play every day if something happens to the other guy. And I think that preparation has been a direct cause of our success. Attitude keeps us prepared. You sit for two, three days, an opportunity comes, you're prepared to succeed. You always got to be ready. I've been in games in the third inning that I'm not expected to play in. If you sit in the corner of the dugout and pout, your at-bat comes up, you're not giving yourself a chance to be successful.

"I've kind of always said that I'm just going to go out and do my work, hit in the cage, do my defensive stuff on the field. I don't have any control over playing time. It's a situation where you're not the guy who's in charge of writing the lineup. There's no use really worrying about it. The only thing you can take care of is making yourself a better player."

Someday Johnson will make a savvy hitting or outfield coach. He pays attention to the game's nuances, in the manner of Greg Maddux, the smartest man in baseball in his illustrious career. He may not study his swing on video, but he'll scout opposing pitchers. On the morning of May 10, 2008, he sat at the clubhouse table while others played cards or ate. He was the only Cub paying attention to a tape of Max Scherzer, that day's young Diamondbacks starter. Scherzer pitched well, but the Cubs still pulled out the game.

The game's smartest players were also the toughest. Johnson offered up one of baseball's greatest names as a role model.

"From books I read and movies I've seen, Ty Cobb, the way he played the game [is a role model]," he said. "It's stories you hear. I'm not going to play cheap. You hear quotes from him about ignoring pain and continuing to push forward. Some hack of a doctor ripped one of his tonsils out due to an infection in his throat. He went out that day playing with blood in his mouth. Who knows if it's legend? But if he did that, why can't players [do it] today?"

Johnson can strive to be as tough and dedicated as Cobb—but nowhere near as nasty in temperament. Nothing wrong with leaving people with a good feeling with a combination of playing hard and an upstanding personality.

Like dog, like man. Shooter and all his retriever kin know how to spread good cheer. Shooter's dad is in good stead.

THE COMIC IS RETIRED

The Ryan Dempster almost every Cubs clubhouse visitor got to know since his arrival in the summer of 2004 would go much further than Lou Piniella, his latest manager, in leading them off-track in the finest misdirection style.

The tape player would start. After about two minutes the visitor realized Dempster had delivered a comic monologue far off the track of the original question. He did the college of comics from his native Canada proud. Rewind time. Eventually Dempster gave the straight answer after enough laughter and shaking of heads. Somehow he had gone to the Johnny Carson ad-lib school and was prepping for an advanced course. Dempster was too clever, too quick, and too glib for anyone, media or teammates alike, to match as he possessed the off-season goal of stand-up comedy. Throw in elaborate pranks committed on fellow Cubs. Fox Sports always called on him to read the Cubs lineup with his Harry Caray impersonation on the Game of the Week, or miked him in the bullpen at mid-game. He was the life of the party.

That was a good way to keep one's sanity: Dempster first coming back from Tommy John surgery, then enduring the roller-coaster life of a closer without razor-sharp control. On the darkest Cubs day—and there were plenty in the mid-2000s—Dempster could be depended upon to brighten the scene with laughs.

But comedians are like the best sportswriters. They can handle serious roles much the same as the scribes can cover politics or disasters, as sportswriters pressed into service during the 1989 World Series' earthquake in San Francisco penned riveting accounts. There's a built-in versatility.

So when the 2008 season opened at Wrigley Field, Dempster still was the funny guy—inside. He kept that quality bottled up. Although he relaxed in his usual card games at the table in the north end of the home clubhouse, conversations by his locker were shorter, more businesslike, to the point. The quips were rationed. No grand pranks were reported, like the time in spring training three years previous when Dempster and accomplices removed all the wheels off fellow pitcher Will Ohman's SUV and stashed them in different parts of Mesa's HoHoKam Park. He was off working out, doing something positive to improve mind and body in every off-the-field moment. Through his exterior, in every muscle fiber, he desired to handle the best dramatic role of his career—great starter. Throwing one inning several days in a row required a loosy-goosy demeanor along with the requisite conditioning. But eight or nine effective innings? The mind had to be clear and focused, while the body had to be fine-tuned like never before.

Ryan Dempster wanted his big-league scouting report to read something other than clubhouse character and comedian.

"I'm still really funny, the funniest man on the team," he said. "My No. 1 priority is getting my work in. There's times and places and everything. People say, 'do Harry Caray, tell us a joke, do something funny.'

"When you start doing that too much, people assume you're never serious. He's a clown. I'm the same person; I still have a good time. There's not a more competitive person than me. I hate when we lose as a team, and I really hate it when I don't do my job. There will be times I pick it [to be funny]. I've done things here and there.

"I think at times we get a lot of demands on our time—interviews, ticket requests. It's easy to handle all those and forget to do your work you need to do to prepare. Ultimately, if you don't do your job, what good are all the interviews and tickets? My off-the-field life, I used to always meet people for a bite to eat, coffee, a drink. I don't have time for that now. I've got to focus on what's important—my family and my teammates, to put the best product out on the field."

Seriously, Dempster went from inconsistent closer to All-Star starter in one season in 2008 as a reward for his efforts. But like the greatest dramatic performers, Dempster knew he couldn't rest on his laurels. The greatest lesson came on an off-kilter October night at Wrigley Field in his last game of the season. His pitches acquired the wanderlust with seven walks in less than five innings before a too-good 1-and-2 serve to the Dodgers' James Loney carried to left-center for a grand-slam homer that set all the wrong tone for the Cubs' second consecutive postseason trip.

If Dempster—who possesses a steel-trap memory for the fine details of his career—used past setbacks as a spur to transform himself into semi-elite starter in 2008, then he'll also employ the nightmare of his division series disaster to push himself much further.

That means the public hardly will hear a Dempster quip in future seasons. If any big leaguer could lift himself even further, putting light years between himself and the embarrassment against the Dodgers, it will be the best athlete ever produced by the hamlet of Gibsons, British Columbia, who used to get himself in trouble with his grade-school science teacher with his one-liners.

They may have to find new descriptions for the determined Dempster of the near future. "Man on a mission," was Cubs media-relations chief Peter Chase's attempt to categorize the 2008 version. "Locked-in" was former teammate Scott Eyre's even better phrasing. Never say "no-nonsense," because Dempster could never restrain himself to the 10th degree, although he called past lapses of control "a brain fart." Even the liberal language parameters of this book probably could not accommodate Dempster's private thoughts for the greatest meltdown of his career.

In the months before that lowlight, he elaborated on his uplifting of concentration for his breakthrough 17–6 regular season that included spring-training runs up Camelback Mountain in Scottsdale and four-mile jogs through the Wrigleyville neighborhood around 10 a.m., before batting practice.

"It's not an easy workout," Dempster said of huffing up the mountain. "All the way to the top . . . I get in these workouts before the season starts, and they get me through tough situations during the season."

But the humorous angle never escapes Dempster even when he's dead serious. One report had him doing his runs adorned in a blond wig to throw off fans' recognition.

"There's always rumors out there," he said with a straight face. "Speculation leads to a lot of things that aren't always true. I'm faster than most people [in Wrigleyville]."

The rigorous workouts had a singular goal.

"I want to leave nothing to chance," Dempster said. "I want every fifth day when I pitch to be physically and mentally ready to pitch that day. *Mentally* means knowing the game plan and trying to execute that plan. It's fine and dandy to have a scouting report on guys, but if you don't execute pitches, the scouting report is crap, it's no good. To me it's important enough to repeat a delivery, take it one pitch at a time.

"I was lucky enough to play with Greg Maddux [2004 to 2006]. If there's anyone who exemplifies the theory of one pitch at a time, it's that guy. Bases loaded, 40,000 fans at Wrigley Field, ultimately it doesn't matter who's the hitter. It's just executing the pitch. Other than that, you can't control what happens other than fielding your position, covering first base.

"I always laugh. Throw a pitch down middle, the guy pops up, you get out of inning, you come in, and everyone says, 'Great job.' You can locate a pitch on the knees, down and away, and the guy breaks his bat, it falls in, everybody says he choked, he didn't make the big pitch. If you don't let the results bother you, great. More important is executing pitches, and I want to do it for six to seven months."

Games against the Dodgers aside, Dempster pretty much executed those pitches over the long run, impressing Piniella so much with his control and endurance that the crusty manager tried to let him complete several games hard on the heels of his conversion from closer. Only a toned physique that shaved off 27 pounds from the previous season enabled him to slog through the heat to the ninth inning. Hailing from the cool maritime climate of western Canada, Dempster was so well-conditioned that repeatedly drawing assignments in the hottest, most sultry conditions in which the Cubs played in 2008 was hardly a bother after Dempster pushed himself in his workouts.

"I always worked out hard, but I never worked out very smart," he said. "What's going to put me in position to be the best starting pitcher I can be? I just like to be well-conditioned. My body feels great, my arm feels great. [In 2007] I started doing the four-mile [pre–batting practice] runs. I'd run with Rich Hill and Neal Cotts. But just because you feel good doesn't mean you pitch good."

The workout has developed into a routine.

"The day after I pitch, I go for a nice, long run to flush the body out," Dempster said. "I lift some leg [weights] and do some core stuff. The next day, I do my bullpen, some interval running, light upper body and shoulder stuff. One thing I did a lot in the winter is a lot of stretching to be flexible. We're not getting any younger. I taper down nearing my start. I'm as strong as I can be on my fifth day."

Dempster can joke about "five and dive" starters working the minimum for a victory. He feels he's just starting to earn his pay at the five-inning mark. Dempster worked at least seven innings in 12 of his 33 starts in 2008.

"People have become content with the stat of a quality start," he said of the new minimum standard of six innings with three runs yielded. "A pitcher will say, 'I had a quality start.' Who gives a shit? Go out there and pitch nine. My goal is to go nine.

"I've been feeling good, my arm feels healthy, and my legs are great. Setup men and closers are being paid millions and millions to pitch those [late] innings, so you don't have many complete games. But that's why you show up at the park [to go nine innings]. Lou knows my body can take it [110 pitches in nine innings]."

"[He impressed Piniella] just being consistent, not settling for anything. The biggest thing is there were a lot of question marks about me going into the starting rotation. I was thankful for the opportunity. I wanted to make it as easy for Larry [Rothschild], Lou, and Jim [Hendry] as possible, so they know every fifth day I'm ready to go out there and pitch and be prepared.

"[Piniella] sees I want the ball every fifth day. You throw 70 percent strikes in the game, you'll have a chance to stay in games."

Four years after his Tommy John surgery, Dempster had regained his velocity, reaching the mid-90s mile per hour range throughout 2008. He also improved his control after an increasingly spotty strike-zone performance as a closer.

"My fastball is the key," he said. "Throwing strike one. If people command a pitch down and away, that's the key. That's the toughest pitch to hit—a fastball down and away. You could have the problem of sometimes not challenging hitters enough. I like to pitch, as opposed to being a power thrower.

"I can throw harder. I'd much rather throw a pitch at 90 percent where I want than 100 percent, not knowing where it's going. I can rear back and throw if I want. I don't concern self with velocity. The hitters tell you how hard you're throwing. I say if you got life on your ball and you're throwing downhill, that's better than throwing a flat 95 mph. Some guys can throw 100 mph, but they get hit around because there's not that life and tilt on the ball. It's all about adding and subtracting [in mph]."

He also tightened up his delivery and featured a new wrinkle as he began the motion—a one-of-a-kind twitching of his glove.

"It's one of those things where I have to preset my split-finger fastball," he said. "[Previously] when I put it in my glove and changed grips, my arm was moving. So this way allows me to take the focus off my arm. I'm moving my arm every time now, whether I'm keeping the split, or throwing the fastball or slider. It doesn't allow the hitter to maybe see changing grips and knowing it's not a split-finger fastball. I just think they're looking for the ball. They don't look at the glove.

"Because I haven't thrown out of the windup for so long, people automatically assume there are a lot more changes. People think they see a lot more."

Dempster had returned to his first love—starting— after a three-year detour as closer mandated out of necessity. Joe Borowski, the gutsy, Everyman closer of the 2003 Cubs NL Central titlists, broke down the following season, with manager Dusty Baker making the ill-advised choice of setup man LaTroy Hawkins as his replacement. Hawkins was wound too tight to handle ninth-inning duties consistently and melted down at all the wrong times in an aborted wild-card run late in the 2004 season. Tried again as closer in 2005, Hawkins bombed out again. Dempster was quickly shifted to closer as Hawkins got out of Dodge, traded to the San Francisco Giants for his own good. Dempster quickly adapted to the pressurized role, setting a team record for saves percentage with 33 out of 35 for the 2005 season. The potential impact of his effectiveness was blunted, however, when the Cubs fell quickly out of contention in August.

Dempster got off to a good start in 2006, carrying over a streak of 19 saves in a row to end the previous season. He saved 7 more through May 1, but like the rest of the Cubs, he fell into a bottomless pit as summer approached. Although he saved 12 in a row at one point in mid-summer, he otherwise was being hit hard with poor control, giving up 77 hits and 36 walks in 75 innings and finishing 1–9 with a 4.80 ERA with 24 saves. He began to hear the kind of catcalls that drove Hawkins, Mel Rojas, Dave Smith, and other big-name failed closers out of Wrigley Field over the previous 15 years. At one point, Baker even dropped him out of the closer's job.

Piniella restored him to full-time closer for 2007 but soon realized Dempster's style was not suited for the job long-term. He even decided to convert Dempster to the starting rotation at midseason, then abruptly changed his mind. Dempster still struggled with command, giving up ill-timed homers while ending up 2–7 with 28 saves and a 4.73 ERA. Still burning in Dempster's memory bank are the batter-by-batter details of another disastrous outing against the Dodgers, having blown a save on Andre Ethier's three-run homer September 6, 2007, at Wrigley Field. The boos as Piniella yanked him were probably the loudest of the season for a blown save, but that experience is not his primary motivation to succeed as a starter.

"In this town, being a closer here is like being a kicker for the Dallas Cowboys who has never won a Super Bowl," he said. "Or been 100 years since they won a Super Bowl. You kick 30 in a row, you miss one and they want a new kicker. It's a thankless job.

"It's not poor me or boo-hoo, it's just reality. It's just the way it is. I closed for 2½ years, and I'm fourth on the [Cubs'] all-time saves list. People always want change, they want someone out of there the minute they blow a save or have a bad outing.

"As reliever, everyone wants you gone, says you suck, and you're not doing your job. You throw ball one in the ninth, you hear 'boo.' Give up a hit, it's 'boo.' The reality is you're not going to save everything. You look at Eric Gagne. Gagne messed it up for everyone else because he saved 84 in a row. Before that if a closer blew two or three in a year they were considered gods. That was unheard of.

Guys are blowing eight or nine a year. I blew three, and that's not good enough."

In addition to several spectacular failures like that Dodgers game, Dempster coughed up games in which he was brought in for a nonsave situation.

"I know there were games I let get away," he said. "There were lapses and I gave up runs. You come in an 8–1 game, they say throw strikes, and give up hits and runs. Next thing you know, after you had a 2½ ERA you have a 4½ ERA and people question whether or not you're good."

Good thing that Dempster had a slightly off-center personality going into the closer's role—and in handling the aftermath of the 2008 playoff failure. Otherwise he might have gone nuts under all the pressure.

"Laughter is the best medicine," Dempster said. "If you're laughing, life is better."

He had a ribald sense of humor and a quicker wit than almost anyone with whom he came into contact from the beginning growing up in British Columbia. *Sports Illustrated* picked up on his desire to be a stand-up comic in 2005, recalling an impromptu Dempster session at a Boston night club on Father's Day 2001.

"It's good to be in Boston," Dempster told the appreciative audience then. "I've noticed the Big Dig [interrupted by cheers] and I've seen the official state tree of Massachusetts, the three-foot orange cone."

He also told how he got the best of Mr. Smethurst, one of his eighth-grade teachers in Gibsons.

"He was trying to discuss the planets," Dempster recalled. "We kept calling it 'ur-ANUS,' and he kept calling it 'UR-anus.' I repeatedly asked him, 'How big is 'ur-ANUS?' Finally he kicked me out."

While in the bullpen, Dempster entertained his fellow relievers with classic movie lines, while throwing back barbs from fans with compounded interest. He's also a master of sight gags. The prank on Will Ohman in spring training 2005 was an all-time great. Lefty Ohman found his Yukon Denali up on blocks outside the clubhouse. One tire was in the shower, while another ended up in the bullpen. Later that season, Dempster rode his bicycle to Wrigley Field, but he did not stop pedaling at the players' entrance. Carrying it down the stairs into the cramped locker room, he alighted the bike and somehow navigated it the entire length of the room through the centimeters of empty space, missing all obstacles in his path before stowing it in the equipment area. He also brought his three labs onto the field for playtime after one 2005 Wrigley Field game. Of course the chowhounds pooped on the playing surface.

Dempster also could have auditioned for a part in the comic musical *The Full Monty.* Different stories have come out of this episode: Shortly after coming back from his Tommy John surgery in 2004, Dempster joined his teammates at Stanley's, a watering hole on Chicago's near North Side. He took up some kind of dare and reportedly streaked around the bar. The pitcher himself never confirmed publicly he had opted for maximum exposure.

"Just say I served people at the bar wearing just an apron," Dempster said.

But perhaps a clue to his inhibitions or lack of the same came in a word-association game he played late in the 2007 season for the syndicated baseball radio show *Diamond Gems.* When asked to describe himself, Dempster replied: "Naked. Lying on a bench. Drinking a piña colada watching the sunset."

The other results of the word association of situations and people were answered instantly without any hesitation or stumbling. Dempster was quicker than his fastball on its best day:

Bases loaded with nobody out in the ninth: "Intense."

Piniella: "Intenser."

Wife Jenny: "The greatest."

Lindsay Lohan: "Problems."

"Stevie Ire" [the misidentification by Piniella of reliever Scott Eyre]: "Split personality."

Ohman: "Quadruple personality."

Barry Bonds: "Best player to ever play the game."

Pitching coach Larry Rothschild: "Terrific."

Drew Carey on *The Price is Right:* "Awesome."

David Letterman: "Funny."

Bob Uecker: "Hilarious."

Johnny Carson: "The best."

Dempster in trouble in the ninth: "Tightrope."

The author of this book: "Persistent."

Rich Hill: "Quirky."

Sean Marshall: "Tall."

Ryan Theriot: "Everything the LSU Tigers exemplify."

Albert Pujols: "Natural hitter."

Jason Marquis: "Doyle Brunson wannabe."

Jason Kendall: "Gamer."

Carlos Zambrano: "Crazy."

Michael Barrett: "Crazy."

Simon Cowell: "Honest."

Paula Abdul: "Emotional disaster."

Even with his exquisite comic timing, Dempster is a veteran of knowing about a time and place for everything. He has lent his humor, but more importantly his time and commitment, to community work. In 2000, only two years after his big-league debut, he donated $10 for every strike-out [totaling $2,090] to the Kids That Care pediatric and cancer fund, established to build a pediatric bone marrow transplant unit in Miami. As a result, *The Sporting News* named him one of 99 "Good Guys" in pro sports.

With the Cubs, Dempster established a Father's Day weekend program in which he hosted families whose fathers and other male members were absent, serving in Iraq. The idea was the brainchild of Jenny Dempster.

"She had an uncle who was shot down in Vietnam," he said. "A quite amazing story. One of her cousins came back [in December 2005] from Iraq. Just talking about it being my first Father's Day, having a baby, what a tough time it would be to be gone. How fortunate we are to be around our family.

"Here are people who miss holidays, birthdays, Father's Day, Mothers Day. What a neat opportunity, to have them out to the park and just kind of relax for a day to enjoy it. When Dad comes back, it would be kind of a neat story to tell him.

The Dempsters and Cubs' community affairs official Mary Dosek arranged for the families to obtain tickets and "Cubs Dollars" to purchase food and drinks.

"We'd take care of all the ins and outs, loose ends, just enjoy the ball game with family," Dempster said.

All this from a man whose own native country is not fighting in Iraq.

"My belief is I'm very, very proud to be where I'm from, to be Canadian," said Dempster. "I'm very patriotic about my country. But the United States of America has allowed me to have an opportunity that very few people in life experience, and I'm very grateful for that.

"In a way, even though I'm Canadian, I feel part-American, just because I've been here so long and been married to an American woman. I have a lot of respect for the country and what it's allowed me to attain and achieve. For me I don't believe in war, but I believe in supporting anybody who's over there doing it. Because those people are true heroes and they put their life on the line every day to provide us a safe place to live, and to be with our families."

Only one Dempster belief seemed to be even stronger. On the first day of spring training 2008, he flat-out predicted the Cubs would win the World Series. The prognostication was logical given the team's talent base, but he did not realize how much the human factor—including his own playoff failings—would come into play.

"I just believe in our team's ability to win any game at any time," he said.

Dempster won't be stopped by his 2008 pratfall. He's just going to have to try harder next time, elevate his locked-in persona far above the level he had ever reached previously.

"If you don't fear your dreams and your expectations, if you're not scared of them, then I don't think they're big enough," he said. "If you don't set them so high that you actually fear how hard it is to get there, then I don't think they're big enough. Those are huge expectations [winning the World Series], those are a huge mountain to climb, but if you're not willing to put in the work to do it . . . "

And if somehow the Cubs could block everything else out in a playoff run, they might find that each daily challenge "is just a baseball game," Dempster added.

"Just remember when you go on the field, you're trying to get a guy out, trying to get a hit, trying to field a ball.

Pressure is not being prepared. If you hit 100 free throws during practice, then get to the free-throw line in a game, you feel pretty good about hitting free throws. If you prepare, the fear isn't there as much."

The Cubs funnyman always has been serious about pitching in a World Series. He already has envisioned it.

"Ever since I was four years old," he said. "Absolutely I want to do it here. You'd need the armored guard here. You wouldn't be able to drive a car within 100 square blocks of this place."

PANIC CITY, A NO-HITTER, AND A TASTE OF CHAMPAGNE

By August 30, 2008, the Chicago Cubs knew exactly where they were going in another month's time. To be sure, a crazy-quilt series of events might drop them into the National League's wild-card berth. The pursuing Milwaukee Brewers, enjoying their first 20-win month since 1992, *could* continue playing at that pace while the Cubs dramatically cooled off. But at 85–50—the franchise's high-water mark above .500 since the 1945 pennant season—and with a 6½ game lead on the Milwaukee Brewers, the Cubs had punched an express ticket to the postseason for the second year in a row, first time since 1907 and 1908.

At once superstitious and cautious, most players express the usual baseball clichés and platitudes about their obvious destination with a month's worth of games yet to be played—and the Cubs had a potentially backbreaking September schedule chock-full of contenders on the road. But occasionally the truth does slip out, and it came from centerfielder Jim Edmonds's mouth after the Cubs split a four-game series at Wrigley Field.

"You get a little anxious," Edmonds said. "You want to get to the playoffs, you want to get started. Everybody's getting a little tired, the season's getting a little long. Day games are wearing on you here. You have to do the best you can to stay focused as a team."

First baseman Derrek Lee professed to not obsessing over the fortunes of the Brewers, who also enjoyed a hot August with a 20–7 record.

"Not so much if you have the lead," he said. "If you're trying to catch someone, you pay a lot of attention. You pay a little attention. They say if you're out in front of the race, if you look behind, you slow yourself down a little bit. You take a peek, but it's not a concern. It's out of control of what you do."

September should bring out the best in players. The climactic month did so for Piniella back in his playing days.

"This last month is a month where you reap the rewards of playing well all summer," he said. "You enjoy the situation and come out to the ballpark with expectations of winning a baseball game and giving yourself a chance to go to postseason and further. I enjoyed it immensely as a player. It should bring out the best in you, the competitive spirit in you. Pressure is only self-inflicted. You have confidence in what you're doing, you have confidence in your teammates, it's a fun time to play, and that's just the way I felt as a player. That's the way our guys feel. Unfortunate thing is baseball is 162 games and you're going to have some rough spots all the way."

Piniella could have been forecasting his own team's upcoming fortunes. The Cubs got to their 35-games-over apogee thanks to late-inning power dramatics—an eighth-inning Aramis Ramirez grand slam on August 28 off Chad Durbin and a seventh-inning Alfonso Soriano blast off Clay

Condrey on August 29. Scant notice was given to the fact the Cubs did little against Phillies starters Cole Hamels and Joe Blanton on those days. But the alarms started revving up when Brett Myers and Jamie Moyer held down the powerful lineup in 5–2 and 5–3 losses on August 30 and 31, the Cubs not collecting an extra-base hit in either game.

Little did the professional and armchair analysts realize how truly significant the lineup slowdown against top starters would prove to be in five weeks' time. A sense of background unease always had been present about the bunch-up of right-handed hitters in the Cubs' lineup, but the seasonlong uptick in runs scored and on-base percentage had masked the nervousness. At this point, though, all that seemed significant was a garden-variety regular-season hitting slump. Such offensive short-circuiting would go on to haunt the Cubs longer than they could have ever foreseen.

Perceived signs of collapse are always close at hand in the Cubs Universe. This time, though, the chief debunker was Sweet Lou himself, full of piss and vinegar after the August 31 setback, when asked if the loss was frustrating.

"Why is it frustrating?" he said. "Why should it be? We're supposed to win every day? I don't think so. We went out and played hard, and got beat. Give them credit.

"Listen, if we could get guys in every time we got men on base, we'd be 162–0. That's not going to happen."

So was Piniella fine with his team's effort?

"What the hell am I supposed to be? Not OK?" he said.

"It's not that easy. I think we've spoiled people and we've gotten people used to it. How many games did we win [in August]? Twenty games? Not bad."

Kerry Wood actually believed the process of "spoiling" fans with winning was positive.

"I think it's a good thing," he said. "I've been on teams where we've lost 96 games. There wasn't really an expectation. We're going to lose, we're going to have a good time at the park. It's a direct result of raising the expectation level of this organization."

Piniella, though, could not put himself in the shoes of the many-times-burned, million-times-careful Cubs fans and media. There were other portents causing the mass skittishness beside the strength being drained from Cubs bats. After six seasons of good health in the rotation, Carlos Zambrano suffered a bout with a "tired arm"—his second encounter with arm problems in 2008—and his first September start was pushed back two days. His absence might have been easier to digest had not flamethrower Rich Harden also come down with what Piniella later admitted, after days of prodding by media, was "discomfort" in his troublesome shoulder. Harden, whose velocity noticeably dropped in the August 29 game, also was prescribed rest with two planned missed starts.

By the time Roy Oswalt and Jose Valverde shut out the Cubs on four singles on September 1—all 27 of their hits over the past three games were singles—more nervousness enveloped the team. The Cubs' left-handed thump in Edmonds and Kosuke Fukudome had totally shut down. Derrek Lee seemed to slap only harmless grounders to the left side of the infield, grounders that proved harmful to Cubs' rallies. He hit into a double play in the eighth inning of a 9–7, 11-inning loss to the Astros on September 2. Lee only needed to lift the ball to the outfield with the bases loaded and nobody out to send home the go-ahead run, yet he produced only a worm-killer instead. Meanwhile, Zambrano excused himself after five innings, telling pitching coach Larry Rothschild that his shoulder was aching again. The panic quotient rose appropriately as Zambrano declined to take an MRI arthrogram test on September 3 as the Cubs were shut out by Randy Wolf, the first five-game losing streak at home of the season.

A 10–2 loss to the Reds in Cincinnati on September 5 brought the panic-mongers out of hiding, the most nervous of which conjured up past Cubs collapses. They looked backward instead of sideways, not noticing that the Cubs maintained at least a four-game lead as the Brewers muscular lineup began tanking just as bad as the Cubs. A three-homer Alfonso Soriano barrage in a 14–9 victory over the Reds on September 6 only temporarily allayed fears, which became morbid the next day when a command-challenged Wood coughed up a 3–1 ninth-inning lead thanks in part to a misplayed game-ending double-play grounder to shortstop Ronny Cedeno. The Cubs had now lost seven of eight, their worst slump of the year. Another one-run loss in St. Louis on September 9 brought mentions of the infamous 1969 debacle, no matter that the slumping Brewers gained not an inch of ground on the Cubs. C. C. Sabathia and Ben Sheets were great pitchers, yet they were by no means the ghosts of Tom Seaver and Jerry Koosman from 1969. Piniella had stuck his head into a mass neurosis, and the only sure cure would have been a smooth, uneventful ride straight to the World Series.

For the first time all season, Piniella purposefully lit into his team, admitting later he used the media just as they had used him throughout the year.

"We're playing like we're waiting to get beat," Piniella said loudly in a two-minute diatribe that could be heard outside his office. "We had many chances today again and we had many chances Sunday against Cincinnati, and it's the same result! If we had played ball like this all year, we wouldn't be here playing for a championship! We'd be playing a spoiler role for somebody else!

"I know we're trying. I've got no complaints about the effort. But you've got to get the job done! We can talk about having fun. We can talk about relaxing. But you've got to get your damn shirts rolled up and go out and kick somebody's ass! That's what you've got to do! Period!"

Calmer the next day, Piniella expounded on the ass-kicking part of his message.

"What's wrong with that?" he said. "What do you put the uniform on for? You put the uniform on to compete and win baseball games, that's what you put it on for. That should be the intended purpose, right? That's all I meant. I didn't get on anybody, I said I was getting effort and I had no fault with it. But you've got to go out and win baseball games. Teams I played on, that won world championships, that's exactly what we did."

Fortunately, the Cubs employed a low-wattage, high-motivation guy named Ted Lilly, who in his unique way knew how to boot some hindquarters from the mound.

Without a 98 mile-per-hour fastball like Rich Harden and the personalities of Carlos Zambrano and Ryan Dempster, it's easy for left-hander Lilly to get lost in the shuffle. He was an important part of the rise of the Cubs in 2007 with a 15–8 record few thought he would record for the $10 million per-season he was being paid. Lilly was best-remembered for heaving his glove, Bad News Bears–style, when he served up Chris Young's homer in Game 2 of the 2007 National League Division Series. That was virtually the only time Lilly had shown emotion on the mound as the anti-Zambrano personality.

"I try to keep my emotions under control as much as possible," he said. "I'm trying to get my job done. I feel like that's the whole reason I'm here."

Projecting ahead to the 2008 postseason, Lilly at first was left out of many pundits' rotations with what was seen

as just fair to middlin' stuff. Yet the soft-spoken Califor-
nian was as tough as a terrier, grabbing onto opponents'
ankles and never letting go. He started out 0–3, but by
August 25 he had more than overcome the slow start with a
13–7 mark. "It's nice," he said of the turnaround. "I'm not
going to stand here and say I'm proud of myself because I'm
doing my job. I'm certainly glad that didn't continue and I
didn't expect it to. That's my duty to go out and pitch well,
no matter what my record."

Lilly often gave up two, three, or even four runs early
in games, but then buckled down, using a crafty curve and
expertly located fastball to rack up surprisingly high strikeout totals that gave the Cubs a chance to catch up and win
those starts. He had vowed to improve his shaky control
when he first came to the Cubs, and came through with
just 55 walks in 207 innings during the 2007 campaign.
Still prone to the home-run ball, Lilly found ways to overcome the hanging curves and come out the winner.

But on September 10 at Busch Stadium, Lilly needed
to come up big. The Cubs bats had been sluggish the previous night in the opener of the three-game series with the
Cardinals, prompting Piniella to send his "go out and kick
somebody's ass" message through the media.

In Lilly's start, the bats again operated at popgun efficiency, without an extra-base hit. However, he didn't need
much run support. He dominated the Cardinals, allowing just one run and five hits in eight innings in his most
impactful outing of the season. In a further display of his
underrated toughness, Lilly barreled into catcher Yadier
Molina while scoring a crucial run, forcing a banged-up
Molina out of the game shortly afterward. Kerry Wood
allowed a two-run homer in the ninth as the Cubs hung
on to win 4–3.

"Unfortunately the idea is not to give up a couple of runs," Lilly explained. "Sometimes you don't have a choice, and you have to minimize the damage that's already been done. You just try to make adjustments. Whatever hasn't been working, find something that will. I don't think there's any one pitch I go to when I'm in trouble. Whatever adjustments need to be made at that time."

Lilly's lockdown outing provided a spark. Harden returned to the mound on September 11, holding the Cardinals to two runs in five innings despite a drop in his velocity. Wood, who had been shaky all season when he got himself in trouble in the ninth, pitched out of a bad jam by getting Albert Pujols to pop up for the final out in the 3–2 victory.

The panic had been unwarranted. While the Cubs struggled, the Brewers matched them loss for loss as their young, cocky hitters went ice-cold. The Cubs led by 5½ games when they got an unexpected three-day break due to Hurricane Ike's delaying of their three-game series with the Astros in Houston.

In a controversial move that provoked bad feelings from Astros fans, Major League Baseball moved two games of the series to Miller Park in Milwaukee. Widespread loss of power and other damage from Ike had made playing in Houston impractical. Although every official up through commissioner Bud Selig knew all too well that Miller Park would turn into a "Wrigley Field North" with its location just 90 miles from Chicago, they had few other options to play the games. Rain had been forecast for other available outdoor stadiums in St. Louis and Atlanta. Domed stadiums had schedule conflicts, including NFL games.

With just 24 hours to sell tickets, 23,441 fans, almost all Cubs rooters, showed up on Sunday night, September

14. The crowd might have been even bigger had not the Chicago area been hammered by two days' worth of flooding rains, including the remnants of Ike, that totaled up to nine inches. Many ticket buyers were distracted by waterlogged basements. The Astros arrived in Milwaukee only four hours before the 7:05 p.m. game time, hopping the first plane to take off from Houston after the hurricane had moved through. Zambrano was sent to the mound after an 11-day layoff with the pregame plan of limiting him to about 90 pitches.

Big Z was focused like never before in his mercurial career. He mowed down the previously hot-hitting Astros with ease, with no seriously hard-hit balls or sensational plays behind him. He was economical with his pitches. The crowd, packed into the lower two decks and bleachers of Miller Park, sensed something special afoot in the seventh and began roaring with every pitch. Zambrano's teammates in the dugout observed protocol and mentioned nothing. Out in the bullpen, the relievers hung on every pitch while pursing their lips.

"When it's going on, unless we're scoring a bunch of runs, the pace is pretty quick due to no hits," said rookie right-hander Jeff Samardzija. "So before you know it, you're in the seventh inning, and that's when you realize what's going on. I didn't hear anybody say anything. I wouldn't say anything. Everyone's just saying he's throwing well and is excited for him. Usually, players don't say too much about it. You can talk plenty about it once it's done."

Zambrano had a no-hitter broken up by the Diamondbacks' Shea Hillenbrand on an infield chopper in the eighth inning of a 2003 road game. He also took a no-hitter into the seventh at Wrigley Field in a 2006 contest, but Jacque Jones lost a fly ball in the sun for a double.

Zambrano would have been pulled from that game anyway because he had passed the 120-pitch mark in the seventh. His high pitch counts and excess of walks usually ruined any thoughts of no-hitters, but on this night Big Z had thrown just 99 pitches by the end of eight innings. Amazingly, the radar gun registered as high as 98 miles per hour for a pitcher who had not worked in 11 days and was coming off shoulder twinges.

"It's just a matter of him not walking anyone, throwing strikes and not giving up a cheap hit," Samardzija recalled later. "The only way it was going to get broken is a broken-bat single here or there. They didn't square a ball all game, so that wasn't going to happen."

Pitching coach Larry Rothschild, who had to ride Zambrano's emotional roller coaster since he first joined the Cubs rotation in midseason 2002, knew his eccentric charge was due for a special night watching him warm up fluidly in the bullpen.

"I don't know, man, my arm is weird, for real," Zambrano said afterward. "Sometimes I give all I have in my arm. I even go back and try to throw harder and I just see 92, 93. And sometimes I just kind of play catch [with Geovany Soto] and see the scoreboard and it's 97, 98."

Two routine grounders to shortstop Ryan Theriot brought up Darin Erstad as the final Astro in the ninth. Here was the juncture at which the best shots at completing Cubs no-hitters had been broken up since the last hitless gem, a near-perfect game by Milt Pappas on September 2, 1972, at Wrigley Field. The Reds' Eddie Milner singled to center with two out against Chuck Rainey on August 24, 1983, at the Friendly Confines. Otis Nixon slapped a ball past shortstop against Jose Guzman on April 6, 1993, also at Wrigley. Still another last-batter spoiler was the Cardinals'

Bernard Gilkey, who on September 25, 1995, sliced a triple into right-center, just out of a diving Sammy Sosa's reach, to mar Frank Castillo's masterpiece.

But Zambrano would leave nothing to chance. He threw a sweeping splitter that broke down and away on a 3-and-2 count as Erstad went fishing, coming up with nothing. Zambrano dropped to one knee, pointed skyward in his usual postinning spiritual thank-you, and then celebrated with a mob of happy Cubs. Minutes later, Zambrano revealed that Pappas told him on several occasions he'd be the next Cub to throw a no-hitter.

Hardly anything could top Zambrano, but Lilly tried the next afternoon at Miller Park. As a still-impressive crowd of 15,158 showed up on short notice on a Monday afternoon with school in session and vacations over, Lilly held the Astros without a hit as the innings wore on. Jim Edmonds helped keep it going with a diving catch of Brad Ausmus's liner to right-center with one out in the sixth.

"There were a couple of guys before the game who let me know that I had a lot of work to do to follow up Z, " Lilly said. "But there's so many things that it takes for a no-hitter to take place, so my expectations were just to go out there and make good pitches and be aggressive."

Lilly's bid for a back-to-back gem really piqued his teammates' interest.

"We were paying a little closer attention to that, just because it had happened yesterday," Samardzija said. "The funny thing, it was kind of the same atmosphere. The fans were into it and cheering every out starting in the fifth. We were just happy to see Teddy throwing so great. They sneaked one hit in there."

The no-hitter should have been broken up by Reggie Abercrombie's shot off third baseman Aramis Ramirez's glove. The ball caromed to shortstop Ronny Cedeno, who futilely attempted to nail Abercrombie at first. But the play was ruled an error. Wrigley Field scorer Bob Rosenberg said a week later he would have ruled the play a hit had he been on duty; the standards must be consistent, Rosenberg added, whether the ruling takes place early or late in a no-hit bid. The debate over the error became academic moments later when Mark Loretta slapped a clean single to right.

That remained the Astros' only hit as Samardzija, Carlos Marmol, and Bobby Howry took over for Lilly after the seventh. The game entered into the record books as the only time a no-hitter was followed up the next day by a one-hitter. Better yet for the Cubs, the dominant outings, accompanied by a spark of hitting to rightfield by the well-grounded Derrek Lee, got the team out of second gear.

The Cubs handed new Brewers ace C. C. Sabathia his first National League loss—after nine wins—the next night at Wrigley Field. After a 6–2 loss to Milwaukee on September 17, the Cubs then pulled off a comeback to rival their rally from a 9–1 deficit against Colorado back on May 30. The Brewers took a 6–2 lead into the ninth on September 18, and had closer Salomon Torres on the mound with nobody on and two out. But Aramis Ramirez doubled, Jim Edmonds singled in Ramirez, and Mark DeRosa singled to bring up Geovany Soto. Even with a batter's dreaded late-afternoon shadows, he jumped on Torres's first pitch to belt a three-run homer into the leftfield bleachers to tie the game.

"I was just trying to get a pitch to hit and he left a fastball up," Soto said of Torres. "I thought he was going to throw a sinker down and in, or at least down and away, and make me hit a ground ball. He left it up.

"It was a bright background and we were in the shade, so once that ball got in the shadows, it was kind of tough to pick up. But I saw that one."

Then, after Kerry Wood escaped a second-and-third, none-out jam in the top of the 12th, Lee continued his revival with a game-winning single up the middle in the bottom of the inning.

"I don't look at it that way," Lee said in response to a question on whether his game-winner was a relief after weeks of clutch failures. "I thought, 'What a day.' Just feels good to win this game. It's a big game.

"I was actually pretty relaxed. I've been pretty good at the plate. It's easier to feel good when your swing feels better."

The sudden Cubs surge and Brewers collapse knocked the Cubs' magic number down to two in a hurry. Lou Piniella became increasingly irritated with questions about the Cubs clinching the NL Central in advance of the actual event and suddenly had to deal with another Zambrano controversy on September 19.

Three days after the no-hitter, Zambrano flew home to Venezuela to deal with the death of his grandmother. He reversed course on September 18, getting to Chicago close to midnight after the long flight. Still, he elected to make his scheduled start against the Cardinals the next afternoon.

The decision was a disaster for both Zambrano and Piniella. He gave up eight runs in 1⅔ innings. Afterward, Zambrano said his legs were not in shape to pitch so soon after the grueling round trip—let alone his emotions being distracted.

Piniella said he would have been hard-pressed to push Zambrano back a day or two.

"Who was I going to start?" he said. "Who would you want me to start?" He had no response when he was given lefty Sean Marshall as an answer. Piniella eventually said he needed to keep Marshall available for middle relief, but the starting of Zambrano under the conditions was a risk that backfired.

Zambrano said he thought about asking Piniella to push his start back at least a day. "It's hard to make that decision, especially in the situation we are," he said.

Another conflict between Piniella and Zambrano had erupted with two out in the second, after Zambrano had given up a double, two walks, and a single, while casting a wild pitch as two more runs scored. Piniella came to the mound to pull him. Zambrano walked off the mound, in violation of baseball etiquette, before Piniella reached him. Piniella pointed to the mound, Zambrano backtracked and gave him the ball.

In his last two starts against the Cardinals at Wrigley Field, Zambrano had allowed 17 hits, including five homers and 17 runs in six innings.

Piniella used the game result to show why he doesn't like talk of clinching the division until it actually takes place.

"It's a little reminder why you don't count your chickens before they hatch," he said. "You people are getting ahead of yourselves. We got plenty of time to talk about clinchings when we get the magic number down to zero. We're still at two. You can say I'm cautious, you can say whatever, but that's the way I've always approached it and that's the way I'll continue to approach it."

But Piniella would talk to his heart's content 24 hours later. A 5–4 victory over the Cardinals on September 20 locked up the NL Central for the second year in a row as

Lilly again came up big, a Troy Glaus three-run homer in the sixth the only blemish on another good performance. The Cubs mobbed Kerry Wood after he got Aaron Miles to fly out to ex-Cardinal Edmonds for the final out, yet the celebration was relatively sedate compared to past Chicago division clinchings in which finishing first was the end-all to every dream. A gaggle of players came back out onto the field minutes after the final pitch, dressed in dark NL Central championship sweatshirts to spray champagne into the bleachers, while several bottles were simply given away for chugging duty to fans in the box seats behind the Cubs dugout. The clubhouse champagne spraying was confined to the north end of the clubhouse. Alfonso Soriano sported a gold wrestling-style belt with a giant *W*, the Cubs' new victory symbol.

"They should be cautious," Piniella, his hair soaked by bubbly, said of nervous fans. "I understand. In the two years that I've been here, I have heard the frustrations of all these Cubs fans. But what the heck can you do? You can't relive the past. You've got to look at the present and look toward the future."

Amid the hysteria about the quest for the Holy Grail of the World Series, fans apparently could not appreciate what they already had.

"We have accomplished something already," Kerry Wood said of two consecutive playoff appearances for the first time since 1907 and 1908. "We have accomplished something already and people haven't mentioned it."

Only a few years ago the big accomplishment was the first back-to-back above-.500 seasons [2003 and 2004] since 1971 and 1972. That could only happen to the Cubs. What would people say if they ever won consecutive World Series? Would they be speechless? Dumbstruck?

After a week's interregnum, sports' longest-running soap opera prepared to move onto a bigger, grander stage to which all the cast of characters had long expected to ascend. No matter what Piniella, Wood, or anyone could say, the unseen pressure increased to ocean-depth levels.

How much the walls would close in would not be felt for a while. As Piniella rested regulars in the season's final week and set up his playoff rotation, debate raged as to whom the Cubs' preferred playoff opponent should be. The Los Angeles Dodgers, bumping along around or just below the .500 mark most of the season, for weeks appeared to be the division series foe. But after the New York Mets began dueling the Brewers for the wild-card playoff berth, the flawed Big Apple team entered the picture. The only redeeming feature of the Mets was ace southpaw Johan Santana. Word then began to filter east that the Dodgers, authors of a late-season charge that won the NL West, were much improved with the recently acquired Manny Ramirez firming up the lineup while their rotation solidified around Derek Lowe and Chad Billingsley. Some pundits suggested that even with Santana, the Mets were a preferable opponent to the Dodgers.

Their emphasis being marking time until the playoffs, the Cubs lost a season-ending series in Milwaukee, enabling the Brewers to win the wild card over the Mets on the final day. Thus the Dodgers were locked in as their opponent, though little concern surfaced with the Cubs safely possessing home-field advantage through the NL playoffs. Little known were the consequences of not taking advantage of Wrigley Field. The Cubs had lost eight straight playoff games in the western time zone, dating back to 1984. They simply had never played well in the big-ballpark, often pitching-rich teams in California. And there was the forgettable two

NLDS games in Arizona, on the same clock as Pacific time when the Cubs played them.

In spite of these background blips, the Cubs prepared to move full speed ahead into October. They possessed, by far, their most World Series–ready team on paper in 63 years. Almost to a person anywhere in the world, Cubs fans prepped for the culmination of a long-deferred dream, just three weeks and 11 wins away.

CANADIAN HARDBALL

Stop by Rich Harden's Wrigley Field locker and you can't really linger.

The right-hander tends toward the soft-spoken, verbally spare side, appearing like an Everyman not even filled out at his listed 6-foot-1, 195 pounds. Harden's friendly and never rude, but he's committed to business and doesn't stick around, disappearing into the weight room or trainer's table for long stretches. This whole thing about a big-market, fishbowl existence as a Chicago Cub is all too new, and probably a bit overwhelming to the right hander who could throw 101 miles per hour and blow away the best hitters like Little Leaguers when both his mechanics and shoulder were in fine tune. No doubt there's bit of a culture shock coming to the big, big city from Harden's former employer—low-profile, low-payroll Oakland—and his hometown, the modest maritime provincial capital Victoria, British Columbia. Harden's father, Russ, even suggested the ever-inquisitive Chicago media give him a little space down the stretch of a season with high expectations.

One day, though, Harden surprised. Suddenly, he produced a strange-looking gizmo to display to you. It is a metal baton with yellow-colored balls of different sizes at each end. It's called a B.O.S. In place of a baseball, Harden holds the B.O.S. as he goes through his delivery in the bullpen to gauge proper mechanics. Its one moving part, inside the baton, tells whether Harden is in proper balance as he follows through by the clicking noise it makes.

Figures that the B.O.S. originated on the West Coast, via Harden mentor Ron Romanick, the Athletics' bullpen coach. But if it works, why not? Baseball always lagged behind in cutting-edge training techniques. Harden has picked up on this kind of advanced thinking. He can't afford not to. He's got both a gift and a burden, not mutually exclusive as 2008 teammate Kerry Wood has understood for a decade. Harden possesses some of the most electric stuff and one of the most balky shoulders in the game. He's got to ride the wave even if he leaves most everyone in baseball behind. By necessity, Harden must self-teach himself about mechanics and kinesiology, to understand how to stay one step ahead of the pain in that shoulder, possessed of all its own moving parts, still a stiff challenge to orthopedists who have long since conquered frayed elbow tendons via the 35-year-old Tommy John surgery.

"I'm open to new training techniques and conditioning," Harden said. "That's why we try all the stuff with the throwing program. Your body's not always going to feel great, it's not always going to feel 100 percent. You're always going to have nagging injuries. A throwing program is the way to get through it. Baseball maybe needs to make a change, start accepting new practices and training methods. There is a lot to it."

Harden is doing everything in his power to avoid being Mark Prior Redux. As if he was dropped from the sky into the Cubs' lap, Prior set to team with Wood channeling lightning through their arms and smiting opponents standing in the way of ending the Cubs' endless walk in baseball's Sinai Desert. But the manna from heaven turned into the ultimate tease, Prior's shoulder deteriorating to the point in 2006 that he took part in a much-satirized "towel drill" in the bullpen in which he held a towel—vaguely suggesting a white flag of surrender—in place of a baseball. If Harden isn't going to hold a baseball, let it be something like a B.O.S. that gives him any kind of edge over the crapshoot that is the health of a power pitcher—one that, in his case, doesn't have the 6-foot-5 raw-boned body stereotype.

There are times when Harden is willing to squeeze some insight to his expanding consciousness about pitching. Ten minutes at the end of the visitors dugout at Miller Park in Milwaukee, five minutes here or there by his locker before he has to go where he has to go. He doesn't waste a word or thought. These sessions, as quick as his fastball at high heat, yield a window into his mental focus. If he could only harness his shoulder and health to the level of perception he has reached about his profession, he could truly be baseball's beast.

"I've always been a firm believer that a lot of power for pitchers comes from the legs, core strength," Harden said. "It's being able to put it all together, being able to get your body to work together, to get your legs to work with your core and shoulder. There's a whole kinetic chain involved. When you push off your legs, your core goes up diagonally into the shoulder, and then you use your arm like a whip."

Indeed, *whip* is the right word. Study Harden's delivery and there's little waste before he turns his shoulder and arm toward the hitter. Imagine the G forces contained within when he instantly cranks it up to full power after not flailing all over the place at the start of the delivery.

"Too many people try to create the velocity too early," he said. "They'll really muscle up and try to throw too hard. When I'm really throwing it up there in the upper 90s, I'm free and easy, and at last minute, I whip my arm through. That's the difference between 92 and 99 mph. At the end, you want to fire it and whip it. It's a great feeling.

"You can still be maximum effort, but still probably expend less effort than someone else who is really muscling up, arms going this way, legs going that way instead of being almost effortless in it. With me you're putting a lot of effort into it, but it's only at the finish."

Harden has continually worked at refining his mechanics for maximum efficiency without wasted effort.

"When I first came into the league, it was a real big deal for me," he said of throwing hard. "It's definitely a really good feeling [to throw at least 100 mph]. I think as a young pitcher you can get too into it, too concerned about it. Try to throw the ball as hard as you can, and throw even harder. It puts a lot of strain on your body.

"The older I get, the more I learn to back off and pitch at a lower velocity. And when I need it, give it a little extra. I've been most successful doing that."

"It's kind of what I've been learning the past three years. Some games I'll dial it up, some games I won't. It depends on the situation. It helps me to save a little bit when I need it. Instead of throwing all one speed, 93 to 95 [mph] on every pitch, you vary the velocity."

Backing off includes replacing a devastating split-finger fastball with a changeup as his second pitch.

"The change puts less stress on the body," Harden said. "With young kids, the curve was more fun. But the change is one of the best pitches in baseball, thrown with the same arm speed as the fastball. The hitters see the same arm speed, but the grip takes off the speed. My change is 85 to 89 [mph]."

Harden's next gauge of success will be proving his gift is meant for mortal man to possess. The bulk of his big-league career has been spent pitching in fits and spurts due to not only the shoulder, but a strained oblique muscle and several other dings. He claims he has never actually injured himself by the act of pitching, with a literal over-reach for a comebacker to the mound having stretched him past the breaking point and, like falling dominoes, caus-ing a myriad of other problems. No matter what the ori-gin of his aches and pains, Harden is baseball's version of fine china—handle with care. The days of being a 33-start, 200-inning pitcher are off in the future, if ever. He has to be given extra rest, and even a cortisone shot, as he expe-rienced almost two months into his first half-season with the Cubs in 2008.

"I spent some time on the DL, pulled my oblique a couple of times, because I created so much torque," Harden said. "I put so much strain on my body, if one part is weaker, you're going to strain it. Another time, I tried to bare-hand a ball coming back to me, and put myself in such a bad position I injured myself. I stretched it and strained my shoulder capsule. It's common in hockey goalies, reaching back and stretching the shoulder. It made it a little more loose and caused impingement with one of my tendons. I had some slack in my shoulder and my tendon was pinched in there. In 2008 [with Oakland] it was the muscle [under-neath his shoulder]. It's nothing to do with the shoulder structure, rotator cuff, or labrum."

Harden's performances are too tantalizing, too dom-inating to not take a flyer on him. Picking up his $7 mil-lion option for 2009 was the Cubs' first act of off-season business after their 2008 campaign prematurely ended. He spoiled both fans and baseball people when he blew through a series of dominating strikeout games, as he demonstrated when he first came to the Cubs in a surprising trade on July 8, 2008. Harden struck out 10 in each of his first three Chicago starts, ranking as the first pitcher since 1900 to whiff 10 or more in his first trio of games with a team. He had a total of 39 strikeouts in his first four Cubs starts and 89 in 71 innings while allowing just 39 hits.

"I'll have a few games where I get a ton of strikeouts and a lot of games where I don't get many," Harden said. "It evens up in the end, I find. I just had a stretch where I did it. That's the way pitching is."

Then the frustration of others sets in when he has to be skipped a turn or two to make sure the sensitive shoulder either can recover from discomfort or is properly rested. Once burned, a million times careful, given the histories of Prior and Wood.

Whether whipping his arm or carefully managing his shoulder, Harden is much happier doing it in Chicago than Oakland. Although a pitching prodigy on a team that had its fair share of the same in the 2000s, eventually he needed to make a change, to get away from the Athletics, who had grown disillusioned with all his time missed, Harden having logged just 72⅓ innings combined in 2006 and 2007. He prefers not to elaborate on his Athletics days and instead just desires to look forward.

His adjustment to the Cubs, its quaint but eccentric ballpark and playing conditions and the giant media market will be ongoing. And it represents almost a world away from his youth days at the western end of Canada, hardly a traditional hotbed for power pitchers.

The reality is that Harden took the side door into hardball. For an old youth-league centerfielder and defenseman who was probably good enough to move on to juniors level in hockey, and who also dabbled in "extreme fighting," he's a pretty good pitcher. No matter in what athletic position, the arm always was electric.

"When he could stand in centerfield at 11, 12, 13, and throw a ball on a line from deep centerfield, you could see it was a gift," said Russ Harden. "It was obvious he had great skill. He also was a great hitter, and the same quick-twitch muscles to give him throwing skill also gave him bat speed."

Off the beaten track in Victoria as far as the normal talent flow into pro baseball, Rich Harden could develop his skills in a semi-vacuum.

"We didn't have a whole lot of scouts scouting us," he said. "Down here, every scout has a radar gun on kids. Being a centerfielder really helped me as a pitcher. I always had to really long-arm it. I got that good spin where I didn't have that carry from the outfield. I'd throw it there on a line.

"I really wanted to pitch. I pitched occasionally, but not in big games consistently. In the 12th grade, at a scouting camp, I pitched the first inning, then they wanted me to play outfield. I only had 91 [mph] on the gun at that age. I just started lifting weights, and I was getting stronger. From there it just kind of progressed. I wasn't flying open, which I had done when I was younger. You're always fighting that. It was a combination of getting stronger and maturing physically. I just kept refining my mechanics and was keeping everything as simple as possible."

Baseball had won out over hockey by the time Harden graduated high school and attended Central Arizona College in 1999.

"As a defenseman, he could have played junior hockey, but at 17 he focused on baseball," said Russ Harden. "He loved to check. He played physically. Teams started dumping the puck into his corner when he was smaller, but he could handle it. He was a real good skater with a good shot."

The younger Harden was low-key from day one. He did not hang on every score and every feat from the majors, whose only outpost was several hours away across the border in Seattle. He was not even aware Wood had struck out 20 in a game back in 1998 after he was asked to put his initial Cubs strikeout feats in perspective.

"He's a low-key guy," Russ Harden said. "Is he a passionate baseball fan? Not particularly. If you're expecting him to be a rah-rah guy, he isn't."

And Harden's status as a student of the game is a personal "evolution," according to his father.

"He's a 'feel' athlete as opposed to Greg Maddux," he said. "When he was in college, he'd try to overpower hitters. If he feels good, he tries to overpower hitters. When Ron Romanick took over, he got Rich thinking of repeating his delivery. He got him to a consistent release point. He was a power guy, but over the last five years, they taught him how to pitch, for him to be able to dial back [velocity]. The best thing that happened to him was Romanick becoming bullpen coach. Ron was willing to share information that helped Rich."

The fireballer now has flown away from the nest and must find a new on-site mentor, or be his own best teacher now that Romanick is nearly 2,000 miles away.

"I worked with Romanick since I signed in 2001," Harden said. "He's had this idea of conserving pitchers' arms by limiting throwing in between starts. He's had this idea for a while. He's always evolving, adding things, subtracting things.

"A lot of the throwing pitchers do in between starts is something you grow up with. It's something you do in college. It's tradition. Baseball's always a game of tradition and one of the last to change. In terms of treatment and injury prevention, the way we go about doing everything lags behind. In other sports they're more willing to try new training methods. With my injuries, we try to limit the throwing. I feel I've responded great to it."

Branch Rickey, a master innovator back in the day, who set up strings framing the strike zone at the Dodgertown camp, might be a kindred spirit of Romanick.

"He's used some cones and pylons set up certain distance, depending on how you feel certain days," Harden said. "You go further or shorter. The overall throwing program is you go out to 180 feet, play long toss, but limit your throws. You're not on the mound every day, either."

He really believes less is often more in pitching preparation.

"The normal baseball routine is if you're not feeling well, you still grind it out and throw 40, 50, 60 pitches," he said. "I've seen a lot of guys get on the mound a couple of times between starts and really grind it out. You're putting a lot more strain on shoulder and elbow. A lot of that has become a kind of mental crutch for guys. I was the same way, and I was reluctant to change at first. I gave it a try and my body responded well.

"[In 2008] I'd be taking a day off after I pitched to let my body recover. For many pitchers, a lot of times you throw the day after. My body responded well. A full day of recovery of not doing anything helps."

More adjustments are in store. Harden has to learn how to pitch in day games in much more sultry weather conditions than he encountered in Pacific-temperate Oakland. Even sitting in the Cubs dugout on an 80-degree late morning in July is an exercise in endurance with the sun's radiant energy beating directly down.

"I've always liked night games," he said. "I've always felt better, it's a little cooler and I feel stronger later in the game."

But with 51 day games legislated at Wrigley Field for now, the Cubs cannot just pitch him at night at home, nor excuse him from duty in such semitropical outposts like St. Louis, Cincinnati, Atlanta, and Florida. The difference in climate is striking. Ken Holtzman, who pitched no-hitters for the Cubs in 1969 and 1971 before being traded to Oakland, recalled how a full schedule of home night games in 60- to 75-degree weather on the West Coast, compared to the humidity of Wrigley Field, was much more conducive to building durability for starting pitchers.

Russ Harden figures his kid will train differently as a Cub, to better manage his energy. But fatherly advice probably isn't needed in this case. Rich Harden's journey isn't so much from team to team or through the brutal 162-game schedule, but up the knowledge scale. And if he ever becomes a brainiac like Greg Maddux, he can boast he always had a better fastball than the Master and knew what to do with it.

16

WOODY

Temporarily alone by his Wrigley Field locker, not a teammate with whom to gab or a media member to pester him, Kerry Wood exulted in the static of a cell phone call.

Toddler son Justin was supposed to leave a message, and Wood, a smile ever widening, pressed his ear like a suction cup to the phone. He didn't quite hear the stream of consciousness from blond-coiffed Justin, turning out to be a spittin' image of the old man. The elder Wood delighted in bringing his son onto the field after games, turning the kid to run loose and ranking perhaps as the first Cub to ever change a diaper at shortstop. On the mound, erstwhile Kid K strikeout whiz-turned-closer Wood is Texas intense, the image long planted in batters' minds that if you flipped him off, you might get his A train under your chin or stuck in your ribs. But by his strategically located locker, best in the clubhouse that permitted quick escape to off-limits areas by the showers and equipment room, Wood displayed the gamut of emotions.

He's at his happiest when family thoughts enter the picture. Remember, he's a decade removed as a raw rookie, a rare man to strike out his age—20 at 20. Now he's a father of two who rigorously keeps himself in shape compared to the baby fat he carried around as Kid K. Several feet from the locker was the main clubhouse table, where card games proceeded and breakfasts and lunches were wolfed down. So there's no shortage of teammates nearby who respect the daylights out of Wood. Occasionally, media types slipped down as far as the locker, where Wood did not mind a few minutes of one-on-one banter, preferably with no tape recorders whirring or notebooks produced. The pitcher's razor-sharp, cutting wit, with visitors to the locker serving as the foil or straight man, was in full bloom here.

The other side of Wood, more radically intense than his mound presence, also has been glimpsed here. After a May 1, 2008, game against the Milwaukee Brewers in which he blew a 3–1 lead in the ninth inning and lost the game with a walk and hit batsman mixed in to the formula, he stewed at his locker in his skivvies, chewing his nails for 15 minutes. Laser beams could have zapped out of Wood's eyes if this was a 1960 American International sci-fi movie. Anger permeated the ballpark anyway. As Wood percolated, Lou Piniella had his biggest blowup of the season in the interview room, reachable via striding the length of the clubhouse, then traversing corridors through a left turn, two right turns, another left, and finally a right distant from the closer's redoubt.

Wood just sat at his locker, transfixed as media— already stunned by Piniella's explosion due to a question about replacing a gimpy Alfonso Soriano for defense in leftfield—gathered around Soriano's locker in the middle of the clubhouse. He waited and waited some more, until the mob finally drifted his way. He had seen other closers in his time, all professionals like Rod Beck, Rick Aguilera,

Joe Borowski, and Ryan Dempster, fess up to their screw-ups by waiting by their lockers for the postmortem to begin. No way was Wood going to mimic a character like Antonio Alfonseca, who shook his six-fingered right hand at media to warn them to stay away when he coughed up a game.

As the reporters and camera operators approached, Wood stood, and backed up against the locker until he was totally blocked in, the questioners numbering more than the throng that surrounded him at the other end of the locker room after his 20-K game. Wood was one of the biggest names in Cubs history and when he did something, it was big news. The questions came in rapid-fire fashion and as he answered, reliving the ninth-inning nightmare, his eyes glistened—a rarely seen Wood emotion. Save for the postgame trauma of Game 7 of the National League Championship Series against the Marlins, when Wood said he had let everyone down, this was the worst experience he had ever had in the majors. He was still learning the closer's craft, he stumbled badly, and he had to answer for it.

A week later, after the hurt of the blown game had passed, Wood could more calmly describe his mind-set, part of the training of a closer—one of the most pressur-ized and often thankless jobs in sports.

These scenes are now past tense in the Cubs club-house. Often called the Mr. Cub of his generation, Wood reluctantly was cut loose after the 2008 season as other ros-ter and payroll priorities overwhelmed general manager Jim Hendry's sentimental side that strongly wanted to keep the pitcher a lifelong Chicago player. The loss was even more keenly felt in the locker room compared to the mound, as Wood's Texas-strong persona and comeback story made him first among Cubs equals.

Chicago's loss was going to be someone else's gain in this case the Cleveland Indians'. Wood's post-Cubs employer added an intelligent, passionate player with powerful self-motivation, a 6-foot-5 old-schooler with just a high-school education who developed into a tremendously self-educated, street-savvy, mature good citizen.

If the Indians got to know Wood as well as his teammates and less than a handful of longtime Chicago media types, they'd like what they'd see. Take, for example, Wood's calm description of his post–blown save mind-set after that Brewers game, part of the training of a closer—one of the most pressurized and often thankless jobs in sports.

"First and foremost, I'm pissed off at myself," he said. "Right after [being upset at] myself, I wasted a solid outing by Zambrano. That sucks when you lose games for teammates who did their jobs all day.

"I had plenty of time to come in here and get whatever I needed out of my system. It's different for every guy. I watched Joe [Borowski] and watching Ryan [Dempster] when they handled it when things didn't go well. Everyone in here feels bad for them, but no one feels worse than that guy. You come in for four minutes and it [a winning effort] gets wiped away. That's the hardest part. Against that team [Brewers] it's even worse.

"The clubhouse is too late [for recriminations]. At that point, you second-guess yourself as you're backing up the bases. I'm not a big second-guesser on pitch selection. You second-guess on location. More so, I'm upset for the guy who pitched for 2½ hours."

But was it tough to stand here as your eyes started to moisten?

"That's the way it goes," Wood said. "I've never been one to have a bad day and not talk to media. It's the worse I felt in a while. It was a big game for us, a big series, to lose in the last inning there is not a worse feeling."

Learning a new role that had been projected as a later-career destination as far back as the turn of the millennium was challenging enough for Wood throughout 2008. But if working as a closer with no margin for error was tough enough, figure the process by which he was merely pitching without pain would have been off the charts.

Never underestimate the near miracle of Kerry Wood taking the mound after what he had been through.

Frustration and derision had been the twin images subscribed to Wood as his shoulder simply was not healthy enough to pitch consistently at the big-league level in 2005 and 2006, the Cubs' hopes tumbling with his declining condition and that of Mark Prior's. The twin prodigies were so good they seemed as if they were dropped from the sky into Wrigley Field.

And they seemed endorsed by similar above-the-majors talent. Nolan Ryan, whose No. 34 Wood wears and whose final no-hitter he witnessed as a teenager, closely observed Wood's between-starts bullpen session in Houston on July 21, 2001. A year earlier, Greg Maddux called Wood's repertoire "as good as anybody's I've seen. It's the whole package when combined. Somebody might have a better fastball than Wood, someone might have a better curve. But when you put the two together, it's the best." Maddux ended up citing Wood and Prior's presence as a major spur to returning to the Cubs in 2004 after an 11-season absence.

How much baseball lightning coursed through Wood's right arm? During his fabled rookie season in 1998, then-manager Jim Riggleman pretty much telegraphed when he would pull Kid K. As Wood worked on his final batter, he'd often finish with a flourish. His final pitch of the game, in the seventh or eighth inning, often reached 98 or 99 miles per hour.

There was a flip side to such power, and it grew increasingly dark. Wood and Prior could not economize on the number of pitches as they ran deep counts on hitters, striking them out, walking them, or having their best offerings fouled off as hitters were unable to center their swings. Man's physiology is scarcely capable of handling such maximum effort in such an unnatural act as pitching, with awkward mechanics only making things worse.

Having recovered nicely from Tommy John surgery on his elbow in the spring of 1999, Wood underwent a second operation on his labrum near the end of the 2005 season. Angered that a partially torn rotator cuff was not properly diagnosed in the process, Wood opted to skip yet another operation when shoulder stiffness returned in 2006, shutting him down on June 6 after just four starts. Taking buddy Borowski's advice from the latter's own experience rehabbing the rotator cuff without surgery, he embarked on a rigorous conditioning program to build up the muscles around the damaged area. The tear would never fully mend, but Wood could compensate by strengthening the overall shoulder area. He also would be in the best physical condition possible. So between workouts and an organic diet discovered by wife Sarah, Wood shaved between 30 and 35 pounds off his frame going into spring training 2007. He lost so much weight that some thought he was trying out for the track team. He didn't look anywhere like the husky Woody of old.

But even though he was in the best shape of his life, the shoulder was still balky. He was shut down after experiencing pain in a game late in spring training 2007.

He still could not throw without pain as Lou Piniella's managerial tenure began. Shuttling between Chicago and his off-season home in Arizona as the regular season got underway, Wood was nowhere near ready to come back. Doubts about continuing began to build until one day in late spring he figured he'd just throw in the towel and go on with the rest of his life.

"I was one day away from quitting," Wood said. "I actually told Sarah that I was already done. After all the conditioning, all the stuff, that was it. I threw on a Friday, came here [Wrigley Field] on the weekend, and my arm was killing me. I was going back to Arizona on Monday, and I'd call Jim [Hendry] on Monday night [to tell him he'd retire]. I called my doctor Monday morning and said I'd see him Wednesday to do [another] surgery.

"I was at my [physical] therapist's place, telling him about it. He said why not just throw again to flare it up, make sure he [the surgeon] doesn't miss anything? I went to throw honestly to flare it up to see everything. I went to throw to make it hurt.

"It felt good."

Wood was shocked, but not tricked. He had felt good before, then the shoulder regressed. This time, however, was different. He had a gift that simply couldn't be taken away.

"I threw again Tuesday, and felt better than on Monday. There was no pain. I changed my mind. I kept throwing and kept throwing, the next thing I was [throwing] off the mound. Then I called Jim and Mark [Cubs trainer O'Neal]. I told them I was ready to do rehab stuff. Within three weeks I [was] back in minor-league games."

Wood's recovery was not quite an otherworldly miracle, yet no single explanation has been narrowed down for the abrupt turnaround in his shoulder's condition. The best guess by Cubs officials was the scar tissue around the 2005 surgically repaired area finally loosened—plus the fact that Wood experienced a positive adrenaline rush when he threw.

On the sultry Chicago night of August 5, 2007, with the storylines of Tom Glavine's 300th victory and Alfonso Soriano's torn quadriceps muscle otherwise dominating, Wood returning to pitch for the first time in 14 months was a voluble sidebar. The fans chanted "Woody, Woody" as he strode in from the bullpen for mop-up duty in the Cubs' loss to the Mets. All the strong spirit that had been more than counterbalanced by the weakness of flesh had not been forgotten by the paying customers.

"I understand people look and respect what I've gone through to come back," Wood said. "A lot of these people out at the stadium started reading about me when I was drafted at 17. They feel like in a sense they've watched me grow up. I've played in the same stadium and they see the same person. They respect more than anything what I've been through, what I came back from, and the effort I gave to get back out there."

Wood was a bullpen regular finishing out the 2007 season, then won the closer's job in a three-headed competition against Carlos Marmol and Bobby Howry the following spring.

"It's a reward for not giving up, not quitting, not throwing the towel in," Wood said. "I was blessed with another chance, and you take advantage of it. You never want to give up regardless of what you do. It shows that there's light at the end of the tunnel. For a long time that light was a train."

Wood's journey went just as authentic Jersey Boy Borowski had predicted almost two years previous. The two pitchers and their wives had become close when Borowski saved a number of Wood's 14 wins in 2003, their mutual efforts coming so frustratingly close to a World Series berth. Borowski said Wood would have periodic setbacks, but eventually would make it all the way back.

"I don't think you can say it was 100 percent," said Borowski, whose own career as a blue-collar closer seemed to end in 2008 with Cleveland. "Nothing's guaranteed. I was going on what I went through and based on what type of person I know Woody was. And if he dedicated himself and put his mind to it, he could do it. I see him every off-season and see how he works; I had no doubt in my mind if he applied it and stuck with it, he'd do it."

Wood did it well enough to earn a National League All-Star berth in his first season as a closer, five years after he was named an All-Star as a starter. Such a feat put him in good company with a select group of pitchers who made the team first as a starter, then as a reliever. They include John Smoltz, Dennis Eckersley, Goose Gossage, Hoyt Wilhelm, Derek Lowe, Luis Arroyo, Bob Stanley, Johnny Sain, Joe Page, and Gerry Staley.

His comeback complete and more than a full season under his belt without pain, does Wood ever wonder why someone who wanted to do everything the right way in both baseball and life had to go through such misery? Who did he flip off to undergo three career's worth of trials and tribulations? He got further reaffirmation when he lost three weeks to a lingering finger blister at midseason 2008 that cost him the chance to actually pitch in the Midsummer Classic in Yankee Stadium.

"You'll never get answers thinking about it that way," he said. "I look at it as it happened for a reason, not why me. When you see Make-A-Wish kids here everyday in the dugout. I got a blister on my finger and I can't play base-ball, but it's not life-threatening."

Wood learned the nuances of closing almost brick by brick. He encountered hiccups along the way, such as an unusual habit—despite otherwise good control—of hitting or walking batters, then overcompensating by throwing extremely hittable pitches that cost him. Like the other aspects of his career, he made improvements with time.

Despite the maturity of his 31 years in 2008, Wood did not like talking about these shakier elements of his ninth-inning work. But that's his traditional pride and stubbornness taking over. For almost his 10 years in the majors, Wood abruptly cut off conversation when his mediocre mechanics—throwing across his body, not using his legs enough—were brought up. But they were so noticeable that former manager Dusty Baker said during spring training 2006 that former players had come up to him to ask why he couldn't make Wood use his legs more in his delivery.

Finally, from the hindsight of his veteran's wisdom, Wood admitted early in 2008 that his mechanics were a problem, having gotten by on pure power early on.

"If you want to play in this game a long time, you have to be smart enough to know what you can do and what your body can handle," he said. "Obviously if my mechanics were better—they weren't great in my rookie year and they weren't great for a while—obviously mechanics can help things. When you have young guys coming up who are invincible, you don't worry about mechanics. You're out there throwing. You've been blessed with a good arm and you know how to pitch. All the mechanics stuff come later."

By all classical measurements, Wood's first season as closer was a success. He saved 34 games in 40 opportunities, despite missing three weeks due to the blister. He held opponents scoreless in 51 of 65 games. Hitters batted just .219 against Wood. And he walked just 18 batters in 66⅓ innings, a stark contrast from the first half of his career as a starter. Then, his mechanics and his power style resulted in Wood averaging around one walk for every two innings. Now he says walks "absolutely" are a mortal sin.

"With the ninth inning of a game on the line, walks kill you," he said. "Make them beat you and don't help them, without making them earn it."

Again, the one throwback to his wilder earlier days were the hit batsmen. Wood hit seven in 2008, harking back to his National League–leading 21 hit batters in 2003. But he could more easily pitch around such off-target serves as a starter. The extra baserunners as a closer sometimes proved fatal. Overall, he was still in the learning process of getting out of his own jams, a crucial quality for any successful closer.

That's Wood's last hurdle to overcome as a closer, but he was still defiant in talking about the issue.

"I was unaware I was the first guy to ever hit anybody in the fuckin' game," he said. "If you hit a guy in the ninth inning, it's a runner on base like a base hit and walk. You can't talk too much about it. It is what it is. When you come into game with a one-run lead, you establish the ball in and away. I'm trying to locate two pitches. The few times I hit the first batter, it doesn't mean the game's over because there's a runner on first. Hitting somebody is the last thing on my mind out there.

"Bases loaded, no outs, I feel I can get out of it. You're four pitches away from getting out of it. Strike the first guy out, then get a first-pitch double play. You're always one pitch away from getting two outs with runners on base.

Guys get in jams all the time, but it's magnified late in the game."

In calmer moments, Wood can be prescient. Back in the summer of 1999, as he rehabbed from the Tommy John surgery, he projected about how he might pitch once recovered. Asked if he would trade in his flirtations with 100 miles per hour for a top speed of 95 but with fine control, Wood said he'd gladly take the latter. Other than the hit batsman, he is not far away from that scenario.

The only way he could consistently get up to his old Kid K velocity these days is by speeding on the expressway. But he does not closely monitor radar guns anymore.

"Usually I get a feel on [velocity on batters'] swings," Wood said. "Every now and then take a peek to see where I'm at [velocity]. If it's just 90, I have to be more careful. I'm more likely to top out at 96, 97. There may be a day where I let it go and it's up to 98, 99. On a consistent basis, it's 94 to 96. As long as I'm pain-free, that velocity will be enough at this level."

The Kerry Wood of baseball maturity has even learned how to throw a sinking fastball. He has simplified his repertoire.

"I'll flip a curve every so often in 'pen," he said. "But I'll stick with the fastball, slider, and occasional cutter."

The array of pitches was much more sensational on May 6, 1998. That dank Thursday afternoon ranked as one of the greatest games ever pitched in big-league history. It may have been the most dominating, with better, more unhittable pitches than seen in most no-hitters. In just his fifth big-league start, Wood used a devastating slider-curve that mimicked the fantasy pitch from the 1949 Ray Milland comedy *It Happens Every Spring* to strike out 20 Houston Astros, making top-notch hitters like Jeff Bagwell, Moises

Alou, and Derek Bell look helpless in the process. The pitch ended up too good to be true for the long run. Wood had to junk it once he came back from the Tommy John surgery because it put too much torque on the elbow.

A decade after the feat, which was celebrated in Chicago on its anniversary, Wood has grown comfortable remembering the game. In his 30s, he now fully realizes why such a strikeout spree matched only in a nine-inning outing twice by Roger Clemens would be considered so special.

The 20-K game seemed both a blessing and a curse. The blessing of the achievement put Wood on the map and ensured his big-league career. The curse—unrelated to the imaginary hexes put on the Cubs overall—was that no human could live up to the game's standards.

Wood takes it as a blessing, but also realizes that expectations of more superhuman performances are unreasonable.

"You're smart enough to figure out you're never going to keep that pace up," he said. "But when you're doing it, you're like, well, you expect to punch out 12 to 15 the next game. It would be the norm. For a little bit of time, you begin to expect it yourself. Reality is, nobody could keep that pace up.

"By far it was the best game I've ever pitched. Obviously it means something to me. I don't really think about it. I think about it about once a year when they bring it up for the anniversary. I'm sure when I'm done playing, when I go on to do something else, I'll think about it. For a while, it was kind of what I was known for. After all the injuries, I'm known for the injuries instead of that game."

In hindsight, Wood realized he had to pay a stiff price for throwing the unnaturally breaking slider-curve.

"I hadn't looked at the tape in a long time," he said. "I've seen guys come into the league who throw hard and have really, really sharp breaking balls. The first thing on my mind is that's going to catch up to them eventually. That comes from seeing it happen to me, it feels like it's inevitable. You hope it doesn't, but it feels like it's inevitable."

Wood never cashed in on the big game. He was invited to appear on the late-night talk shows, but declined. Then and now, he eschews a high profile off the field.

"That's just not me," he said. "I don't talk about myself to my teammates. It would be hard to go on Letterman and Leno and talk about me. I was just never really a person to talk about it. It's just who I am. Obviously I was thrilled with the game and I was in shock with all the attention I was getting. After it happened, all I wanted to do was work and stay under the radar, and that was impossible."

Wood is still guarded about his off-the-field life. Only a couple of media types have his cell-phone number, which isn't worth much anyway. He doesn't particularly care to gab on the phone. Make no mistake about it, he's no hermit with Sarah, Justin, and daughter Katie. "People see me out, it's not that big of a deal to see me out," he said. However, Wood was particularly incensed when his address was published and his house was displayed in a newspaper photo. He's had a car stolen when it was valet-parked and a dog kidnapped from a dog-sitter.

Canines are a favorite Wood conversation topic. Kerry and Sarah Wood are dog lovers. They once were overwhelmed by fans when they took their pooches to "Wiggly Field," a dog park about a mile south of the ballpark. Before the Cubs banned such visits, Sarah brought Toby, their Jack Russell terrier, and Stella, a fawn-colored pug, to the ballpark to wait for Kerry by the family room down the

leftfield line. Toby, unfortunately, was high-strung, endemic
to his breed and could not be kept when the Woods became
parents.

"He was great dog, but just wasn't real good with
kids," he said. "He was just a growler. We got a great home
for him. Stella's great with the kids, but she just has really,
really, really bad breath. I'm on the road so it was tough on
my wife with two kids and two dogs."

While the Woods dote on their dog, they also love the
city of Chicago. They already have steered fund-raising for
the community via an annual charity bowling tournament
in which the majority of Cubs teammates have attended. In
the first three years from 2004 to 2006, more than $1 mil-
lion was raised for Children's Memorial Hospital. In 2007,
Wood directed the $300,000 proceeds to Derrek Lee's Proj-
ect 3000 effort to fight an eye disease that afflicted Lee's
preschool daughter, Jada. And in 2008, the bowlers generated funds for the Chicago Public Schools' Organic School
Project, which taught students the food cycle from farm to
plate. Students would cultivate a garden and be educated
on healthy lifestyles and environmentally sound practices.
Choosing such an academic program was the logical next
step from the organic meals that Sarah Wood obtained to
aid in her husband's weight loss in 2006 and 2007.

"It's something we both believe in, especially since we
had kids," Wood said. "Kids that [preschool] age are wild
enough as it is, and food has an effect. We don't know a lot
of stuff that's in food that companies have put in for years
and years and years. There are a lot of health problems.
These problems are starting younger and younger kids—
diabetes and different illnesses.

"I think it's something we as a family decided to keep
our kids off the junk food, the Cokes, juices, and snacks.

They still have snacks and things, but it's organic and natural. There's a correlation the way your body feels, the energy level you have [with food consumed]. They talk about 'brain food,' so it has an effect on how you learn and how you process things."

Wood's 2008 event got some unintended publicity. The top celebrity guest was Mark Cuban, by then the people's choice to purchase the Cubs in a drawn-out sales process that began on Opening Day 2007.

But Wood insisted he was not subtly helping Cuban buy the team through his appearance at the benefit.

"He's a fan of Chicago sports, a fan of the city," he said. "He's into giving back to charity and giving back to community. He was willing to be a part of it. We e-mailed back and forth. I met him at the dugout when he threw out the first pitch of a game. The sale was the one thing we didn't talk about. I gave him that respect. That's probably all he gets asked about. I talked to him on a personal basis."

If Cuban—who grew up a Pirates fans—could bid on the Cubs, why not some real true-blue rooters like the big Chicago expatriate colony in Hollywood? Why couldn't the likes of Bill Murray, Joe Mantegna (who co-wrote and starred with Dennis Franz in the original 1977 play *Bleacher Bums*), Bill Petersen, and Gary Sinise put together a group?

"I've met them, but they are more fans who enjoy coming in [on their breaks from production]," Wood said. "Maybe they're not interested, they're all still working, they're still busy."

Not too busy or well-appointed enough to watch Wood fulfill his greatest dream?

He missed out on it in 2008, logging just a meaningless inning in an NLDS against the Dodgers that did not even have a whiff of a save situation. Too bad. As a closer he could have made an image he first envisioned in the spring of 2002 come to life.

You see, Wood would not have minded throwing the final pitch that ended the Cubs' preposterous walk in baseball's wilderness. Back in 2002, sitting in an alfresco section of a Mesa, Arizona, sports bar with Sarah listening in, he was given a scenario of a starter, working the bottom of the ninth at Yankee Stadium in Game 7 of the World Series.

"I can't wait to be in that situation," Wood said at the time. "You want the ball in that situation, just like the shortstop wants to make a diving play in the eighth.

"Let's do it, let's strap it on, let's see who's better today."

Of all the deserving pitchers in recent Cubs annals whom you wanted to have the ball in that situation, Wood has to be No. 1. Greg Maddux would be a decent 1a, and right behind him would be Rick Sutcliffe.

Like Maddux and Sutcliffe, Wood won't have the chance to be the best-remembered game-ending pitcher in Cubs history. There's a tremendous sense of loss in his story, but there's also a moral to be told.

Perhaps the World Series isn't the end-all to these long-deferred Wrigley Field dreams. Maybe the greatest satisfaction is in the chase, the striving, the overcoming of odds, and how one comports himself in the process. The story of Wood, the eternal Cub despite a new uniform by necessity post-2008, is the No. 1 evidence of that fact.

EPILOGUE

Cubs fans are the real stewards of their team.

Through a seven-decade period of largely incompetent ownership and front-office management, they've been the rock of the franchise. Sure, they stayed away in droves for much of the 1950s and 1960s, and again in 1981, when a panicky Bill Wrigley—worried over a $40 million inheritance tax bite—ordered the trading of what few player assets he had left. But they were never further than their TV sets, a Sunday doubleheader, a Sandy Koufax duel with Ken Holtzman, or a visit by Willie Mays and company. And they were always ready to return en masse on a moment's notice if the Cubs showed any signs of life.

The late, great Cubs announcer Vince Lloyd recalled his astonishment when he got ratings figures for both the Cubs and the White Sox when they shared WGN-TV in the early 1960s, when the Cubs were a College of Coaches–addled embarrassment while the Sox were contenders under manager Al Lopez. Playing only daytime baseball, the Cubs drew the higher video numbers.

Fans sent the message to the befuddled Phil Wrigley for years. They didn't like his inept ownership and desired some night games by staying away to the point that the Cubs were the worst draw in the National League, as attendance plummeted near to the 600,000 mark in the nation's then second-largest city on four occasions during the 1960s. Crowds plummeted into the hundreds for some late September weekday games. A prime example of the fact the fans would not play hooky to watch bad baseball during the week came on Friday afternoon, August 20, 1965. With the Cubs mired in eighth place in a 10-team NL, the Wrigley Field doubleheader with the Houston Astros drew just 7,936. Yet exactly one week later, on August 27, the Braves—playing out their final, lame-duck season in Milwaukee and drawing worse than the Cubs—attracted a good gate of 20,723 for an 8 p.m. County Stadium game with the Chicagoans. The crowd was heavily sprinkled with Cubs fans. Some 77 busloads of fans made the trip up Interstate 94. In those days, Cubs rooters would rather drive 90 miles at TGIF time to watch their team, in their free time, instead of sneaking out to the Friendly Confines in the afternoon.

Phil and Bill Wrigley, their compliant minions, and the succeeding Tribune Company ownership never realized the sleeping giant in their control and the positive effects on image and pocketbook if they had a consistent contender. In 1969, Vince Lloyd told general manager John Holland that the Cubs would draw more than 2 million annually if they won year after year. Holland, who kept his job through 19 years, numerous 90-defeat seasons, and two record-setting 103-loss campaigns by paying fealty to Phil Wrigley, refused to believe him. He and his master had a massive deficit of imagination and comprehension, let alone courage.

On at least two occasions the fans protested, with Phil Wrigley writing back defending his positions as if he was scripting an ad for his gum company. In 1959, the fans knocked the owner for his "stand-pat" management and lack of night games; Wrigley fired off a response to the *Chicago Daily News* suggesting one letter-writer ought to find other leisure-time pursuits if he got so worked up over the Cubs. In 1971, a triumvirate of Cubs players, fans, and the traditionally soft Chicago sports media ganged up on increasingly senile manager Leo Durocher, who had Wrigley under his spell. The owner placed an ad in Chicago newspapers insisting the "dump Durocher clique" might as well give up as Leo the Lip would remain as manager.

A generation-plus later, the fans would not be so kind to a Wrigley. They don't have to worry. The gum magnates along with bottom-line Tribune Company execs like Stanton Cook, John Madigan, and Don Grenesko are long gone. So is the archconservative, old-fashioned, overcautious Andy MacPhail. The Cubs' bar has been dramatically raised, and the fans expect nothing less than a World Series victory.

That's why the likes of Valparaiso, Indiana, rooter Karen Nelson termed the three-game 2008 division series flop against the Dodgers "a disaster of biblical proportion." The succession of the near-miss World Series team in 2003, new manager Lou Piniella's proclamation that the Cubs will win, and a 97-victory season that seemed to promise an express ticket to the Fall Classic ensured there's no turning back in the fans' mind-set—ever.

But the Cubs Universe, having endured a long, hard off-season after the astounding '08 playoff debacle, still must endure too many accoutrements left over from the losing decades. It's bad enough the fans are still caught in a stereotype branding them as partygoers and tourists who merely visit Wrigley Field for a good time, don't care if the Cubs win, and don't even know the score. None other than President Obama, now the nation's No. 1 White Sox fan, made just such an off-hand statement during his '08 campaign. Worse yet, fans must endure continual explanations for the endless Cubs walk in the baseball wilderness centered around billy goats, curses, black cats, and Steve Bartman. The media-fueled hex-fest, simmering during the 100th-anniversary championship season in '08, boiled over after the NLDS. Accompanying it are age-old bromides that the Cubs are losers and will never win a World Series.

This time, though, the fans are fed up and won't accept the hex-mongers force-feeding them nonsensical explanations for Cubs failures. That's why they universally panned Cubs chairman Crane Kenney's recruiting of Rev. Father James L. Greanias of St. Iakovos Greek Orthodox Church in Valparaiso, Indiana, to spread holy water in the Cubs Wrigley Field dugout before Game 1 of the NLDS. "He said, 'I'm a devout Catholic, and I'm not superstitious, but if there is anything there, I want to take care of it,'" Greanias said.

On the same day, Northwest Indiana also represented the origin of yet another attempt to bring a billy goat into Wrigley Field to lift the supposed curse. Instead of the usual Sam Sianis of the world-famous Billy Goat Tavern, this time it was Jimmy Gerodemos, proprietor of the Hobart Country Lounge in Hobart, escorting his goat Tito via limousine to the ballpark, where they were denied entrance, the same fate as frequently befell Sianis and his beasts over the decades.

During and after the NLDS flop, the usual "Cubs are cursed" columns, talk shows, and network TV sidebars fed the need to be clever, whimsical and sarcastic at the expense of accuracy. Typical was *Daily Herald* sports columnist Mike Imrem, who grew up with the Cubs, writing after the collapse his latest of many entries attributing curses for the Cubs' failures. Imrem and his colleagues should know better, but they can't help themselves.

"There are no curses, jinxes, or hexes," Imrem penned after Game 3.

"Except when it comes to the Cubs, that is.

"Some sort of supernatural force must be at work for a baseball franchise to go as long as the Cubs have without winning a world championship."

After several times linking curses to Ryan Dempster's seven-walk outing in Game 1 and the Dodgers' acquiring Manny Ramirez, Imrem concluded the column while supposedly glorying in Cubs futility.

"Hey, Cubs fans, maybe it's time to just take pride that the Cubs went a century without winning a World Series.

"That's a record for futility that doesn't figure to be matched as long as any of us are around. Perversely speaking, a parade and a party are in order.

"Just be careful a black cat doesn't stroll in front of your float."

But Imrem wasn't finished. Two weeks later, writing about general manager Jim Hendry's stature among all Cubs general managers, he resorted again to the occult.

"All thought they were strong enough to overcome the curses, jinxes, and hexes that inflict this organization. All thought they were ghostbusters. All were wrong."

The columnist's angle is clear—he's trying to be witty. But the more the curse angle is repeated, like anything else the more it's perceived to be true. Interestingly, Imrem never suggested Hendry's predecessors might have been underqualified or inept, hired by equally inept owners or team presidents all falling prey to human failings rather than some bewitching spell.

Fortunately, enough fans and other media see through such superficial and misleading attempts to explain away the Cubs. The strongest rebuke was by Al Yellon, Cubs fan since 1963, leftfield bleachers season-ticket holder, and proprietor of the popular BleedCubbieBlue.com. By day a staff director at Chicago's ABC station WLS-TV, Yellon wrote this essay on his site.

"Fred Merkle's curse. Goats. Black cats. Bartman. These are things that you haven't seen me discuss much here—because what do they have to do with baseball? To me, they seem the lazy mass media reporter's crutch for trying to explain the inexplicable.

"Think about it. There are a number of other teams, both baseball and other professional sports, that have had championship droughts of decades—some now broken—and never did you hear about such frivolous things. Only the Red Sox had one (and JUST one)—the 'Curse of the Bambino'—and that wasn't real, it was the invention of a Boston sportswriter, Dan Shaughnessy in the 1980s. The White Sox (88 years, now broken), the Indians (60 years), the Giants (54 years) in baseball; the New York Rangers (54 years, now broken), the Blackhawks (47 years) in hockey; the Detroit Lions (51 years) and the Chicago/St. Louis/ Arizona Cardinals (61 years), all teams with long title droughts—no excuses, no cutesy little stories, nothing.

"So why do the Cubs have these? Why are we the *only* team with a sports drought that has it shoved down our throats? It can't be simply the length of the drought—the White Sox drought was nearly as long before it was broken. Part of the answer lies in what I said above—laziness on the part of mass media reporters and columnists. Not wanting to delve into the real problems, they fall back on something easy, something they've heard of.

"These things have been part of Cubs lore and I think they shouldn't be. We need to leave them in the dust and focus on management and players. This is a call to reporters, columnists, and yes, team management.

"Stop the cute stuff. Ignore it. Be done with it. I am."

Yellon found an unlikely ally in *Chicago Sun-Times* columnist Greg Couch, who also grew up a Cubs fan. Couch believes all the woe of previous decades must be written off since the Cubs only in the Piniella era have been seriously trying to win.

"For years, the smelly billy goat story with the Greek curse has been fun to tell to your friends, date, kids," Couch wrote. "Of course, BG, or Before Goat, the Cubs already hadn't won the World Series in 37 years.

"Details. Why let them get in the way of a fun tale?

"Well, somehow, the story has become a very real problem for the Cubs. Instead of something to laugh about at a tavern, it has morphed into an excuse for why the Cubs never win a championship, and then into a marketable part of the team's charm. The Cubs have actually become fictional characters themselves.

"For fans who have been duped by the worst-managed franchise in sports history, that goat has become the acceptable reason for their heroes' failure. For the suits running the team, it has become a great way to sell tickets without bothering to pay for a good team. And for the media, it has become the easiest of all explanations.

"Cheap, inept management? Nah. Just a goat."

Unfortunately, Lou Piniella's voice on the subject surprisingly is not loud enough. When informed of the Greek

priest's irrigation of his dugout, Sweet Lou became the ultimate naysayer to only a limited audience of writers.

"There's no curses here," he said. "I don't know how
many times I have to answer about curses. Who did it?
Crane graduated from Notre Dame. He might have had
somebody from South Bend . . . I don't believe in those
things. I really don't. I've said it many times. Good pitching,
good defense, and timely hitting. Those are the ingredients
that win baseball games. I saw it a little bit on TV. I saw the
sprinkling. The other guy's praying, too. God doesn't care
about a baseball game."

Only the World Series that Piniella vowed to win with
the Cubs can put a brake on the cottage industry of curses.
To think the whole thing started as a publicity stunt, then
was forgotten for a quarter-century.

Original Billy Goat's Tavern proprietor William Sianis
may have been an urban goat-herder, but his No. 1 role
was publicity hound for his saloon, in 1945 located near
Chicago Stadium on Chicago's near West Side. Sianis's
use of his billy goat Murphy and the pair's ejection from
the 1945 World Series got the intended effect—publicity
in most Chicago papers at the time. But as the years proceeded, the story and the concept of the curse Sianis alleg-
edly put on the Cubs for the ejection was largely forgotten.
Baseball Digest editor John Kuenster, a *Chicago Daily News*
beat writer covering both the Cubs and White Sox in the
1950s and 1960s, does not recall the goat/curse story written about through the endless Cubs losing seasons of his
era. During this time, William Sianis busied himself trying
to promote himself at other venues. He tried to smuggle
the goat in a hearse into the Republican National Convention in Chicago one year. In 1959, he plotted to bring the
goat to old Comiskey Park for the World Series between

the White Sox and Dodgers. But Bill Veeck caught wind of the plan. Although he was the Baseball Barnum promoter, Veeck knew a stunt that went too far. He warned Sianis to stay away because the police's ballpark detail was on the lookout for him.

Mike Royko, the Babe Ruth of columnists for the *Chicago Daily News,* and *Chicago Tribune* lead sports columnist David Condon inadvertently combined to revive the goat/curse story around 1970, when William Sianis died and the Leo Durocher–led Cubs suffered through a series of late-season collapses. Both heavy drinkers and regulars at Billy Goat's, by now relocated to Michigan Avenue steps away from the city's newspapers offices, Royko and Condon picked up on the 1945 curse story to work in their whimsical entries on the Cubs.

Condon went so far as writing an entire column on the attempts of Sam Sianis, nephew of William Sianis, to bring billy goat Socrates into Wrigley Field on July 4, 1973 to officially lift the '45 curse. The younger Sianis hired a similar publicity craver, a limo driver named Fabulous Howard, to take him and Socrates—whom Condon claimed wintered at Oakland Athletics owner Charlie Finley's Indiana farm—to the ballpark, where security men and Chicago police barred their path. The first-place Cubs came from behind that day minus the goat on Ron Santo's 10th-inning homer, but three days later began an outrageous 6–29 slide that knocked them out of the NL East lead and all the way down to eight games under .500 to officially end a contending era headed by Santo, Billy Williams, Ernie Banks, and Fergie Jenkins. The massive collapse in the wake of excluding Socrates, of course, provided years of grist to the media satirists.

Eventually, Sam Sianis got successor goats admitted to Wrigley Field on Opening Day 1982—first under Tribune

Company ownership—and during the playoffs in 1984 and 1989. A group of Wisconsin seminarians served as the first copycat goat herders into the ballpark on May 4, 1994. Seeking to reverse the "hex" of the Cubs' 12-game home losing streak from the start of the season, the men and goat failed at first to gain entry. But through Ernie Banks's help, the goat was admitted through the big "wagon gate" doors in rightfield, paraded all along the warning track and then down the third-base line to home plate as a retinue of photographers and TV camera operators followed. The Cubs broke their losing streak via a 5–2 win as rookie Steve Trachsel, angered that his warm-ups were disrupted by the passing goat and company, took it out on the Cincinnati Reds. Again, more grist to suggest a connection between the goat and curses.

All played for laughs while the team continued losing overall. But supposedly Cubs diehard fan Royko—the only man who battled Mayor Richard J. Daley to a standstill with his riveting exposé columns—could have helped out the situation rather than his typical satire involving curses and alter ego character Slats Grobnik. His last-ever column before his 1997 death pinned the cause of the Cubs' decades of losing on their slow pace of signing African-American players in the 1950s. In fact, the Cubs continued to lag behind on adding color to their organization the remainder of the Wrigley family ownership. With the sports departments of Chicago newspapers largely neutered of tough commentary and peeking-by-the-curtains style in relation to the Cubs' foibles, Royko's freedom and stature on Page 3 could have really turned the heat on Wrigley through well-placed columns on management ineptitude and latent racism. Here's a story Royko missed: In the mid-1970s, African-American Cubs pitcher Ray Burris had a casual conversation outside Wrigley Field with a white woman who headed up his fan club. A management toady spotted the chat and warned Burris never to be seen talking to the woman again. Burris also recalled how the mossified front office sent a detective on the road to monitor the behavior of Cubs players of color, lest they consort with females of fairer races.

Had Royko exposed such blatant racism, he might have embarrassed Phil and Bill Wrigley that they might have been forced to sell to a more progressive, Cubs-fan owner. After all, ol' man Wrigley couldn't have tolerated Jesse Jackson picketing Wrigley Field any more than the presence of a billy goat in his box seats.

Fortunately, the 21st-century Cubs don't require such shock treatment. All the fans desire is for media to cut out the curses/goats obsession and simply provide some oversight to ensure the team is managed like the top-market, baseball-pacing franchise both Crane Kenney and Lou Piniella insist it is. No more letting an Andy MacPhail slide by, simply because he confided in beat writers via group proclamations while allowing the team to rank second-to-last in front-office staffing and middle of the pack in farm-system expenditures. Exposure of the latter two demerits required more legwork than merely dashing off an essay on farm animals and felines hexing the Cubs.

The fans cannot be taken for granted anymore. Management learned the hard way via sold, but unused, bleacher seats near the end of the disastrous 2006 season. They could not have avoided hearing the postseason 2008 anger. Now the players themselves have an obligation. They have to block out the crazy curses talk—inevitable given the temptations of all the ink-stained wretches and microphone jockeys—and the other kinds of pressure that seems to trip them up in October.

In fact, the players owe the fans. There cannot be any more statements such as what was uttered by the otherwise upstanding Derrek Lee in the morguelike Dodger Stadium locker room after Game 3 of the 2008 NLCS. When asked if the fans should be mourning the latest disaster more than the players, Lee demurred.

"They shouldn't take it harder than we do," he said. "We're the ones out there scratching and clawing. I don't think they can take it any harder than we're taking it.

"I don't know what to say to the fans, I really don't."

That comment really set off Hoosier rooter Karen Nelson, no doubt speaking for countless fans.

"We don't deserve to feel worse than they do?" she exclaimed. "They get paid millions of dollars to play a stupid game, have fans ogle over them, and bow down to them, and yet all we get in return is countless criticism for being loyal and hopeful?"

If it's emotionally possible, the players have to dig down deep in themselves to dedicate future playoff efforts to the fans. What's wrong with winning the World Series for the fans? Without such stout backing, they in essence would not have their jobs and their lifetime financial security. Dedicating themselves to the fans would be the best clutch effort of their careers, and well worth it.

And Lou Piniella, maestro of this revival effort, has to be even more flexible as he moves past normal retirement age still in charge of the Cubs. Sweet Lou must at least tolerate the "cerebral" part of the game for the first time in his 47-year career. It's as much mental preparation as the simplest pregame stretching routine. If Piniella has to descend more often from his Wrigley Field office—where he sequesters himself most of the time other than batting practice—and use his considerable reputation to get in players' heads positively, so be it. Respect, if not fear, precedes Piniella. He should use those qualities to the max.

Not all fans have the life flexibility of this book's researcher, Patrick Roach, who in his early 20s has a lot of time to wait for a Cubs World Series winner.

"Eddie Vedder's "All the Way" sums it up best when it states, 'Don't let anyone say that it's just a game,' " Roach said. "For Cubs fans, well, we really do live and die with the team. I still recall dropping to my knees, resting my face in my palms, and bawling as an eleven-year-old in 1998 when Brant Brown dropped a routine fly ball with two outs in the bottom of the ninth in Milwaukee. You know the rest of the story. Three runs scored—erasing the Cubs' 7–5 lead and drastically affecting the National League wild-card race with just three games remaining. That was the first time I lost sleep over the Cubs. It wouldn't be the last. When the Cubs won the division in 2003 on a brisk, beautiful fall day, however, I shed tears of a different kind. Witnessing Sammy Sosa, Moises Alou, and Dusty Baker hug it out made all the prior agony and pain seem worth it.

"When you are a Cubs fan, the highs are so high, and the lows are so low. The Cubs have invented new ways to lose over the years. Some are cruel and unusual. But we fans keep coming back. Whether they deserve it or not, we continuously return in the spring optimistic. We don't boo our players (apologies to LaTroy Hawkins). We are the punch line in jokes, yet we still hold our heads high. We are a proud breed despite not having a World Series trophy to point to. We have put up with a lot. Sure, the Cubs went to the postseason four times between 1998 and 2008, but the faithful deserve more than just an opportunity to crowd Wrigleyville's taverns. We *need* to be world champions.

"When players sign with the Cubs, they have an opportunity to become the legends that saved Cubdom. They are not just playing for themselves and their teammates. They are playing for the child in all of us that chose to believe in something bigger than his or herself. For a century now, Cubs fans have given a lot, yet they have received very little. It's time to reverse this trend. After all, we deserve it."

ACKNOWLEDGMENTS

NOBODY CAN COMPLETE A BOOK BY HIMSELF. IT TAKES A TEAM EFFORT, and the rookie of the year for *Sweet Lou* is not a big leaguer, but Loyola University student Patrick Roach. A fanatical baseball fan, Pat crunched numbers like an assembly line, pulled vintage articles out of seemingly thin air on the Internet, and contributed his own essays to this project. We enjoyed our alfresco meetings on summer evenings by the Ernie Banks statue near Wrigley Field's main entrance. There are worse ways to make a living. Hey, sports departments, hire this guy, you'll get your money's worth and then some.

This era of player-press relations is supposed to be fraught with conflict. But with time, patience, and proof that you know the game, a good reporter can break through those barriers. I'm appreciative to some of the pillars of the Cubs clubhouse, namely Kerry Wood, Derrek Lee, and Ryan Dempster, for taking time regularly to share their insight about their own games and their team. Many of their teammates were similarly helpful in shorter doses. The majority of big leaguers belie the stereotype of being arrogant, egotistical, and distant. Good relationships are a two-way street. Other than being the best at their game and handsomely compensated for their efforts, big-league athletes are indeed human and put their pant legs on one at a time, just like everyone else.

The Cubs media relations staff of Peter Chase, Jason Carr, and Dani Holmes was helpful on a daily basis and in facilitating access. Special thanks does go out to former media relations officials Sharon Pannozzo and Katelyn Thrall for helping foster an atmosphere where I could build up one-on-one clubhouse relationships. Even with somewhat diminished access compared to a decade ago, including less for the manager, who often is limited to group interviews, baseball is still the last bastion of daily access where a reporter can really get to know the athletes.

Thanks also go out to all colleagues and friends for their encouragement and insight. Even without a World Series championship at this deadline, covering the Cubs does not lack for stimulating news taking place every day.

And, finally, the book wouldn't take the form it has without the pronouncements of Lou Piniella. I'm sure there were many times Sweet Lou would have preferred to do anything else other than answer my question when I'd pull him aside after his main group interview sessions. But to his credit, he stopped for a minute or two and provided answers that were as honest as could be found in baseball today.

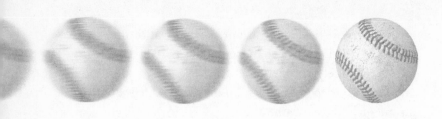

INDEX

ABOUT THE AUTHOR

GEORGE CASTLE HAS COVERED THE CUBS AND MAJOR LEAGUE BASEBALL SINCE 1980 for a variety of newspapers and magazines, and for the *Times of Northwest Indiana,* the Chicago area's fourth-largest daily newspaper. An author of eight books, he hosts and produces a weekly syndicated baseball show, *Diamond Gems,* which is broadcast on 35 to 40 affiliates in 14 states and podcast on the YourSportsFan.com sports site. Castle has become a multimedia purveyor of Cubs inside information and analysis that has been unmatched, using a network of close clubhouse and front-office relationships to continually produce scoops and informative pieces that outflank other media. He has gotten to know—and gain the trust—of almost all of the important figures in the franchise. Castle has also appeared on a wide variety of network radio—including ESPN, Sporting News, and Sirius—and local sports-talk radio programs. He was tapped by producers as one of the historical experts on the Cubs for *Wait 'Til Next Year: The Saga of the Chicago Cubs,* the HBO 2006 special on the team. He lives in the Chicago area.